THE FIRST MEASURED CENTURY

AN ILLUSTRATED GUIDE TO TRENDS IN AMERICA, 1900–2000

Theodore Caplow
Louis Hicks
Ben J. Wattenberg

The AEI Press

Publisher for the American Enterprise Institute

WASHINGTON, D.C.

2001

Cover photo: *In 1926, Mrs. Ida Zahler and her eleven children arrived in New York City from Switzerland. They continued their journey to a farm in North Canton, Ohio, where they joined Mr. Zahler. Courtesy of UPI/Corbis-Bettman.*

Inside front and back covers: *Chicago's Hull House was home to a group of university-educated women devoted to charitable work on behalf of immigrants living in the poor, inner-city neighborhood depicted in these maps. In 1893, the women conducted an in-depth, door-to-door survey of their immigrant neighbors, gathering information on socioeconomic characteristics such as ethnicity and wages, which was eventually converted into these detailed color-coded maps. Courtesy of the University Library, Department of Special Collections, University of Illinois at Chicago.*

Available in the United States from the AEI Press, c/o Publisher Resources Inc., 1224 Heil Quaker Blvd., P.O. Box 7001, La Vergne, TN 37086-7001. To order, call 1-800-937-5557. Distributed outside the United States by arrangement with Eurospan, 3 Henrietta Street, London WC2E 8LU, England.

Library of Congress Cataloging-in-Publication Data

Caplow, Theodore.
    The first measured century: an illustrated guide to trends in America, 1900–2000/Theodore Caplow, Louis Hicks, Ben J. Wattenberg.
        p. cm.
    Includes bibliographical references and index.
    ISBN 0-8447-4137-X (alk. paper) — ISBN 0-8447-4138-8 (pbk.: alk. paper)
    1. United States—Social conditions—20th century—Statistics. 2. United States—Economic conditions—20th century—Statistics.
    I. Hicks, Louis. II. Wattenberg, Ben J. III. Title.
    HN60 .C38 2000
    306'.0973'0904--dc21

00-049580

The AEI Press
Publisher for the American Enterprise Institute
1150 Seventeenth Street, N.W.
Washington, D.C. 20036

Printed in the United States of America

Contents

Chapter 4. Family

Chapter 8. Health

Chapter 9. Money

Chapter 12. Crime

Preface

This is a book about social change in the United States during the twentieth century. It relies on statistical trends to tell that awesome story.

The twentieth century was the first century that could be measured in a systematic manner. Those who saw it coming included President James A. Garfield who, while still a congressman in 1869, observed in a speech to the U.S. House of Representatives:

> The developments of statistics are causing history to be rewritten. Till recently, the historian studied nations in the aggregate, and gave us only the story of princes, dynasties, sieges, and battles....

> Now, statistical inquiry leads him into the hovels, homes, workshops, mines, fields, prisons, hospitals, and all other places where human nature displays its weakness and its strength. In these explorations he discovers the seeds of national growth and decay, and thus becomes the prophet of his generation.

Alas, President Garfield was assassinated in 1881 and did not live to see much beyond the earliest flowering of his prescient observation. As it turned out, we never stopped hearing all about "princes, dynasties, sieges, battles," as well as the other great historical anecdotes, personalities, and moments of the ensuing years: the Titanic; the Hindenburg; Elvis; Lindbergh; Challenger; December 7, 1941, and June 6, 1944; the Roaring Twenties; Einstein; Madonna; the Zapruder film; O.J.; and Monica.

But, as Garfield surmised, we developed a second way of seeing history. During the twentieth century, Americans became the most energetic measurers of social life that ever lived. They measured everything that had been counted before, such as population and the size of the government's territory and army. And they pioneered the measurement of facets of American life that had never been systematically counted before, such as crime, love, food, fun, religion, and work.

This tradition of counting and measuring social conditions gradually spread to virtually every nook and cranny of life in America. Numerical thinking became the discourse of public life. Complicated statistics about arcane matters of national policy permeated presidential debates. The numbers that fill the news—the Gross National Product, the Consumer Price Index, the unemployment rate, the teenage pregnancy rate, the poverty rate, and so forth—were inventions of the American twentieth century. This was the first measured century in human history.

Of course, measurement in the social sciences does not yield certitude. The measurers, the social scientists, the politicians, the advocates, and the activists often disagree about what the data really mean. But, on balance, the explosion of numerical investigation has indeed offered great value: an imperfect measure of accountability, an imperfect way of problem-solving, and an imperfect way of seeing that many things we thought were so, weren't.

The panorama of the American twentieth century presented in this volume unfolds as a series of key trends, each explained in a one-page essay illustrated by one or more colored charts on the facing page. *The First Measured Century* was designed as a tool for teachers and students, journalists and bureaucrats, managers and consultants, social scientists and housewives, and everyone else who wants a better understanding of American society.

The selection of information was as objective as we could make it. We have focused on significant aspects of the nation's experience without favoring any particular viewpoint. We have tried to exclude our own biases, leaving value judgments to the reader. We have offered partial explanations for many of the individual trends, but we have not advanced any general theory to explain them as a whole. However, we encourage readers to think through their own interpretive designs based on the data. (It is not so hard to become an expert.)

Some trends have been omitted for reasons of space. Social change in a complex society has innumerable facets. In other cases, information we would like to include simply does not exist. Although much more data about American society is available today than in 1900 or even in 1970, huge gaps remain.

To maintain readability, we have kept in-text references to a minimum. But every number and every numerical statement in the text or in the charts is based on a credible source and can be traced back to that source by using the notes at the back of the book.

This book also serves as the companion volume to the three-hour PBS television documentary "The First Measured Century," a prime-time special by the producers of the PBS discussion series *Think Tank*. Unlike many companion volumes, this book does not re-package the television program into a coffee-table picture book. It is a comprehensive reference book. Indeed, the data presented here formed the spine of the PBS documentary. We believe it can add immeasurably to the value of the television program, not least because it presents far more data than could be included in a dramatic television rendering. This works in reverse as well: teachers might consider course presentations based on both the book and the program.

A special feature of this book is the inclusion of the first published results from "Middletown IV." In 1929, Robert and Helen Lynd published the groundbreaking *Middletown: A Study in Cultural Change* based on their research during the 1920s in Muncie, Indiana. In 1978, Theodore Caplow led a team of social scientists that replicated and extended the Lynds' original work. In 1999, The First Measured Century Project commissioned partial replications of the Middletown study to provide long-term data on certain topics not covered by official statistics. The research team, directed again by Theodore Caplow, used the same survey instruments in the same place with the same wording as the Lynds used seventy-five years earlier. For many of the topics in these surveys, these data are the longest time series existing in the world. More extensive findings from Middletown IV will be published in journal articles.

We are much indebted to Howard M. Bahr, Bruce A. Chadwick, and Vaughn R.A. Call of Brigham Young University for conducting the High School Survey and Community Survey of Middletown IV. In particular, we wish to acknowledge crucial support provided by Brigham Young University for the preliminary analysis of the survey data.

Many other people helped in the preparation of this volume. We particularly want to acknowledge the research assistance of undergraduates at St. Mary's College of Maryland: Michelle Adkins, Christa Childers, Megan Duffy, Katherine Maxim, Doan Nguyen, Patricia Richman, Emily Sherman, and Erika Wilson. Pauline Poirier, a recent alumna of St. Mary's College of Maryland, worked hard in the final months of the project to pull it all together. We are also grateful for the office space, administrative support, and library resources provided by St. Mary's College of Maryland. Terry Leonard and Rob Sloan, reference librarians at St. Mary's College, searched energetically for obscure, but valuable, materials. We also wish to thank AEI interns Jill Abraham and Aimee Record, and University of Virginia graduate student Stephanie Lake. Ann Ramsey and Elizabeth Olson, both from New River Media, and Hans Allhoff of AEI prepared the photographs and captions. Mark Mazzetti, Douglas Anderson, Randolph Stempski, and Robert Milt of AEI helped gather information for the book.

Many scholars read all or part of the manuscript, identifying errors and suggesting improvements. We thank them all: Karlyn Bowman, Randall Collins, Helen Daugherty, Murray Foss, Andrew Greeley, Pamela Hicks, Ronald Hicks, Marvin Kosters, Michele Lamont, Steven L. Nock, Elizabeth Osborn, Curt Raney, John Weicher, and James Q. Wilson.

Scholars at the U.S. Census Bureau reviewed those parts of the manuscript that relied on Census Bureau data. Their careful reading led to many improvements. We are grateful to the Census Bureau and, indeed, to the federal government's entire statistical apparatus.

None of those acknowledged is responsible for any errors the book may contain. Those are the sole responsibility of the authors, who would be grateful to hear from discerning readers about errors of commission or omission, so that they may be addressed in future editions.

Juyne Linger, our editor at AEI and fellow student of U.S. statistics, dramatically improved our manuscript in many ways. We are indebted to her for the careful attention she lavished on this work. We are also grateful to the publications staff at AEI—particularly Virginia Bryant, Kenneth Krattenmaker, Montgomery Brown, and Kathryn Burrows—who worked tirelessly to produce this book on a tight schedule.

Only the most enthusiastic support of the idea for this volume by AEI management made it possible. Simply put, without the encouragement and initiative of President Christopher DeMuth and Executive Vice President David Gerson, there would be no book.

Nor would there be one without the generous support of the Donner Foundation.

Chapter 1
Population

Immigrants on Atlantic liner SS Patricia *in 1906, a peak year of immigration. Photograph taken by Edwin Levick on December 10. Courtesy of Library of Congress.*

The American population nearly quadrupled during the twentieth century. The annual rate of population growth fluctuated until about 1960, when a distinctly lower growth rate ensued.

Rapidly falling death rates, massive immigration, and a "baby boom" in midcentury caused the American population to expand at an extraordinary rate, *doubling in the first half of the century and almost doubling again in the second half* (see upper chart). At the same time, the world population grew by almost the same factor of four. Thus, the American population constituted about the same fraction of the world population—4.5 percent—in 2000 as it did in 1900.

Most of the decline in death rates occurred in the early part of the century, primarily among children. Immigration rates were also highest in the early part of the century. The baby boom, which lasted from 1946 to 1964, added 76 million babies to the U.S. population.

While the population increased steadily throughout the century, the annual rate of growth varied (see lower chart). The smallest increase occurred from 1918 to 1919, when more than 100,000 U.S. soldiers died during World War I (see page 206) and more than half a million Americans died from a virulent strain of influenza that swept the nation (see page 136). The growth rate slowed again after Congress enacted restrictions on immigration in 1921 and 1924. A sharp drop in birth rates during the Depression caused a significant decline in the population growth rate. Despite these variations in the growth rate, however, the U.S. population continued to increase every year—even during World War II, despite battle deaths, diminished fertility due to the deployment of millions of soldiers, and a sharp drop in immigration. Fertility rates also fell dramatically after the baby boom, but immigration helped sustain a population growth rate of about 1 percent a year through the end of the century (see pages 84 and 14).

If these trends in fertility and immigration persist, the American population will continue to grow in the early twenty-first century, although at a diminishing rate. The U.S. Census Bureau's "middle series" projection indicates a population of 300 million in 2011.

Size of the U.S. Population
Millions of people

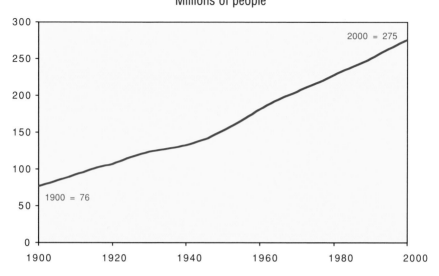

Population Growth Rate
Percentage increase over previous year

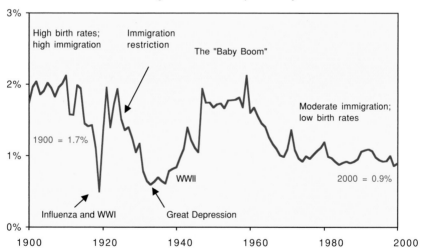

The life expectancy of Americans increased dramatically, first for infants and children, then for adults.

Life expectancy at birth increased by twenty-six years for males and twenty-nine years for females during the century (see upper chart). Driven principally by a decrease in infant (up to age one) mortality, most of this improvement occurred by 1950 (see page 134).

At midcentury, many experts believed that any gains in extending the lives of mature adults would come very slowly. This did not turn out to be the case. Life expectancy increased at age sixty, age seventy, and all intermediate ages (see page 136). In 1950, a sixty-year-old white female could expect to live to be seventy-nine years old. Her counterpart in 1996 could expect to live to be eighty-three years old—a four-year increase in expected life length (see lower chart).

The female advantage in life expectancy at birth increased throughout the century. The difference ranged from about three years in 1900 to nearly six years in 1996. The relative increase was even greater at later ages. This widening margin was often attributed to safer and less frequent childbearing, but that does not explain the existence of this gender gap to begin with. No one fully understands why women are more durable than men, but the fact is unmistakable.

These trends in life expectancy are based on data for white Americans. The life expectancy at birth for nonwhite Americans was thirty-three years in 1900—*fifteen years lower* than the life expectancy of forty-eight years for whites. This gap declined throughout the century, narrowing to seven years by 1996.

Longevity of White Americans
Life expectancy at birth in years

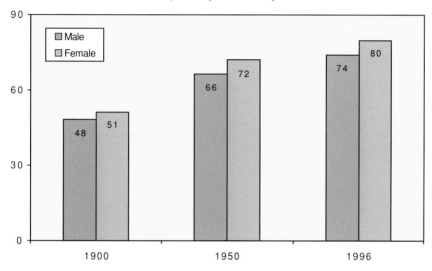

Average expected life length at age 60

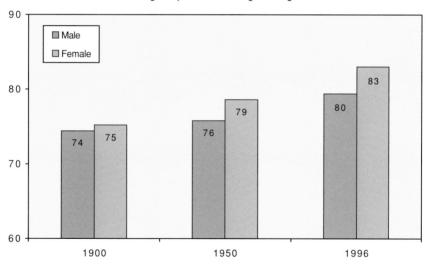

The proportion of children and adolescents in the population declined, while the proportion of older people increased throughout the century.

These two phenomena follow mechanically from the falling birth rate and rising average length of life. As the birth rate falls, the ratio of children to adults necessarily diminishes and the average age of the population rises. As people live longer on average, the proportion of the population at older ages necessarily becomes larger.

Because the decline in the birth rate was almost continuous (with the exception of the baby boom) and the lengthening of lifetimes fully continuous, the proportion of children and adolescents in the population decreased steadily from 44 percent in 1900 to 29 percent in 1998. If the birth rate declines further or remains stable and average lifetimes continue to lengthen, the youthful component of the population will continue to decrease. The Census Bureau's middle series projection indicates that children and adolescents will constitute barely a fifth of the population by 2020.

These changes at both ends of the age spectrum did not have much impact on the relative size of the intermediate group between the ages of twenty and fifty-nine. This segment represented roughly 50 percent of the population throughout the twentieth century, and this is not expected to change much in the twenty-first. That percentage is important because it represents a ratio of 1:1 between people of working age, the great majority of whom are economically active, and their individual or collective dependents.

The Changing Age Structure
Percentage of the population in each age group

Ages 0–19

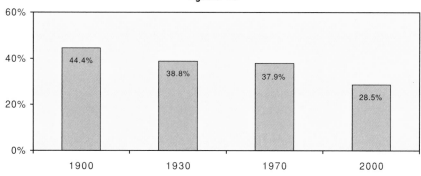

Ages 20–59

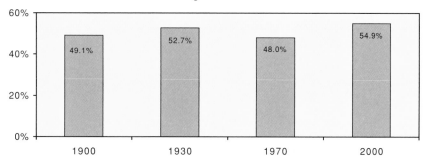

Ages 60+

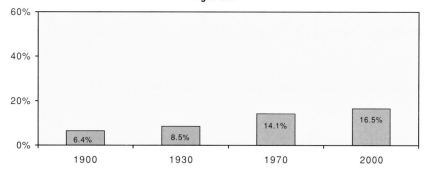

During the first half of the century, the proportion of centenarians in the population declined, but in the last two decades of the century that age group increased more than any other.

This is one of the most puzzling trends in this book. From 1900 to 1950, the proportion of the population that had attained or surpassed the age of one hundred years declined with each census. While life expectancy was increasing dramatically at younger ages, the number of centenarians per million Americans dropped from forty-six in 1900 to fifteen in 1950. One possible explanation is that the centenarians of 1900, who were born in 1800 or earlier and had much less schooling than the centenarians of 1950, were more likely to be misinformed about their own birth dates or to overestimate their ages. A second possibility is that more members of the 1900 cohort had experienced a healthy rural upbringing whose benefits lasted a lifetime. A third possible explanation is that the huge influx of young migrants and the large number of births during those years caused the total population to grow much faster than the population of centenarians, thereby effecting a decline in the number of centenarians per million population.

The number of centenarians per million population was roughly the same in 1975 as in 1900. By 2000, however, the number had escalated to 262 per million. According to Census Bureau estimates, 72,000 centenarians were alive in 2000—enough to fill a fair-sized city.

Unlike *life expectancy,* which changes from year to year, the human *life span* (maximum longevity) seems to have been fixed throughout history. Despite the claims made for the exceptional longevity of Russian Georgians or Bolivian mountaineers, there is no reliable record of any human surviving past the age of 122.

Centenarians
Number per million population

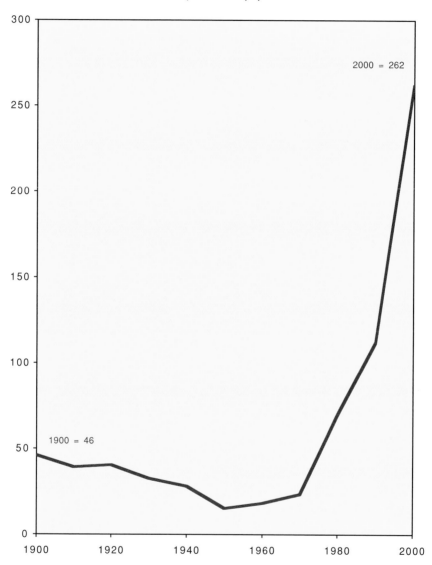

2000 = 262

1900 = 46

As the nation grew, the share of the population living in the Northeast and Midwest declined, while the share residing in the West grew rapidly and the South remained the most populous region.

In 1900, the majority of Americans lived in the colder sections of the country, the Northeast and Midwest (see upper charts). By 1990, the majority lived in the West and South, areas of relatively mild winters and hot summers (see lower charts). The spread of household air conditioning after World War II played a key role in this transformation.

A significant portion of this population shift can be traced to the exceptional growth of California. In 1900, 1.5 million people resided in the state, making it the twenty-first largest in the nation. By 2000, California's population had grown to 33 million, making it almost as large as the next two most populous states (Texas and New York) combined.

Although the Census Bureau considers Texas a southern state, Texans often argue that it is a western state. If Texas were included with the western states, the West would have been the most populous region of the country at the end of the century.

Population Drift
Percentage of total population in each region

Midwest

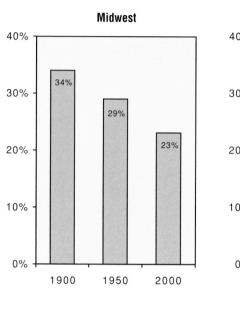

Northeast

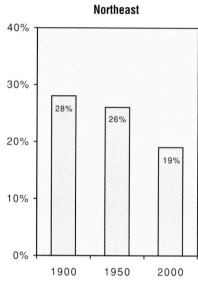

West

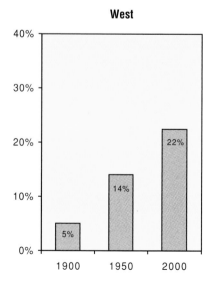

South

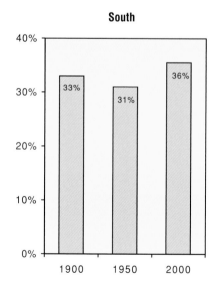

At the beginning of the century, the American people were mostly rural. At the end, they were largely urban. Most of these urban dwellers lived in the suburbs.

The migration from rural areas to the cities and from cities to the suburbs changed the face of the nation at least as much as the movement between regions. At the beginning of the century, 60 percent of the population lived in or around places with fewer than 2,500 inhabitants, and most were involved in farming. In 1990, only 25 percent lived within or in the vicinity of such small communities, and very few had any connection with farming (see page 26).

The cities grew rapidly during the first half of the century, as rural people left the land and the immigrants of the early 1900s flowed into the cities (see upper chart). The combined population of the ten largest American cities in 1900 was slightly more than 9 million. The ten largest cities of 1950 had about 22 million residents. Because so many people left the cities for the suburbs during the second half of the century, most cities experienced little growth and many actually lost population. The ten largest cities of 1998 had about the same combined population as those of 1950.

The growth of the nation's suburbs, in contrast, continued throughout the century. The share of the U.S. population that lived in the suburbs doubled from 1900 to 1950 and doubled again from 1950 to 2000 (see lower chart). Frequently, the suburbs of one city expanded until they encountered the suburbs of another, creating urban corridors such as those that connect Chicago and Milwaukee or San Jose and San Francisco. Some of these corridors combined to create even larger configurations. At the end of the century, an urban corridor extended more than 700 miles from Norfolk, Virginia, to Portland, Maine.

Urban and Rural
Percentage of total population

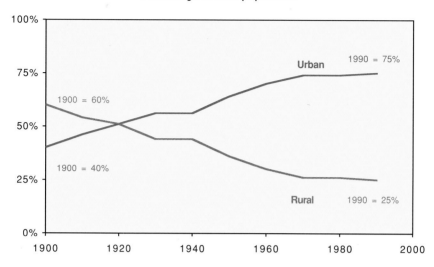

Population Living in the Suburbs
Percentage of total population

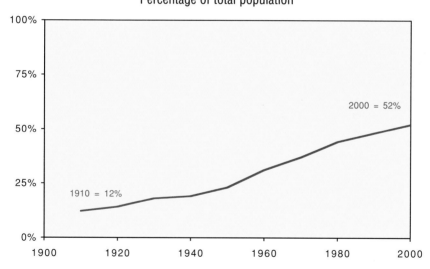

From the founding of the Republic in 1789 until 1880, the great majority of immigrants were from Northern and Western Europe (especially Great Britain, Germany, Ireland, and Scandinavia). Most of the Irish and some of the Germans were Catholic, but the great majority of new Americans were Protestant. In the great wave of immigration that began around 1880, the newcomers came predominantly from Southern and Eastern Europe (especially Poland, Russia, and Italy). They were Catholic, Jewish, or Eastern Orthodox, and concern that they were changing the national character ultimately led to stricter controls on immigration, which prevailed from 1924 to 1965.

The Immigration Act of 1965, which eliminated ethnic and racial restrictions on immigrants, engendered major change in the U.S. population. "The bill will not flood our cities with immigrants," said one of its sponsors. "It will not upset the ethnic mix of our society." But the new law produced very different, largely unanticipated consequences.

The ensuing surge of immigration was dominated by new arrivals from the Western Hemisphere, especially Mexico and the Caribbean islands, and from Asia, particularly Korea, Vietnam, the Philippines, and China. A substantial number of Muslims immigrated to the United States. For the first time since the end of the illegal slave trade in the 1850s, a sizable contingent of immigrants came from sub-Saharan Africa. In 1998, barely 3 percent of immigrants came from Britain, Germany, Ireland, and Scandinavia.

The bar representing 1965–1998 on the graph includes about 3 million illegal foreign residents who took advantage of an amnesty offered by Congress to obtain legal residence between 1988 and 1991. It does not include 5 million others who, according to the Immigration and Naturalization Service, entered the country illegally or overstayed temporary visas between 1965 and 1998 and were not legalized. The largest number of them came from Mexico, but many other countries were represented.

Origins of Legal Immigrants to the United States
Millions of immigrants in each category

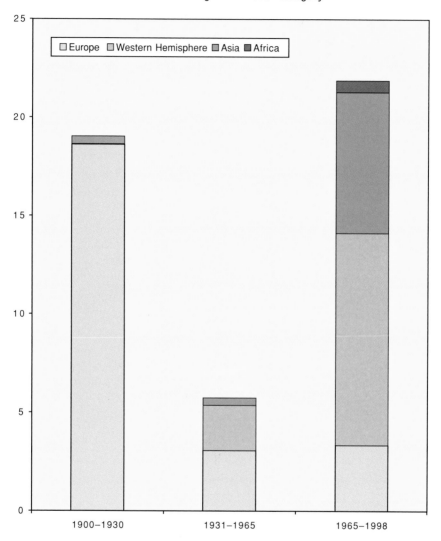

The size of the foreign-born population in the United States fluctuated in response to changing immigration policies.

During the twentieth century, the nation recorded its highest *percentage* of foreign-born residents—14.7 percent of the U.S. population—in 1910. Although the foreign born constituted less than 10 percent of the population in 1999, they represented the largest *number* of foreign-born residents—nearly 26 million—in U.S. history.

These foreign-born residents differed significantly from the nation's native population. Compared with natives, the foreign-born population included fewer children and adolescents and more young adults. Hispanics and Asians constituted 68 percent of the foreign born but only 9 percent of natives.

The educational level of the foreign born was distinctly lower: 35 percent of foreign-born adults did not have a high school education compared with only 16 percent of natives. The employment rate of the foreign born was similar to that of natives, but their earnings were much lower. More than a fifth of the foreign-born population was classified as poor compared with an eighth of the native population. As a group, the foreign born used more than a proportionate share of social services.

These circumstances were not permanent, however. As individual immigrants remained in America, their social and economic well-being tended to improve rapidly. At the close of the century, for example, immigrants who came to the United States in the 1990s had very low rates of home ownership, but foreign-born residents who arrived before 1970 had a *higher* rate of home ownership than natives.

Foreign Born
Millions of people

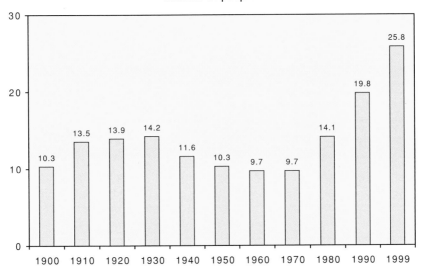

Percentage of total population

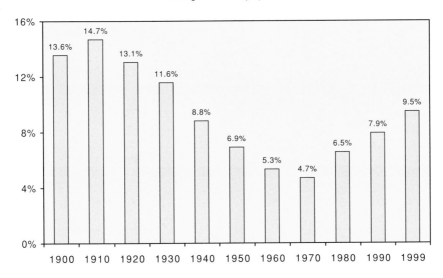

The federal government officially recognizes four population groups that are entitled to the benefits of minority preference programs: (1) American Indian or Alaska Native; (2) Asian or Pacific Islander; (3) Black; and (4) Hispanic.

There is nothing rational or scientific about this classification. By mixing genealogy, geography, culture, and personal history, it produces many anomalies. Based on an arbitrary rule developed to meet the property requirements of slavery, blacks are defined as people with even a small fraction of African ancestry. Through a series of compromises worked out under the reservation system, American Indians are people with some minimum percentage of tribal ancestry (the percentages vary from tribe to tribe and change from time to time). Asians and Pacific Islanders are people who were born anywhere in Asia or the unrelated Pacific Islands (such as Guam) or who have an unspecified percentage of Asian ancestry. Hispanics are people who have Spanish surnames or who grew up speaking Spanish, regardless of ancestry or skin color. Each of the four groups includes many individuals who are indistinguishable from non-Hispanic whites, but for administrative purposes, they all belong to official, legally protected minorities.

From 1800 to 1900, the proportion of such minorities in the population fell from about 20 percent to 13 percent. In 1900, minorities were predominantly black, with a thin scattering of reservation Indians, Chinese and Japanese in California, and people of Mexican descent in the Southwest. From 1900 to 1950, the relative size of the minority population remained about the same.

Thereafter, immigration created an entirely new situation. From 1950 to 2000, the Asian proportion of the American population rose about twentyfold and the Hispanic proportion about tenfold. The American Indian proportion tripled, not because of immigration or increased fertility, but rather because of increased self-identification. As a result of political activism and fuller recognition of Indian treaty rights by the federal courts, American Indian ethnicity acquired much greater prestige. After 1970, more people of full or mixed tribal descent described themselves as American Indian. In 2000, an estimated 28 percent of Americans belonged to an official, legally protected minority group.

Increase in Minorities
Percentage of total population

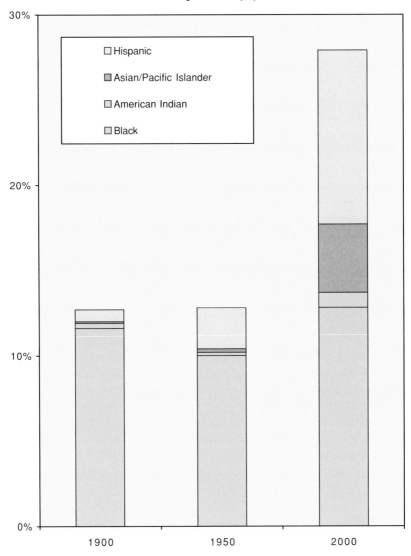

Minority migrants from the rural South and minority immigrants from Latin America and the Caribbean settled predominantly in large cities.

Almost all of the residents of the ten largest American cities of 1900 were non-Hispanic whites. Less than 4 percent of these urban residents were black. The Asian, mostly Chinese and Japanese, city population was too small to register on the chart. The category of Hispanics had not yet been invented for statistical purposes, but their numbers were negligible outside of the Southwest and there were no large cities in that region.

In 1900, about 90 percent of the black population resided in rural areas of the South. A northward migration to the cities began around 1900 and intensified during World War I and World War II. By 1950, about a fifth of the combined population of the ten largest cities was black. In their magisterial study, St. Clair Drake and Horace Cayton described the huge black community in Chicago as "a metropolis within a metropolis." Except for modest-sized populations of Hispanics in Los Angeles and New York City, very few Hispanics lived in the ten largest cities in 1950.

Between 1950 and 1990, southern blacks continued to move to large cities. By 1990, they accounted for nearly a third of the combined population of the nation's ten largest cities. Blacks constituted a majority of the population in Baltimore, Detroit, and New Orleans. The Asians and Hispanics who entered the country in large numbers after 1965 also favored the large cities, as did American Indian migrants. By 1990, the share of these newer minorities in the ten largest cities was equal to that of blacks and nearly as large as the proportion of non-Hispanic whites. The combined minority residents of Washington, D.C., Los Angeles, and New York City represented 73 percent, 64 percent, and 61 percent, respectively, of the populations of those cities. In each case, however, the surrounding suburban areas had substantially less minority representation than the central city.

The cities that were the ten largest in the United States also changed during the century. As residents of the big cities of the Northeast and Midwest moved to the suburbs or migrated to the South and West, only three of the ten largest cities of 1900—New York, Chicago, and Philadelphia—remained among the nation's ten largest in 1990. Rapidly growing Sunbelt cities such as Houston, San Diego, and Phoenix joined the list of America's ten largest, replacing cities such as St. Louis, Boston, and Cleveland.

Ethnic Composition of the Ten Largest Cities
Percentage in each group

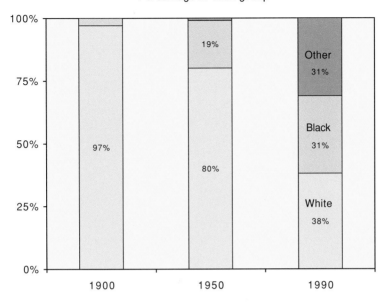

Ten Largest Cities
By population size

1900	1950	1990
New York City	New York City	New York City
Chicago	Chicago	Los Angeles
Philadelphia	Philadelphia	Chicago
St. Louis	Los Angeles	Houston
Boston	Detroit	Philadelphia
Baltimore	Baltimore	San Diego
Cleveland	Cleveland	Detroit
Buffalo	St. Louis	Dallas
San Francisco	Washington, D.C.	Phoenix
Cincinnati	Boston	San Antonio

Chapter 2
Work

The majority of the male labor force shifted from material extraction to material processing to working with people and information.

Throughout history, most men were engaged in primary occupations such as farming or fishing, while a few craftsmen made artifacts and a handful of priests, scribes, and officials worked with their heads rather than their hands. The Industrial Revolution broke that pattern, transforming millions of farmers into factory workers. In Great Britain, the first country to industrialize, factory workers outnumbered farm workers by 1840. In the United States, a comparable shift in the occupational balance occurred shortly after 1900. This shift from the primary occupations of material extraction to the secondary occupations of material processing continued for more than half a century. By 1970, the proportion of the labor force engaged in primary occupations had declined to less than 5 percent.

The subsequent shift from secondary work with tools and materials to tertiary work with information and people, already under way in 1900, gathered momentum throughout the century and by 1970, more men held white-collar than blue-collar jobs. The proportion of the male labor force employed in tertiary occupations—professional, technical, managerial, clerical, and service work—more than tripled during the century, from 21 percent in 1900 to 58 percent in 1998.

An upgrading *within* each of these categories became apparent after 1960, when the ratio of upper white-collar occupations (professionals, managers, officials, technicians) to lower white-collar occupations (mostly clerks and salesmen) increased significantly, as did the ratio of upper manual occupations (craftsmen and skilled artisans) to lower manual occupations (machine operators and laborers).

The long-term shift from digging, riveting, and hammering to filling out forms, negotiating agreements, and writing software continued unabated. Even in straightforward industrial production, computerization expanded the need for administrative activities while minimizing the demand for physical labor. Blue-collar workers were increasingly found at desks rather than workbenches.

Men's Occupations
Percentage of male workers employed in each economic sector

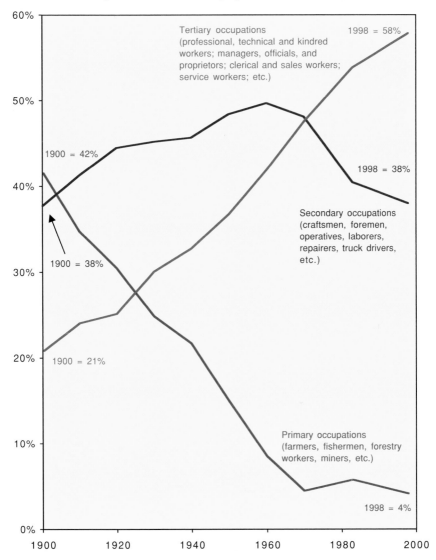

Tertiary occupations
(professional, technical and kindred
workers; managers, officials, and
proprietors; clerical and sales workers;
service workers; etc.)

1998 = 58%

1900 = 42%

1998 = 38%

Secondary occupations
(craftsmen, foremen,
operatives, laborers,
repairers, truck drivers,
etc.)

1900 = 38%

1900 = 21%

Primary occupations
(farmers, fishermen, forestry
workers, miners, etc.)

1998 = 4%

The decline of the farm population reflects a long process of attrition driven by huge technical advances in agriculture.

During the first half of the century, the number of farms in the United States did not change markedly. Thus, the number of farms at midcentury—5.4 million—was only slightly lower than the 5.7 million farms that were operating in 1900. But from 1950 to 1997, when the last Census of Agriculture of the century was published, the number of farms—and farm operators—declined sharply, from 5.4 million to 1.9 million.

The principal cause of this reduction was the rapid improvement of agricultural productivity as new methods and machinery were introduced. From 1900 to 1997, the yield of wheat per acre tripled, while the time required to cultivate an acre of wheat decreased from more than two weeks to about two hours. At the same time, the yield of corn per acre increased fivefold, while the time required to cultivate an acre of corn declined from thirty-eight hours in 1900 to two hours in 1997.

These gains in productivity were the result of several kinds of technological advances, jointly applied. Tractors began to replace horses for planting and harvesting soon after 1900. Their speed, power, and efficiency increased from year to year. By about 1950, tractors wholly replaced the horses, donkeys, and mules that had served farmers for millennia. Chemical fertilizers and pesticides, unknown in 1900, accounted for about 5 percent of farm production costs in 1950 and about 20 percent by the end of the century. At the same time, the agricultural experiment stations of the grain-producing states worked continuously to improve the hardiness and yield of crops by selection, hybridization, and, later, genetic engineering.

Large-scale farmers were better able than small-scale farmers to take advantage of these new methods and superior products as they became available. They were also better able to protect their farms from the vagaries of temperature and rainfall that beset all farming operations. Unable to compete, many small-scale farmers were forced to give up their farms. In addition, many less efficient farmers were pushed off the land during the periodic crises brought on by droughts, floods, high interest rates, and price fluctuations. Others left the farms to pursue job opportunities that emerged in rural areas as industrial and commercial enterprises decentralized. As a result of these trends, between 1950 and 1998, the number of Americans employed in agriculture declined by 53 percent, while the size of the average farm more than doubled.

At the end of the century, the surviving farm operators were a distinctive population—overwhelmingly white (98 percent), male (92 percent), and middle-aged or older (their average age was fifty-four). The great majority had lived on the farms they owned and operated for ten years or more. But only about half of them worked full-time at farming; the others also had jobs in town.

Farm Operators
Millions

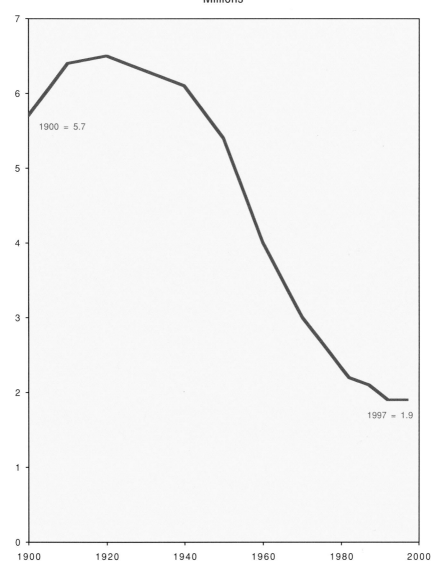

1900 = 5.7

1997 = 1.9

Occupational safety improved significantly throughout the American economy. In coal mining and railroading, two of the most dangerous occupations in the United States, total work accidents declined precipitously during the century. Work injuries showed a similar trend in most other occupations.

At the beginning of the century, men still loaded hundred-pound pigs of iron into boxcars without any kind of mechanical assistance. Frederick Taylor, the father of scientific management, became famous by teaching them how to do it faster. Serious injuries were routine.

The factories of that era were typically dark, cluttered, poorly ventilated, and filthy. Men worked in searing heat at furnace doors and in icy drafts a few yards away. At the end of the day, covered with grease and grime, they returned to homes that had no running water.

In the course of the century, more men found white-collar jobs, and the physical conditions of blue-collar work got better in every way. These improvements were driven primarily by changes in production technology. Workers were moved farther from harm and given much better protection when they were close to danger. Forklifts and conveyors took over the heavy lifting. Safety devices were added to every type of machinery. Factories were cleaned up and air-conditioned. Automatic monitoring systems were installed to warn of dangerous conditions.

Other factors that influenced the decline of industrial accidents were the expansion of tort liability, which exposed the makers and owners of industrial equipment involved in accidents to expensive litigation; the inclusion of workplace safety as a bargaining issue with unions; and government-imposed safety regulations.

Employee Fatalities: Coal Mines and Railroads
Annual Number Killed at Work

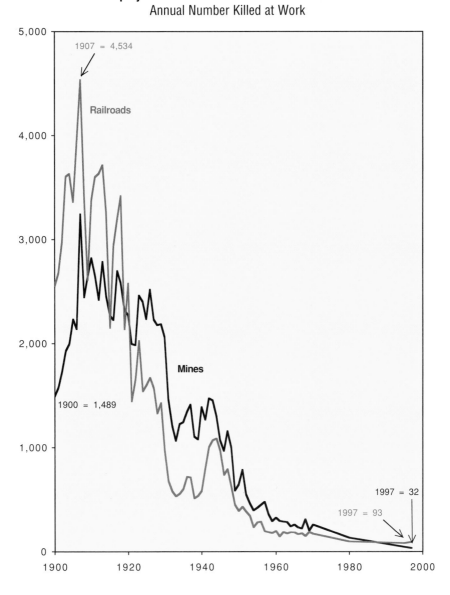

1907 = 4,534

Railroads

1900 = 1,489

Mines

1997 = 32

1997 = 93

Propelled by advances in technology, the ratio of engineers to population increased steadily. The comparable ratio for lawyers and physicians, however, remained largely unchanged until 1970, when it began to rise markedly.

The supply of engineers per thousand population increased in every decade, driven by technological progress and increasingly complex production processes. Most engineers were middle-level employees of large enterprises. At the end of the century, a bachelor's degree was still sufficient for licensing in many engineering specialties.

The relative supply of lawyers was more responsive to trends in social policy than to technological progress. Because requirements for entry were raised during the first half of the century and the size of law schools was effectively restricted, the ratio of lawyers to population was slightly lower in 1970 than in 1900. The number of lawyers per thousand population nearly tripled between 1970 and 1998, however, largely in response to the widening role of governments and a boom in litigation.

The relative supply of physicians declined early in the century, primarily as a consequence of the 1910 Flexner Report, which brought reform to the standards and curricula of U.S. medical schools and closed marginal schools. As a result, the number of physicians per thousand population remained almost unchanged from 1920 to 1970. Licensing requirements continued to be raised until certification in some specialties involved eight or more years of formal training. Most physicians were independent practitioners. The restriction of supply in the face of increasing demand gave physicians the highest average incomes of any occupational group. Such restrictive policies were largely abandoned after 1970 in response to public pressure, as well as massive new funding from the Medicare and Medicaid programs (see page 152).

Engineers, Lawyers, and Physicians
Per thousand population

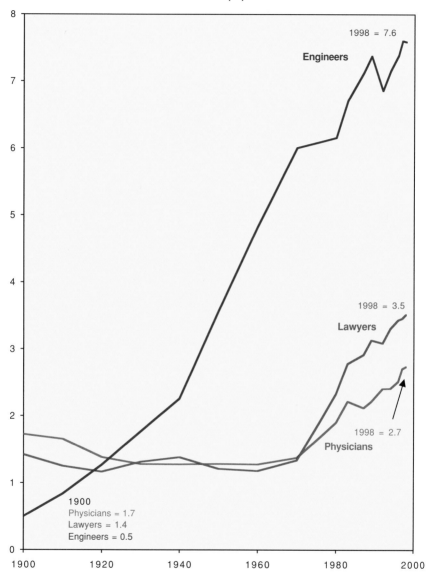

1998 = 7.6

Engineers

1998 = 3.5

Lawyers

1998 = 2.7

Physicians

1900
Physicians = 1.7
Lawyers = 1.4
Engineers = 0.5

The proportion of American men who were in the labor force declined.

The labor force participation rate of adult men gradually decreased from 86 percent in 1900 to 75 percent in 1998. The century's peak labor force participation rate—88 percent—occurred during World War II.

The decline in labor force participation was most conspicuous for men aged sixty-five and older. Two of every three were working or looking for work in 1900. By 1998, only one of six was so engaged. The decline was steep and steady, and it was well under way before the introduction of Social Security and subsequent expansion of private pension plans. This precipitous decline ended in the late 1980s, but whether this portends an increase in the labor force participation of men aged sixty-five and older was still not clear at the end of the century.

The withdrawal of younger men from the labor force can be traced to a variety of factors, including the following: (1) increased involvement in full-time higher education; (2) the availability of income support for people with mild disabilities; (3) military and civil service pensions awarded after relatively short service; (4) early retirement from corporate employment; (5) illicit gains in the drug trade and other criminal activities; and (6) a wider distribution of investment income.

Education, marriage, and race had striking effects on labor force participation rates. Only 7 percent of male college graduates under sixty-five were out of the labor force in 1998, compared with 25 percent of men in the same age group who had not finished high school. Married men of any age were more likely to be in the labor force than single, divorced, or widowed men. Black men had a lower-than-average participation rate, but Hispanic men had a higher-than-average rate.

The Shortening of Men's Working Lives
Percentage of adult men in the labor force

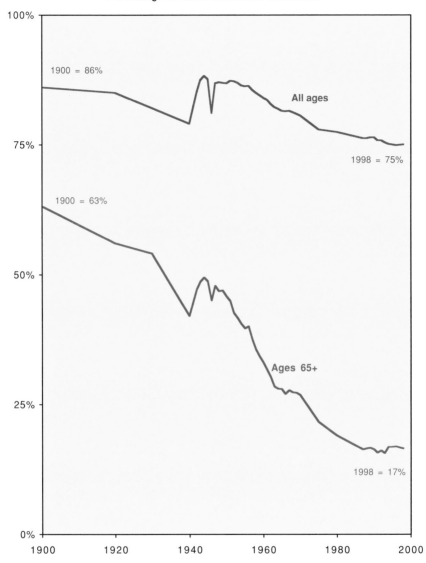

1900 = 86%

All ages

1998 = 75%

1900 = 63%

Ages 65+

1998 = 17%

Daily and weekly work hours declined until World War II, but annual work hours continued to decline moderately throughout the century.

In 1890, the typical factory work schedule was ten hours a day, six days a week, for a total of sixty hours. Thereafter, it fell steadily, reaching thirty-five hours per week in 1934. Expecting this trend to continue, most observers anticipated the advent of a twenty-hour workweek. It never happened. The average factory work-week climbed to forty-five hours at the peak of production during World War II, declined to forty hours after the war, and remained at that level until the early 1980s, when it began to inch upward. By 1999, the average manufacturing employee worked about forty-two hours per week.

The hours of office workers were slightly shorter and much more comfortable in 1900. While factory workers ate lunch at their machines, office workers came in later and went home for a long lunch at midday. Saturday became a half-day for both groups after 1920 and disappeared from most work schedules around 1960. Office workers continued to come in later and work shorter hours throughout the century.

Retail store employees always had heavier-than-average schedules. Thirteen-hour workdays were common in retail stores in the early years of the century. At the end of the century, retail employees worked shorter hours, but they were often required to work on weekends and holidays.

Unlike weekly and daily hours, annual work hours continued to decline slowly because of longer vacations, more sick and parental leave, and time off for obligations such as voting, jury duty, and military reserve service.

Average work hours are calculated for full-time or full-time-equivalent workers and do not include the steadily increasing numbers of part-time and seasonal workers or multiple jobholders. Taken together, these workers constituted about a third of the U.S. labor force at the end of the century.

Work Hours in Manufacturing
Average hours per week for full-time workers

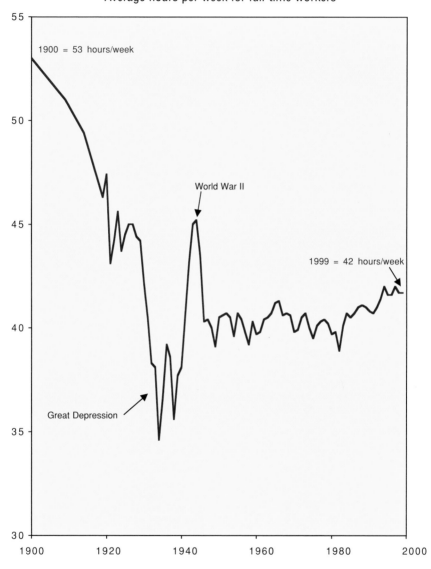

1900 = 53 hours/week

World War II

1999 = 42 hours/week

Great Depression

The massive entry of women into the paid labor force would have been impossible without a drastic reduction in the time that most women spent on household tasks such as cleaning, cooking, baking, sewing, washing, ironing, and other domestic maintenance activities.

Among the married women interviewed in Middletown (Muncie, Indiana) in 1924, only 22 percent had held a full-time job at any time during the preceding five years. The corresponding figure for 1999 was 83 percent.

The chart, based on the community survey conducted by Robert and Helen Lynd in 1924 and on the replications of that survey by Theodore Caplow and his team in 1977 and 1999, tells the story. In 1924, 87 percent of married women spent four or more hours doing housework each day. By 1977, the comparable figure was 43 percent. By 1999, it had plummeted to 14 percent.

This remarkable reduction was the result of the mechanization and simplification of housework. A variety of innovations—vacuum cleaners, central heating, gas and electric stoves, refrigerators, freezers, microwave ovens, blenders, dishwashers, washing machines, dryers, and many smaller devices—led to the mechanization of housework (see page 98). Prepackaged meals, wash-and-wear fabrics, supermarkets, and fast-food restaurants greatly simplified household tasks.

If anything, the figures understate the reduction of housework that actually occurred. In 1890, about two-thirds of business-class wives in Middletown had full-time servants. By 1924, only one-third of business-class wives in the Middletown sample had full-time servants. In 1999, only one of the 397 women in the community survey had full-time help at home.

Daily Housework in Middletown
Percentage of Middletown housewives in each category

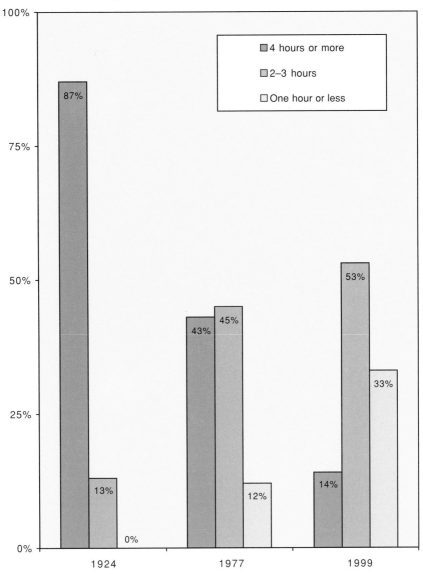

Legend:
- 4 hours or more
- 2–3 hours
- One hour or less

1924: 87%, 13%, 0%
1977: 43%, 45%, 12%
1999: 14%, 53%, 33%

Married women entered the paid labor force in large numbers.

In 1900, only 6 percent of married women worked outside the home, usually when their blue-collar husbands were unemployed. Among wives with children at home, very few worked at all. Almost half of single women held jobs, but they usually stopped working when they married or, at the latest, when they got pregnant, and most never worked for pay again. About a third of widowed and divorced women worked, typically out of economic necessity. Never-married women with children were virtually unknown.

The labor force participation rate of single women peaked in World War II and then declined as large numbers of them pursued higher education. The sharp jump in their work force participation in 1967 is a statistical artifact reflecting an increase in the defined minimum age of the labor force from fourteen to sixteen years old. In the early 1970s, the labor force participation rate of single women began a steady rise to nearly 70 percent by 1998 (see chart at upper left).

The labor force participation rate of widowed, divorced, and separated women remained fairly stable until 1940, when it began a gradual rise to nearly 50 percent (see chart at upper right). These women were considerably older on average than those in the other three groups, and many had income sources such as survivors' benefits or alimony payments.

The steady movement of married women into the labor force began around 1920, spiked during World War II, and never abated (see chart at lower left). In 1998, more than 60 percent of all married women living with their husbands worked for pay outside the family home. Their labor force participation was only slightly lower than that of single women and considerably higher than that of widowed, divorced, and separated women.

Data on the labor force participation of married women with children under age six go back only to 1950, but the rise since then has been sharp (see chart at lower right). Their labor force participation rate increased more than fivefold, from 12 percent in 1950 to 64 percent in 1998, helping to create an entire industry of paid day care in the process.

Labor Force Participation of Women
Percentage of each group in labor force

Single

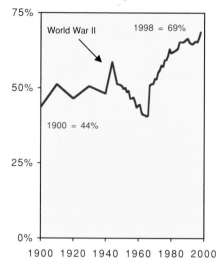

Widowed, Divorced, or Separated

Married

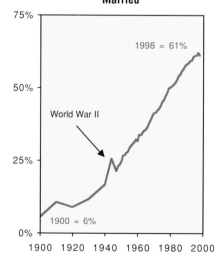

Married, with Children under Age 6

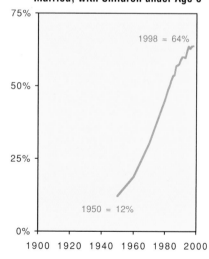

In 1936, a Gallup poll asked a national sample, "Should a married woman earn money if she has a husband capable of supporting her?" By overwhelming majorities, both men and women said she should not. In 1972 and later years, the *General Social Survey* asked an almost identical question: "Do you approve or disapprove of a married woman earning money in business or industry if she has a husband capable of supporting her?" By overwhelming majorities, both men and women approved.

Although the questions were the same, the context of the responses changed. In the early part of the century, as the Lynds' Middletown studies demonstrate, the income of a married man was ordinarily adequate to support his family at the accustomed level of his occupational class. Women, moreover, carried an enormous burden of housework (see page 36). At that time, the employment of women was associated with lower family status. The wives of business and professional men rarely worked outside the home. But the intermittent unemployment of factory workers, even in prosperous times, forced their wives to take jobs outside the home when their husbands were idle. A woman who worked while her husband was employed was often thought to be taking the job of another family's breadwinner.

By the end of the century, the situation had changed dramatically. Except for men in the top professions, the income of a married man was ordinarily not adequate to support a family at the usual level of his occupational class. The burden of housework had been substantially reduced. Many women received education appropriate to professional work and expected to work even after they married and had children. The employment of women ceased to be associated with lower family status, and became the modal pattern in middle-income families and widespread in upper-income families.

Attitudes toward Married Women Working
Percentage of respondents

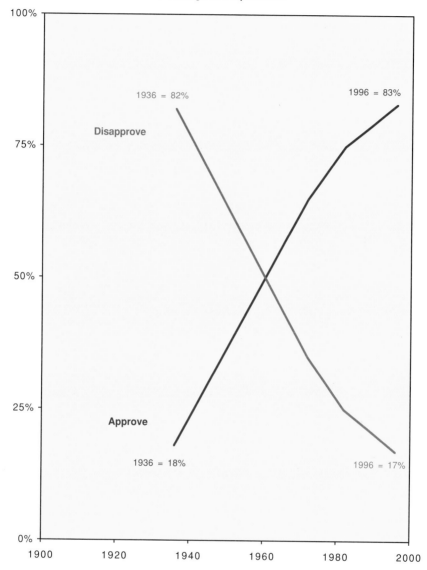

1936 = 82%

Disapprove

1996 = 83%

Approve

1936 = 18%

1996 = 17%

The concentration of working women in a few occupations diminished as they found employment throughout the economy.

In 1900, three out of four working women were engaged in domestic service, farming, or factory work, particularly in the nation's textile mills and shoe factories. A third of working women were domestic servants. Teaching and nursing were the only professions generally open to women; female managers and officials were rare.

During the first half of the century, the concentration of women in farming and domestic service was replaced by a new concentration in clerical and sales jobs, still poorly paid but more comfortable and respected. The proportion of women in factory work declined from a quarter to less than a fifth of the female labor force.

By the end of the century, farming, domestic service, and factory work had become less important for working women. The largest number of women were still in the traditional female occupations of clerical work, sales, teaching, and nursing, but an almost equal number had found more diversified employment throughout the economy.

Women constituted about half of all managers, administrators, and officials in the economy; nearly half of college teachers; more than half of psychologists and accountants; and more than a fourth of lawyers and physicians. Although circumstances were changing at the end of the century, men still predominated in the upper reaches of these occupations.

Women's Occupations
Percentage of the female labor force

Farming and Domestic Work

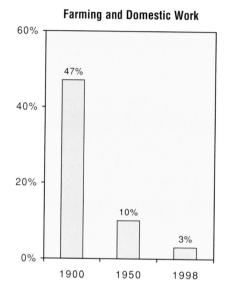

Factory Work

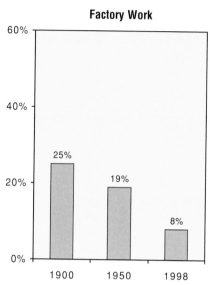

Clerical and Sales Work

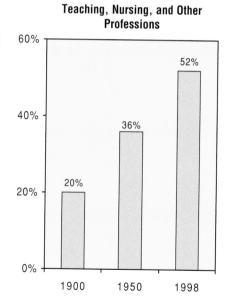

Teaching, Nursing, and Other Professions

Women and blacks were represented only marginally in law, medicine, and engineering until 1970, when they began to move into these influential professions.

At the beginning of the century, only about one of twenty physicians, one of a hundred lawyers, and one of a thousand engineers were female. After 1970, however, women flooded into law schools and medical schools, and many moved from the lower rungs of those professions into more prestigious specialties. Even in engineering, the number of women increased dramatically. By 1998, women constituted 29 percent of lawyers, 26 percent of physicians, and 11 percent of engineers.

In 1940, the earliest year for which reliable information about the racial composition of individual occupations is available, there were approximately four thousand black physicians, one thousand black lawyers, and three hundred black engineers in the entire country.

After the civil rights revolution of the 1960s, the situation changed somewhat. There were proportionately fewer black physicians in 1970 than in 1940, but three times as many lawyers and twelve times as many engineers. Still, they constituted less than 2 percent of their respective professions, and the doctors and lawyers served primarily black clienteles.

Between 1970 and 1997, however, black representation in medicine, law, and engineering roughly doubled. Equally important, most black physicians treated patients of all racial and ethnic backgrounds, and many black engineers worked for large firms. Some black lawyers still served mostly black clients, but many others did not.

At the end of the century, the proportions of women and blacks among students preparing for medicine, law, and engineering were higher than among active practitioners. As a result, the post-1970 trends were set to continue for many years to come. The sharp growth of Hispanic and Asian-American representation in the major professions, which occurred later than for women and blacks, will also persist far into the next century.

Female Physicians, Lawyers, and Engineers
Percentage of each profession

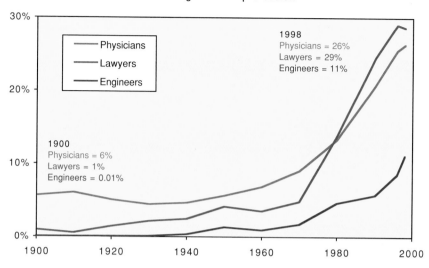

1998
Physicians = 26%
Lawyers = 29%
Engineers = 11%

1900
Physicians = 6%
Lawyers = 1%
Engineers = 0.01%

Black Physicians, Lawyers, and Engineers
Percentage of each profession

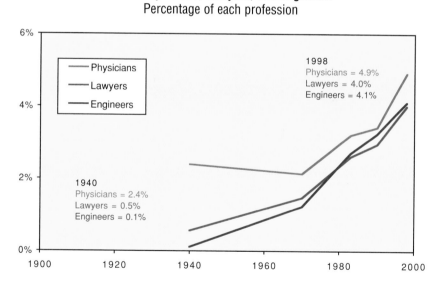

1998
Physicians = 4.9%
Lawyers = 4.0%
Engineers = 4.1%

1940
Physicians = 2.4%
Lawyers = 0.5%
Engineers = 0.1%

The unemployment rate fluctuated with the business cycle and military manpower needs.

In the first half of the century, the unemployment rate oscillated from a low of 1.4 percent in 1918–1919 to a peak of 24.9 percent in 1933 and then to another low of 1.2 percent in 1944. After 1950, these fluctuations became less severe as the business cycle moderated (see page 244).

Before and after the Great Depression, unemployment was largely a blue-collar affliction. Nearly two-thirds of the male factory workers in a sample of Middletown families interviewed by the Lynds had at least one spell of unemployment during the first nine months of 1924. *None* of the white-collar employees in the sample had that experience.

At the end of the century, blue-collar workers had about twice the unemployment risk of white-collar workers. Within the white-collar group, sales and clerical personnel had about twice the risk of managers.

Education, race, and age generated differences as well. High school dropouts had about twice the unemployment risk of high school graduates, who in turn had about twice the risk of college graduates. Blacks had about twice the risk of whites. Men younger than age twenty-four had about twice the risk of men older than twenty-four. These relative differences tended to persist even as the rate of unemployment fluctuated.

Unemployment Rate
Unemployed persons as percentage of the civilian labor force

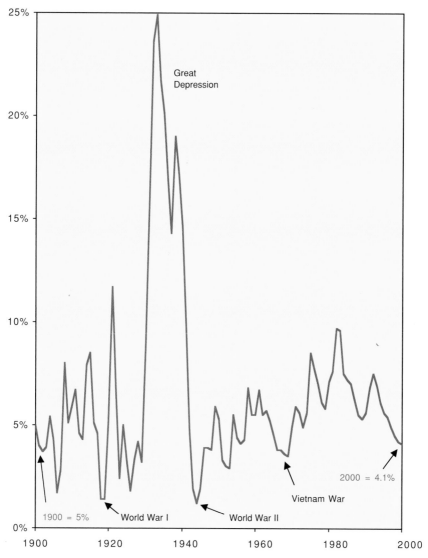

The unionized share of the labor force peaked in midcentury. The union base moved from the private to the public sector.

The unionized share of the work force quadrupled from 1900 to 1920 despite heavy legal restraints on union activities. It peaked after World War I and then declined steadily until the advent of the New Deal. The National Labor Relations Act of 1935 legalized collective bargaining and installed orderly procedures for organizing unions. The immediate result was the recruitment of millions of new union members. They constituted about a quarter of the civilian labor force from 1950 to 1970. After 1970, the unionized portion of the labor force declined steadily.

The incidence of strikes followed a less regular but roughly parallel trend. From 1945 to 1970, hundreds of major strikes involving a substantial share of the labor force occurred every year. The strikes of recent years involved no more than two-hundredths of 1 percent of the labor force in any given year.

In the heyday of organized labor, union strength was concentrated in heavy industry, construction, mining, and railroading. In the latter decades of the century, the biggest unions represented government workers such as teachers, postal employees, police officers, and garbage collectors, although pockets of strength still survived in the private sector. At the end of the century, about half of all government employees were unionized, compared with only one in ten workers in the private sector.

The decline in the unionized share of the labor force can be traced to many factors. The federal government effectively addressed important union issues by assuming much of the responsibility for workplace safety, creating and enforcing wage and hour rules, offering incentives for worker training, requiring notice of plant closings, providing a public pension system, and supervising private pension plans. Public distrust of unions grew in response to scandals that connected unions to organized crime. But the most important sources of the decline in the unionized portion of the work force are probably rooted in fundamental changes in the world and U.S. economies. These include the globalization of the labor market, along with the continual restructuring of U.S. enterprises through automation, mergers, downsizing, outsourcing, expanded fringe benefits, and the extensive use of part-time and temporary workers.

The Rise and Decline of Labor Unions
Union members as percentage of the civilian labor force

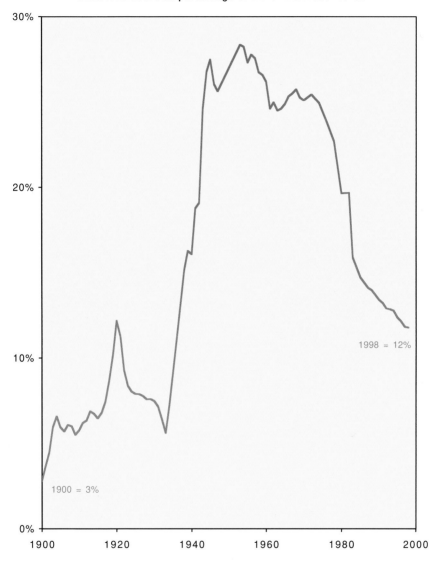

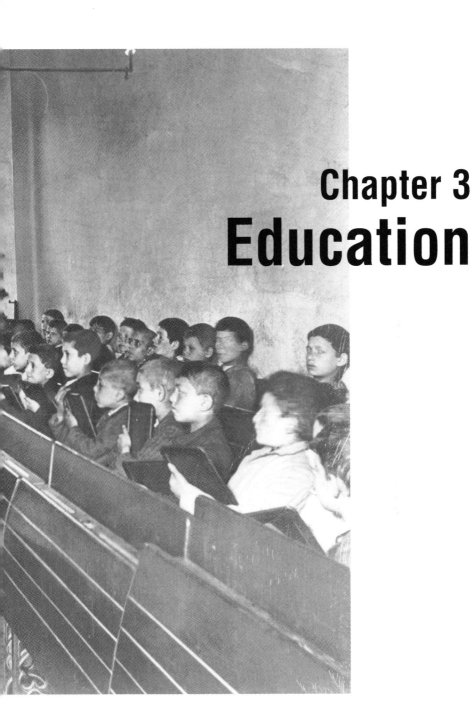

Chapter 3
Education

In this crowded Manhattan classroom, students watch their teacher. Pupil-teacher ratios declined throughout the century. Photograph taken by Jacob Riis circa 1886. Courtesy of Corbis-Bettmann.

High school and college graduates were rarities in 1900. Their numbers rose impressively during the hundred years that followed.

Few American adolescents completed high school in 1900, and only one in fifty finished college. By the end of the century, more than 80 percent of adults had completed high school and a quarter of the adult population had graduated from college.

The annual number of male college graduates increased more than fivefold from 1946 to 1950, when millions of veterans took advantage of the G.I. Bill of Rights to go to college. Another steep rise was associated with the educational deferments available during the Vietnam War.

These trends represented a massive upgrading of the nation's human resources— one that enabled and sustained technological progress, the expansion of knowledge in every field, the continuing shift from blue-collar to white-collar occupations, and the adjustment to an increasingly complex social environment.

The chart refers to all adults aged twenty-five or older, but the educational attainment of those aged twenty-five to thirty-four was even higher. In 1998, 88 percent of this younger group had graduated from high school, and 28 percent had completed four or more years of college.

Educational Attainment
Percentage of population aged 25 and older

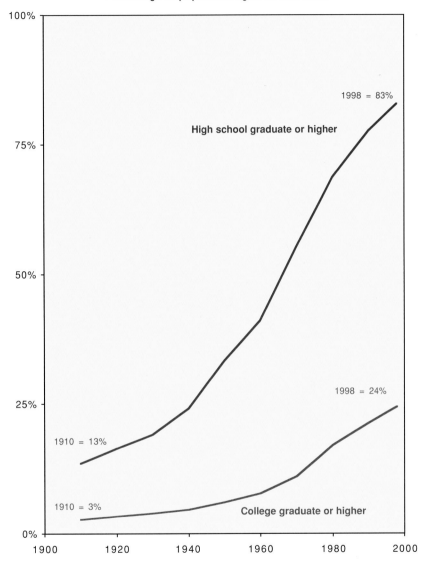

High school graduate or higher

1998 = 83%

1910 = 13%

College graduate or higher

1998 = 24%

1910 = 3%

Women's share of bachelor's and advanced degrees trended upward throughout much of the century.

Women predominated among high school graduates in 1900, earning 60 percent of the diplomas issued that year. Men were less likely to graduate from high school because so many of them entered the full-time labor force before or during their early teens. As the chart at the upper left indicates, the proportion of high school diplomas awarded to women declined to about half by the end of the century.

While women received a majority of high school diplomas in 1900, post-secondary education was still reserved primarily for men. Women earned only 19 percent of bachelor's degrees in 1900, but their share doubled to 40 percent by 1930 and remained at about that level in 1940. After World War II, however, the female share of bachelor's degrees dropped sharply as male veterans flooded into colleges and universities under the G.I. Bill. Not until 1970 did women's share of college degrees surpass the pre-World War II level. After 1970, however, women's percentage of college degrees rose briskly, reaching parity in the early 1980s. As the chart at the upper right indicates, women received more than half of all bachelor's and first professional degrees by 1990.

The chart at the lower left shows the female proportion of master's and first professional degrees. This includes not only the academic master's degrees but also the major professional degrees such as M.D., D.D.S., M.B.A., and J.D. As with bachelor's degrees, the female share was depressed as a result of the G.I. Bill, but by 1990, women received a majority of these degrees as well. In 1996, women received 56 percent of master's degrees in education, 41 percent of medical degrees, 44 percent of law degrees, and 38 percent of business management degrees.

The trend for academic doctorates was parallel, but women still constituted a minority of recipients at the end of the century. The doctoral degrees shown in the chart at the lower right are all academic, such as the Ph.D. in English. Women were awarded only 6 percent of all doctorates in 1900. This proportion peaked at 15 percent in 1930, then fell and remained below that level for more than forty years. After 1970, women earned a steadily larger share of doctorates, but men still predominated in most fields of advanced study.

Although women's share of college and advanced degrees dipped in midcentury, the *number* of women earning degrees at each level increased from decade to decade without interruption.

Gender Balance of Graduates
Female recipients as percentage of each group

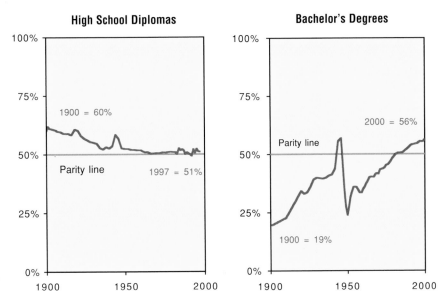

High School Diplomas

1900 = 60%

Parity line

1997 = 51%

Bachelor's Degrees

2000 = 56%

Parity line

1900 = 19%

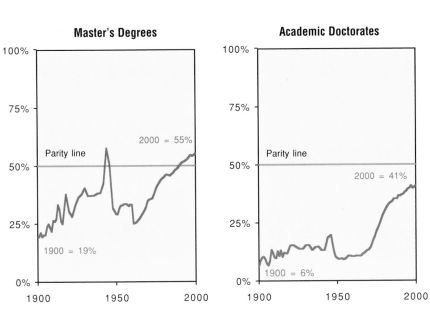

Master's Degrees

2000 = 55%

Parity line

1900 = 19%

Academic Doctorates

Parity line

2000 = 41%

1900 = 6%

The pupil-teacher ratio in the nation's public elementary and secondary schools declined by nearly half during the century.

In 1910, a teacher in a public elementary school taught a class of thirty-four pupils, on average. By 1998, each teacher had only nineteen pupils. The reduction in the pupil-teacher ratio was even greater in the high schools, where the average class declined from twenty-eight students in 1910 to fifteen students in 1998. The spread of special education classes, which are relatively small, contributed to the decline in the pupil-teacher ratio. Despite some reversals in this trend during the baby boom years and in particular localities, the overall movement toward smaller classes was unmistakable.

During the early part of the century, when the U.S. public school system was complacently regarded as the best in the world, pupil-teacher ratios were much less favorable than in the last decades of the twentieth century, when criticism of the same public schools was widespread. Perhaps the most authoritative survey of the educational performance of the public schools was *A Nation at Risk*, the 1983 report of the National Commission on Excellence in Education.

During the latter decades of the century, studies of the relationship between class size and student achievement were inconclusive. But reductions in class size may be desirable nonetheless. Because cultural changes, judicial decisions, and administrative policies curtailed their personal authority, teachers at the end of the century may have had more difficulty managing fifteen pupils than their predecessors had controlling and holding the attention of twice that number.

Pupil-Teacher Ratio in Public Schools
Number of pupils per teacher

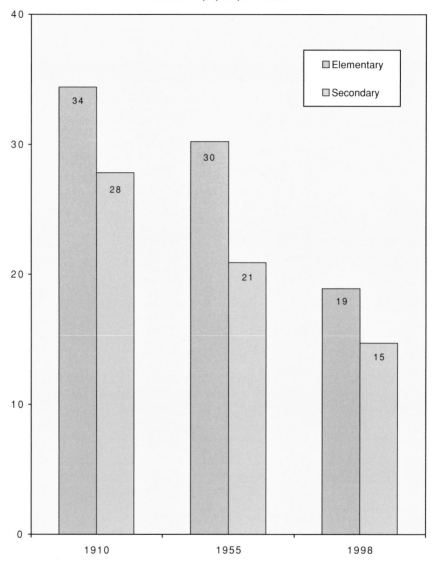

Preschool enrollment remained very low throughout the first half of the century but increased rapidly during the second half.

The traditional starting age for American elementary school children is six years. Kindergartens add an extra year of more or less formal schooling, beginning at age five. The concept and name of this extra year were imported from Germany, where the original kindergartens enrolled children at age four.

Most kindergartens are operated in conjunction with an elementary school where pupils go directly into the first grade. While enrollment in the first grade is legally compulsory, enrollment in kindergarten is usually optional, although school systems may strongly encourage parents to take that option.

Most nursery schools accept toilet-trained children at age three or older, although the distinction between preschools and day-care centers that accept even younger children is not always clear.

The majority of nursery schools are privately owned and operated, some for profit and some not. Until the latter decades of the century, most were small and informal, but the vast increase in the number of working mothers, together with the advent of the Head Start program and federal day care subsidies in the 1960s, enlarged and formalized many nursery schools.

Before 1965, enrollment in preschools never exceeded 10 percent of the total population of children aged three and four. But more than a third of that young population were enrolled by 1980 and more than half were enrolled in 1997, on schedules ranging from two or three hours once or twice a week to full-time attendance.

Preschool Enrollment
Millions of pupils

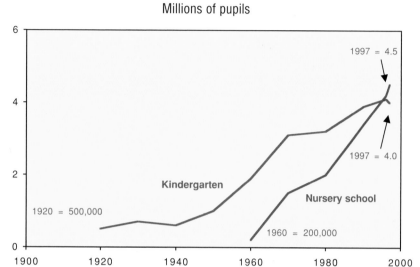

1997 = 4.5

1997 = 4.0

Kindergarten

1920 = 500,000

Nursery school

1960 = 200,000

Proportion of Young Children in Preschool
Percentage of children ages 3 and 4 years enrolled in nursery school

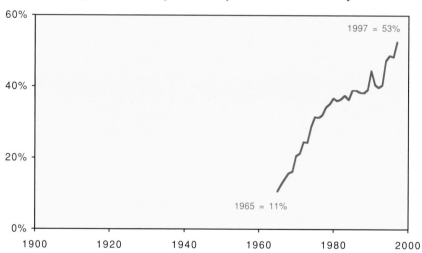

1997 = 53%

1965 = 11%

Enrollment in private elementary and secondary schools peaked in 1960 and then declined through 1990, when enrollment began to increase again.

By 1900, every sizable city in the United States had private as well as public elementary and high schools. Although private schools attracted a relatively small share of the school-age population, they provided an important alternative to the public schools for diverse segments of the population. The peak years for private schooling in America occurred in the wake of the Supreme Court's 1954 decision mandating desegregation of public schools. Hundreds of school districts in the South essentially shut down rather than integrate. White children attended hastily arranged private "academies." This "massive resistance" began to diminish after 1965. Changes in laws affecting the racial composition of public schools also bolstered private school attendance outside of the South.

For affluent families, a small number of expensive boarding schools provided a unique kind of adolescent life and privileged access to selective colleges. Most of these boarding schools were founded under religious auspices for either boys or girls. By the end of the century, however, nearly all of them were coeducational, less religious, and active in recruiting nonaffluent, especially minority, students. Originally, some of them offered six or seven years of instruction, but a four-year course became standard.

Another group of boarding schools was designed for students with special interests or problems. These include private military academies and private residential schools for students with behavior problems and learning or physical disabilities.

All large cities and suburban areas had a few private day schools that offered the same advantages as expensive boarding schools, but in a nonresidential setting. Providing education from kindergarten through high school to students from affluent families, many of these schools retained their single-sex character.

The largest category of private day schools operated under religious auspices and inculcated both religious and secular teachings. Besides Catholic schools, by far the most numerous, this group comprised Christian (Protestant fundamentalist), Jewish, Adventist, and Quaker schools, among others.

As recently as 1970, the pupil-teacher ratio in private elementary schools was twenty-seven students per teacher. By 1998, the pupil-teacher ratio was only sixteen students per teacher. The comparable figures for public elementary schools were twenty-four pupils per teacher in 1970 and nineteen pupils per teacher in 1998. By then, public elementary schools had lost the advantage in class size that they enjoyed in 1970. For various reasons, however, average per pupil expenditures were lower in private schools than in public schools.

Private School Enrollment
Students in private school as percentage of all students

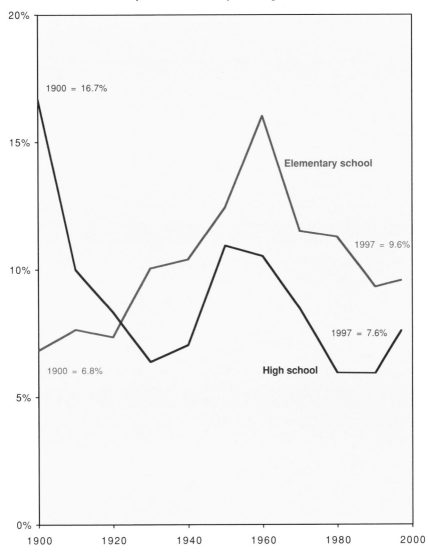

1900 = 16.7%

Elementary school

1997 = 9.6%

1900 = 6.8%

High school

1997 = 7.6%

Tuition at Harvard, measured in constant dollars, nearly quadrupled during the first seventy to eighty years of the century, then doubled during the last two decades alone. The chart shows the trend in tuition only. When dormitory charges, meals, books, and incidental expenses are added, the total bill for a year at Harvard in 1997 came close to the median after-tax family income.

Some other private colleges were even more expensive. Public colleges had considerably lower tuition rates, but their charges also escalated sharply during the last two decades of the century, outpacing inflation from year to year.

Although tuition and fees accounted for less than a fifth of the budgets of public institutions and less than half of the budgets of private institutions, they were much more amenable to institutional control than other sources of income such as government grants and private gifts.

The recent rise in the cost of operating a college or university can be attributed to a number of factors: (1) unpredictable fluctuations in the distribution of student choices among fields of study; (2) a dramatic increase in the regulatory and reporting requirements imposed by government agencies; (3) competition from Medicaid and prison-building programs for state support; (4) the continuing exponential expansion of scholarly knowledge; and (5) the successive addition of mainframe computers, minicomputers, and personal computers to the equipment needs of libraries, classrooms, and offices.

These rising costs were met in large part by increases in tuition and fees. A complex system of scholarships, part-time employment, parental loans, and subsidized and unsubsidized student loans filled the gap between what colleges charge and what students and their families can afford to pay.

Harvard College Tuition
Constant 1999 dollars per year

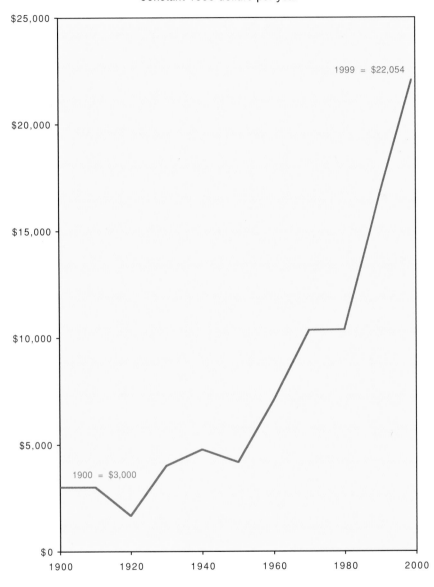

The number of graduate degrees awarded more than quadrupled after 1960, and graduate education became the normal path to the lucrative professions.

Graduate education programs proliferated in virtually every profession. In the nineteenth century, business proprietors managed their own enterprises with a small staff of clerks and managers. By the closing decades of the twentieth century, many corporate management jobs required a degree from a graduate business school.

In many fields, professional credentials became synonymous with graduate degrees: dentists needed a D.D.S.; veterinarians needed a D.V.M.; lawyers needed a J.D. In fields where beginning practitioners required only a bachelor's degree, professional advancement often hinged on acquiring graduate education. Architects added an M.Arch. to their B.Arch. Teachers added an M.Ed. to their bachelor's degree. Computer programmers went back to school for an M.S. in computer science. Military officers traditionally received bachelor's degrees in engineering, but after World War II, they went to graduate school while on active duty, acquiring master's and doctoral degrees in various fields. Indeed, whole academic fields were created to meet the needs of professions for graduate degrees: "national security studies" for military officers and "international relations" for State Department bureaucrats.

The desire for graduate degrees also permeated fields of endeavor whose practitioners scorn bureaucracy as such—art, music, and creative writing, for example. Aspiring artists and writers pursued M.F.A.'s, while musicians often got M.M.'s.

The top of the academic food chain, the Ph.D., was reserved for most of the century for academic subjects. Even this changed as the Ph.D. became a job credential outside the academy. Economists sometimes needed Ph.D.'s to work for banks. Physicists sometimes needed Ph.D.'s to work for telephone companies. A president of the Modern Language Association suggested that the solution to a glut of English Ph.D.'s was to redesign the degree so that it would become the professional credential for screenplay writing, magazine editing, and other language-related occupations.

Still, American graduate education is the envy of the world and one of America's most successful exports. At the end of the century, foreign students received 40 percent of doctorates in biology, 50 percent of doctorates in physics and chemistry, 55 percent of doctorates in mathematics, and 60 percent of doctorates in engineering.

Graduate Degrees Conferred
Thousands of each type of degree per year

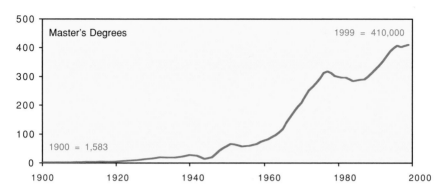

Master's Degrees

1999 = 410,000

1900 = 1,583

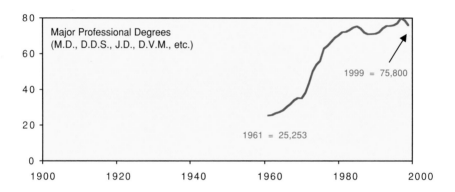

Major Professional Degrees
(M.D., D.D.S., J.D., D.V.M., etc.)

1999 = 75,800

1961 = 25,253

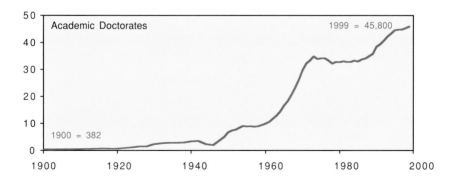

Academic Doctorates

1999 = 45,800

1900 = 382

Chapter 4
Family

Two Barry sisters and Beverly Lawrence
stare in amazement as they learn of
American biologist Alfred Kinsey's
findings on female sexual behavior.
Photograph taken August 20, 1953.
Courtesy of UPI/Corbis-Bettmann.

The marriage rate was lower at the end of the century than ever before. The average age at first marriage, which fell to an all-time low during the baby boom, climbed to an all-time high by the close of the century.

The marriage rate generally rose and fell with the business cycle. The 1990s, with conspicuously low marriage rates in years of unprecedented prosperity, were exceptional. The marriage rate is conventionally calculated as the annual number of marriages per one thousand unmarried women over the age of fifteen. Unmarried women may be single, widowed, or divorced. A rate based on unmarried men would produce a similar pattern.

The highest rate observed since the beginning of the national series was 118, registered in 1946 as millions of soldiers left the armed services and embarked on married life. Until the 1990s, the lowest rate was 52, registered in 1931, when the Depression abruptly lowered the incomes and living standards of most of the American population. As the upper chart shows, that record was broken in 1995, when the marriage rate dropped to 51. In 1996, the rate fell to 50.

The married proportion of the adult population fell from 66 percent in 1980 to 59 percent in 1997—about the same percentage as in 1931. Part of this decline reflected an increase in the number of elderly widows, the result of an aging population in which women had greater life expectancy, and part was attributable to an increase in the average age at first marriage.

In 1900, as the lower chart shows, the typical young groom was almost twenty-six and his bride was four years younger. For the next half century, couples approaching the altar grew steadily younger and the age difference between bride and groom diminished. In 1960, the bride was just over twenty and the groom was under twenty-three. This trend reversed around 1970, and by 1996, the grooms were somewhat older than their counterparts in 1900, while the brides were substantially older.

One out of three men and more than one out of four women in their early thirties were unmarried in 1997, compared with fewer than one in ten in 1900. Still, between 80 and 90 percent of Americans got married during their lifetimes.

Marriage Rate
Number of marriages per thousand unmarried women per year

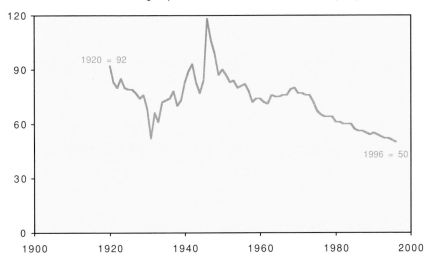

1920 = 92

1996 = 50

Marriage Age
Median age at first marriage

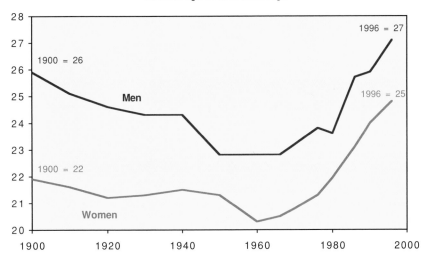

1996 = 27

1900 = 26

Men

1996 = 25

1900 = 22

Women

At the beginning of the century, very few women were sexually active before marriage. By the end of the century, most of them were.

Large-scale research about sexual activity in the United States did not begin until Alfred Kinsey's 1948 study, *Sexual Behavior in the Human Male,* and a companion volume about females published in 1953. Before that time, the subject had been in the closet. Thus, most of the quantitative information about sexual activity in America during the first half of the century is based on retrospective interviews with middle-aged and older people. To make matters worse, some of Kinsey's sampling methods and interpretations were questionable.

After the Kinsey era, research about sexual activity flourished. In *Kiss and Tell: Surveying Sex in the Twentieth Century,* Julia Ericksen refers to hundreds of sex surveys. But as she points out, this collective effort was impeded by ideological conflicts, linguistic ambiguities, unrepresentative samples, and the tendency of ordinary people to give less than truthful answers about sensitive matters.

Nevertheless, the trend shown in the chart is supported by sufficient evidence. Although the data on which the chart is based are neither uniform nor precise, there is little doubt about the general pattern the chart displays. It indicates that at the beginning of the century, most American women entered their first marriages as virgins. At the end of the century, about one-quarter of them did. In the second half of the century, some of this difference may have reflected the tendency of women to marry at later ages than they did earlier in the century. But from 1900 to 1960, the increase in premarital sex occurred at the same time as a *drop* in the average age of first marriage.

At each point in time and at any given age, the percentage of men with premarital sexual experience was significantly higher than the corresponding percentage of women, and the percentages of black men and women with premarital sexual experience were higher than the corresponding percentages of white men and women.

Premarital Sexual Activity
Percentage of 19-year-old unmarried white women with sexual experience

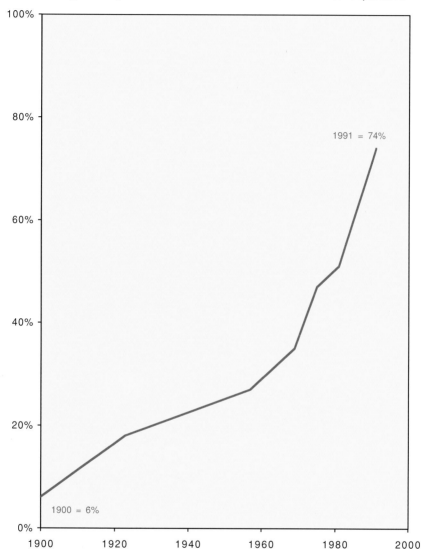

1991 = 74%

1900 = 6%

The cohabitation of unmarried couples became common in the last decades of the century.

Cohabitation was considered disreputable ("living in sin"), often illegal, and quantitatively unimportant throughout most of the century. It became legal around 1970 with the removal of statutory restraints such as false registration laws, which prevented unmarried couples from checking into a hotel, and customary restraints, such as the refusal of landlords to rent to unmarried couples. As the chart indicates, by 1998, more than 7 percent of all American couples were cohabiting. Their actual numbers increased eightfold, from 523,000 couples in 1970 to 4.2 million in 1998.

While the chart represents a time series of cross-sections, data from longitudinal surveys provide a more in-depth look at this trend. The 1987–1988 *National Survey of Families and Households,* for example, found that 44 percent of those who married between 1980 and 1984 had cohabited with someone beforehand. The 1995 *National Survey of Family Growth* found that 51 percent of women aged thirty to thirty-four had cohabited before marriage or were cohabiting at the time of the survey. At the end of the century, a large proportion of newlyweds lived together before the wedding with the full knowledge of their relatives and friends. Many cohabiting couples rented an apartment or purchased a house together with no more difficulty than married couples.

For some couples, cohabitation was something like the "trial marriage" advocated by family reformers in the 1920s. If the trial was successful, the couple married within a few months or years. Unsuccessful unions were terminated more quickly.

Like other types of familial behavior, the propensity to cohabit was influenced by age, ethnicity, and education. Those most likely to cohabit were young adults, non-Hispanic whites, and people who never graduated from high school.

Cohabiting Couples
Percentage of all couples

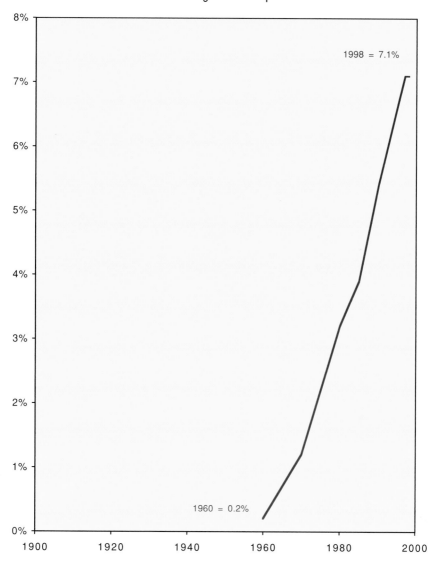

1998 = 7.1%

1960 = 0.2%

Extramarital sexual activity followed a downward trend.

The declining incidence of extramarital sex may seem implausible to television viewers who see a world of wholesale promiscuity in which marital fidelity is the exception rather than the rule. The data tell a different story. The earliest bars in the chart are based on the original Kinsey studies, published in 1948 and 1953, which have been challenged on the grounds of defective sampling. But studies of marital adjustment conducted between 1929 and 1950 produced similar results. The remaining bars on the chart, based on the 1992 *National Health and Social Life Survey*, show an unmistakable decline in extramarital sexual activity during the latter part of the century, especially among married men.

The trend might be explained by the fact that the average older respondent in the sample had been married longer and therefore had more exposure to extramarital temptations. But that explanation would not hold for female respondents. For example, many more women who reached twenty-one around 1968 reported extramarital relationships than those who came of age a decade earlier.

According to the 1992 *National Health and Social Life Survey*, the most authoritative study of American sexual practices, "The vast majority of men and women report that they are monogamous while married or living with a partner. Over 90 percent of the women and over 75 percent of the men in every cohort report fidelity within their marriage, over its entirety."

One likely source of the declining incidence of extramarital sex is the increasing ease of divorce, which allows people to leave unsatisfying marriages.

Married Persons with Extramarital Sexual Experience
Percentage of each cohort

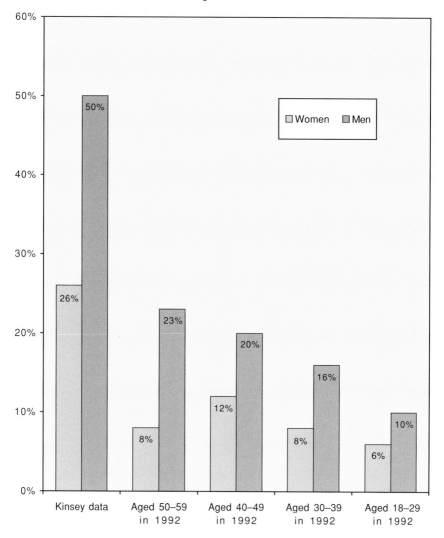

Tolerance of premarital sexual activity increased steadily, but tolerance of extramarital sex remained extremely low.

These conclusions about the level of tolerance for premarital and extramarital sexual activity are based on data from the *General Social Survey,* an omnibus inquiry that was first administered to a national sample of Americans by the National Opinion Research Center in 1972 and repeated annually or biennially thereafter. The two questions charted here were asked sixteen times between 1972 and 1996, with remarkably consistent results. Although the series is regrettably short, it is long enough to confirm the public's growing tolerance of premarital sexual activity and steadfastly low tolerance of extramarital sexual activity during the last quarter of the century.

The proportion of respondents expressing full tolerance of premarital sex ("Sex before marriage is not wrong at all") rose from 27 percent in 1972 to 44 percent in 1996 with some variability along the way, as shown in the upper chart. During the same interval, the proportion of respondents expressing unqualified intolerance ("Sex before marriage is always wrong") declined from 37 percent to 24 percent.

The trends in attitudes toward extramarital sex shown in the lower chart are very different. The proportion of respondents expressing full tolerance of extramarital relations ("Sex with a person other than one's spouse is not wrong at all") never rose above 4 percent during the twenty-five-year period. In fact, the level of tolerance for extramarital sex seems to show a downward trend, never exceeding 2 percent between 1988 and 1996, but the percentages are too low for the trend to be considered reliable. The proportion of respondents expressing unqualified intolerance of extramarital relations ("Sex with a person other than one's spouse is always wrong") rose from 70 percent to 78 percent during the quarter-century.

Attitudes toward Premarital and Extramarital Sexual Activity
Percentage expressing each opinion

Sex before Marriage

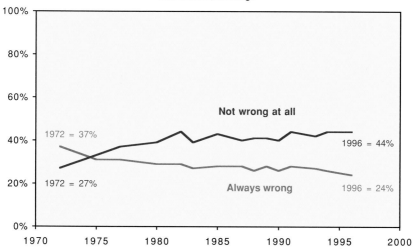

Sex with Person Other than Spouse

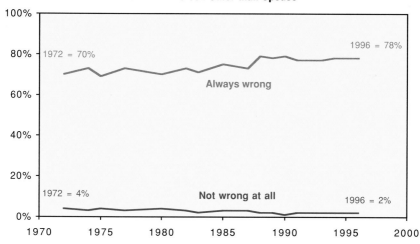

The divorce rate rose unevenly but substantially from 1900 to about 1967, when the introduction of no-fault divorce led to a doubling of the rate during the subsequent decade to a level that was sustained through the closing years of the century.

The U.S. divorce rate (divorces per thousand married women in a given year) approximately doubled from 1900 to 1960, when the national divorce rate stood at nine. During that time, divorce typically required an innocent spouse as plaintiff and a guilty spouse as defendant, except in Nevada, which typically required the legal fiction of residence in that state. Then, between 1967 and 1975, no-fault divorce laws, which allowed divorce by mutual consent, were adopted throughout the United States. The divorce rate promptly rose to twenty in 1975 and, except for a slightly elevated rate from 1978 to 1985, remained at about the 1975 level for the subsequent two decades. The National Center for Health Statistics has not published this series for the years beyond 1996. If the 1996 level of divorce is maintained, however, approximately four of ten marriages contracted in 2000 will end in divorce.

The typical pattern of divorce did not change perceptibly after 1975. The median duration of marriages broken by divorce was about seven years; about half involved children. The propensity to remarry declined somewhat, but the large majority of divorced persons eventually remarried. Almost half of all marriages involved at least one previously divorced partner. Second and third divorces were not uncommon, and most of them were followed by remarriage as well.

American opinions about divorce were curiously divided. While many survey respondents—a majority in some surveys—disapproved of divorce in general and wanted the process to be made more difficult, those same respondents generally condoned particular divorces that involved their relatives and friends. By 1998, a number of states, beginning with Louisiana, were experimenting with "covenant marriages," which gave couples the option to be married under a special statute whereby they gave up the right to an easy divorce.

Divorce Rate
Divorces per thousand married women per year

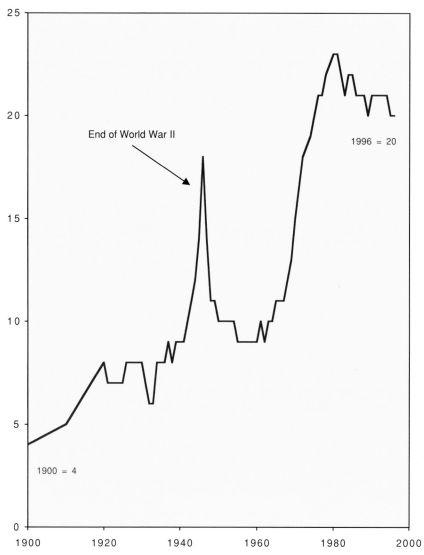

End of World War II

1996 = 20

1900 = 4

The decline in the share of U.S. households maintained by a married couple proceeded slowly until 1970 and accelerated thereafter.

Married couples headed 80 percent of U.S. households in 1910 and 71 percent in 1970; by 1998, however, married couples maintained just 53 percent of all households. In addition to the rise in unmarried cohabitation, this trend had two major components: an increase in the number of people, especially older people, who lived alone; and an increase in the number of families maintained by one person, usually the mother.

At the end of the century, a substantial majority of the white population continued to live in households maintained by married couples. In 1998, women maintained just 21 percent of white families with children under age eighteen. That is a significant proportion, but it hardly signifies the collapse of the traditional family pattern.

The pattern was quite different for the black population. Among black families with children under age eighteen, only 38 percent were headed by two parents in 1998. Mothers maintained a majority—57 percent—of these families.

As single-parent families became more prevalent, so too did the number of people living alone or with unrelated individuals or in institutions (at colleges or in the military, for example). Between 1970 and 1996, the number of Americans who did not live with relatives more than tripled from 15 million to more than 40 million.

Another way of looking at these trends is to examine the erosion of private support for a large part of the population. In 1910, nearly all married women obtained their subsistence from the earnings of their husbands, nearly all young children from the earnings of their fathers, and many older people from the earnings of their adult children. By the end of the century, the majority of married women were no longer wholly supported by their husbands; millions of young children and their mothers were supported by the government; and most older people lived on some combination of their own savings and government contributions, without significant support from their children.

Households Headed by a Married Couple
Percentage of all households

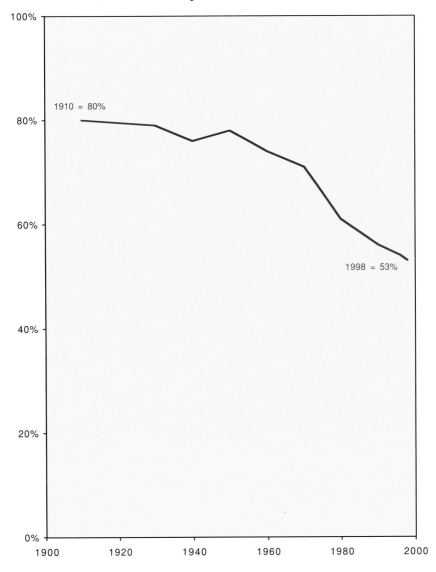

The proportion of the population that is married varied considerably, with the lowest points occurring at the beginning and the end of the century.

The proportion of white women who were married at any given time rose irregularly from a low of 57 percent in 1900 to a high of 70 percent at the peak of the baby boom in 1960. The percentage began to decline after 1960, and by the late 1990s, it was again approaching the level of 1900.

During the first half of the century, the share of black women who were married differed little from that of their white counterparts. But the incidence of marriage among black women began to fall before the baby boom was over, and the gap between black and white women widened significantly. Although the proportion of black and white women who were married differed by no more than 4 percentage points during the first half of the century, the gap expanded to 21 percentage points by 1998. This disparity was even greater for young women. Among twenty-nine-year-old women, for example, 52 percent of blacks but only 19 percent of whites described themselves as "single—never married" in 1990. Proportionately more black women than white women reported themselves as separated, and significantly more as widowed or divorced, particularly at older ages. The marital characteristics of Hispanic women, recorded separately only since 1970, were closer to those of white women than of black women.

The trends displayed in this chart, combined with trends in nonmarital births and cohabitation, suggest that by the end of the century, the black population of the United States had entered uncharted territory with respect to the pattern of their personal relationships and the composition of their households. But it is equally clear from the chart, and from a substantial volume of additional data, that similar trends were under way in the rest of the American population, both white and nonwhite, with long-term consequences that are difficult to predict.

Married Women by Race
Married women as percentage of all adult women

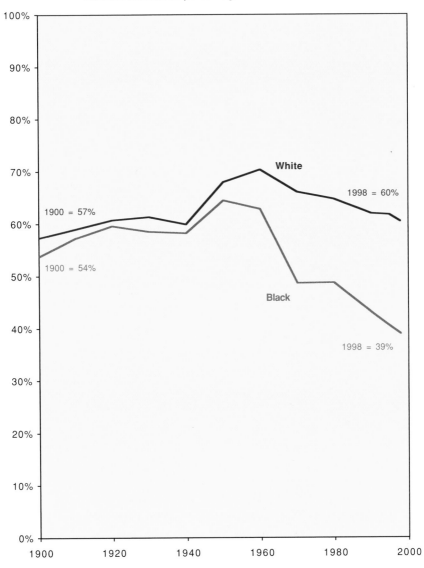

1900 = 57%

1900 = 54%

White

1998 = 60%

Black

1998 = 39%

Women's fertility declined during the early decades of the century, increased during the baby boom, and declined sharply thereafter.

Early in the century, the total fertility rate stood at 3.8 children per woman, down from about 8 children per woman in 1790. The total fertility rate is an artificial measure of the average number of children that women have during their lifetimes. Specifically, it is the average number of children that a woman would have if, throughout her childbearing years, she experienced the prevailing fertility rate for each age group. A total fertility rate of 2.1 represents the generation-to-generation replacement level, under current mortality conditions. At that rate, a woman would produce one daughter who survives to childbearing age, yielding neither population gain nor loss over time, apart from immigration.

The total fertility rate of 3.8 children per woman in the first decade of the twentieth century was part of a longer-term decline that began during the nation's industrial revolution in the nineteenth century and continued until 1930, hovering near the replacement level during the decade that followed. The baby boom brought the rate up to a peak of 3.8 children per woman in 1957, but an even sharper decline in fertility ensued after 1960. The rate dipped slightly below the replacement level in 1972 and remained in that zone thereafter, reaching a record low of 1.8 in 1976, and then rising slightly in subsequent decades. During the last quarter of the century, the fertility of U.S. women remained below the replacement level.

The total fertility rate of nonwhite women was about one child greater than that of white women in the early 1900s, 4.9 versus 3.6 children per woman. The fertility gap narrowed in the decades that followed, but returned to a difference of one child more per woman from 1953 to 1966. In subsequent years, however, the nonwhite-white gap in women's fertility narrowed steadily. In 1997, the fertility rate for nonwhites was 2.2 children per woman compared with 2.0 for their white counterparts.

Most of the reduction in fertility was accomplished technically by contraception and the advent of legal abortion. Condoms were the most common method of birth control for married couples in 1935. Oral contraceptives replaced condoms as the modal form of birth control by 1973. By the end of the century, surgical sterilization was the most common method of birth control for married couples.

Reliable statistics about abortion in the early part of the century are impossible to obtain. The gradual state-by-state legalization of abortion accelerated suddenly in 1973, when the Supreme Court struck down most restrictions in its *Roe v. Wade* decision. The number of legal abortions began a steep climb, reaching about 1.5 million in 1980, then declining somewhat to 1.4 million in 1996. The principal effect of abortion was to reduce the number of nonmarital births; more than 80 percent of abortion patients were unmarried.

Total Fertility Rate
Lifetime number of children per woman

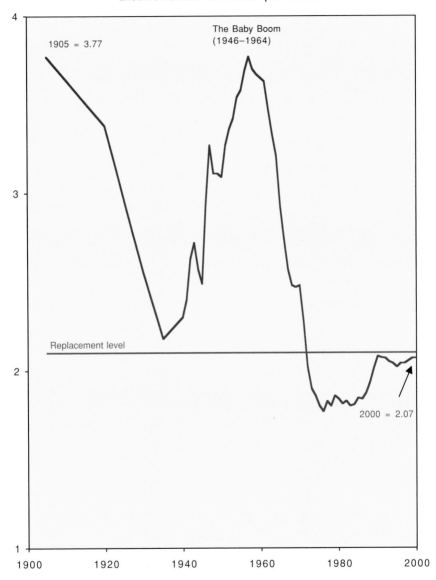

The Baby Boom
(1946–1964)

1905 = 3.77

Replacement level

2000 = 2.07

Births to unmarried women increased sharply after 1960.

What used to be known as illegitimate births in the first half of the century came to be called out-of-wedlock or nonmarital births during the second half. This evolution in terminology mirrored a massive change in social and legal norms: sanctions were no longer imposed on unmarried women who bore children, and the ancient stigma of bastardy was no longer recognized by law or public opinion.

Nonmarital births were always more common among black Americans than among whites, but as recently as 1950, the great majority—83 percent—of black mothers were married, with a husband present. The trend in the second half of the century changed significantly. Less than a quarter of black infants were born to unmarried mothers in 1960, but the comparable figure for 1997 was 69 percent.

The rise in white nonmarital births was even more startling because there was little history of even partial tolerance in this sector of the population. Until the 1960s, young women who became pregnant outside of marriage were encouraged to stay in special institutions and give up their infants for adoption. Before the advent of reliable contraception and legal abortion, any nonmarital pregnancy was considered unintended and unwanted.

This began to change in the 1960s, when intentional childbearing by unmarried women came to be tolerated, if not fully approved. By 1997, 26 percent of white infants were born to unmarried mothers, up from only 2 percent in 1960. The parents of a considerable number of these infants eventually married.

In the 1990s, the rate of pregnancy among teenagers declined significantly, particularly among blacks. From 1991 to 1997, the birth rate among women aged fifteen to nineteen declined 15 percent. This trend may well presage a decline in nonmarital births.

Nonmarital Births
Percentage of all births

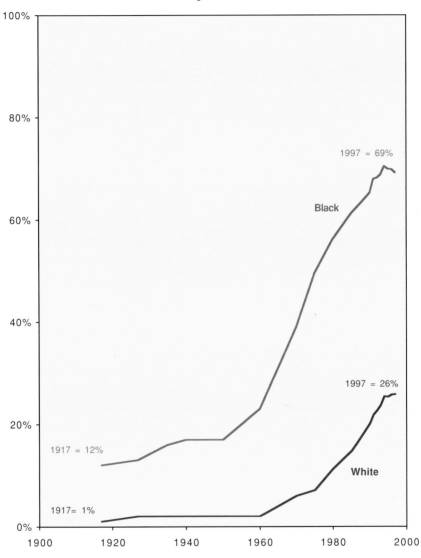

The time and attention that American parents devote to their children increased significantly.

The steady and impressive increase in the number of hours, excluding family meals, that both mothers and fathers spent with their children each day emerged from the Middletown community surveys of 1924, 1977, and 1999. The three surveys were based on random samples of married couples with children under age eighteen.

In the 1999 survey, 83 percent of fathers reported spending an hour or more each day with their children, up from 60 percent in the 1924 survey. Among Middletown mothers, 71 percent indicated that they spent two or more hours with their children every day, compared with only 45 percent of those surveyed in 1924. The change from 1924 to 1999 becomes even more impressive in light of the increased employment of married women, along with the lengthening of the school day and school year.

The simplest explanation for this change is that both men and women spent fewer hours on the job and much less time doing housework (see pages 34 and 36). As a result, they had much more free time in 1999 than in 1924 and slightly more in 1999 than in 1977.

But other factors were involved as well. The Middletown surveys provide abundant evidence that the generation gap—the cultural divide between parents and children—was much wider in 1924 than it was in 1990. Most of the 1924 parents had grown up in rural areas before the era of the automobile and the radio. Most had not finished high school. The world of their children was relatively strange to them. By contrast, most parents in 1999 had the same urban background and outlook as their children. They watched many of the same television programs and followed the same sports. Despite many areas of disagreement and conflict between parents and children, they did not have the fundamental communication problems that earlier generations experienced. Moreover, parents at the end of the century were encouraged by the educational system and the media to take parenting seriously in ways that would never have occurred to their great-grandparents.

Average Daily Father-Child Contact in Middletown
Percentage in each category

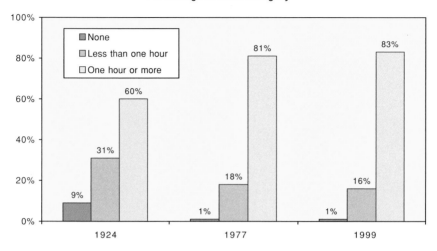

Average Daily Mother-Child Contact in Middletown
Percentage in each category

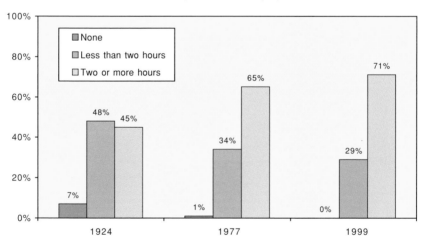

Chapter 5
Living Arrangements

U.S. households became smaller.

In 1900, barely one in a hundred Americans lived alone, and half lived in large households of six or more persons. These living patterns changed dramatically, however. Between 1900 and the end of the century, the share of Americans living alone increased from 1 percent to 10 percent, while the proportion residing in households with six or more people declined from 50 percent to 10 percent.

One reason for the trend toward smaller households was the gradual disappearance of live-in servants and elderly parents and other relatives from family households. But the most important factor was that women had fewer children (see page 84). Although very large families were not uncommon at the beginning of the century, they were exceedingly rare at the century's close. As late as 1940, one of nineteen births was an eighth or later birth. The comparable figure at the end of the century was one of every 219. While the baby boom of the 1950s raised the birth rate far above the level of 1940, it did not permanently restore the pattern of large families.

As the increasing availability of contraception, sterilization, and abortion gave women effective control over childbearing, they chose to have fewer children. Reinforcing that choice were factors such as the influx of women into the labor market, rising health and educational costs, the increased incidence of divorce, ideological considerations associated with the women's movement, and concerns about the putative effect of large populations on the environment.

Population by Household Size
Percentage of population living in each size household

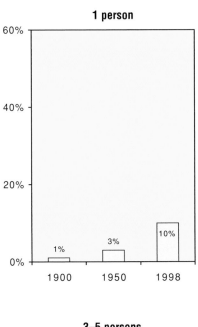

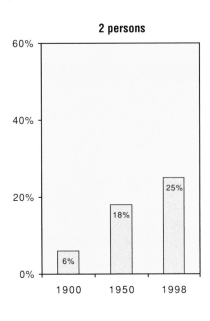

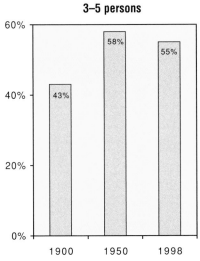

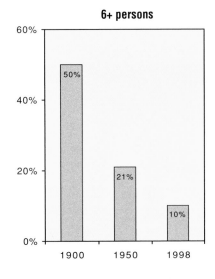

Construction of new housing surged after World War II, and Americans' preference for single-family detached homes remained strong.

Housing is one of the most cyclical of all industries, as shown in the sharp fluctuations in new housing starts per thousand population each year (see upper chart). During World War I, the Depression, and World War II, housing starts dropped to near zero. After World War II, however, the surge in housing construction was unprecedented.

The widespread development of suburban housing that got under way in 1946 was inspired by the typical American pattern of rural settlement, where each farmhouse stands alone on its own ground, with its own barns and sheds, surrounded by its own fields and woods, often out of sight of any neighbors.

The typical suburb consisted almost entirely of single-family detached houses surrounded by their own lawns, gardens, and sheds, and centered on lots that provided at least minimum separation from neighbors, even in low-income and middle-income districts. In more affluent suburbs, houses often reached baronial scale.

The average new house of 1998 was a relatively large edifice: it typically had two or more stories, three bedrooms, two and a half baths, central heating, central air conditioning, a working fireplace, and a garage. With 2,190 square feet, it was 46 percent larger than the average new house in 1970.

Although the single-family share of new housing fluctuated, the preference for the single-family detached house was relatively stronger at the end of the century than at the beginning (see lower chart). In 1998, single-family detached houses constituted 79 percent of new housing compared with 65 percent in 1900. The familiar pattern of so-called "suburban sprawl" and peripheral strip development reflects this preference and its requisite low settlement density and heavy traffic density.

New Housing Starts
New dwelling structures per thousand people each year

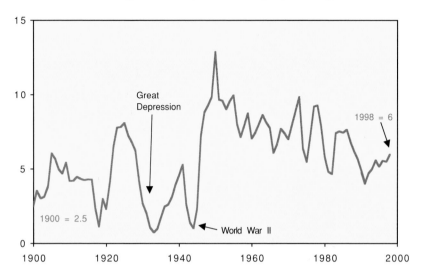

Single-Family Detached Houses
Percentage of new dwelling structures

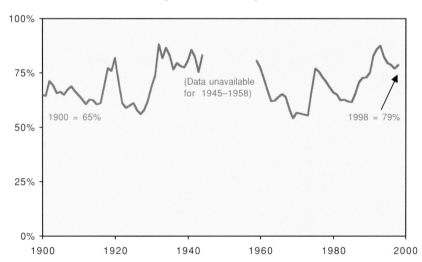

Home ownership and the use of purchase mortgages increased, as did the quality of owned housing.

Home ownership rose substantially from the beginning of the century to the onset of the Great Depression, when the trend was checked by widespread fore-closures, reduced incomes, and the virtual cessation of homebuilding (see upper chart). The decline would have been even greater without the intervention of the federal government, which began to regulate lenders and guarantee residential mortgages that met certain qualifications.

The upward trends in home ownership and mortgage usage resumed during the economic boom years after World War II, when veterans became eligible for fed-erally guaranteed mortgages on favorable terms. By 1960, more than three in five nonfarm dwellings were owner-occupied, and more than half of them were mort-gaged (see lower chart). Home ownership rose more slowly after 1960.

Because the quality of owned housing greatly exceeded that of rental housing, Americans enjoyed a higher quality of housing when they purchased their homes. Owned units had fewer structural defects than rental units, along with many more useable fireplaces, separate dining rooms, garages, and other amenities. In 1997, for example, 62 percent of owned units but only 35 percent of rental units had a dishwasher, while 60 percent of owned units but only 40 percent of rental units had central air conditioning.

Seventy percent of white householders owned their homes in 1997, compared with 45 percent of black householders and 43 percent of Hispanic householders. Even greater differences in home ownership were related to family structure: 82 percent of married-couple families owned their homes in 1997, but only 47 per-cent of female-headed families (no spouse present) did. Home ownership also var-ied strongly with age: only 18 percent of people under age twenty-five owned their homes, but substantial majorities of adults over age thirty were homeowners.

Home Ownership
Owner-occupied homes as percentage of all homes

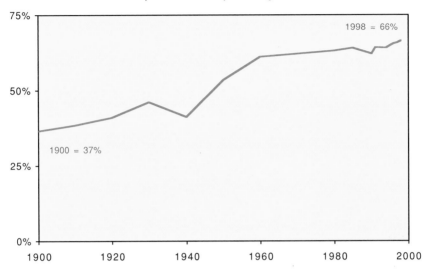

1998 = 66%

1900 = 37%

Homes Mortgaged
Mortgaged homes as percentage of all owner-occupied homes

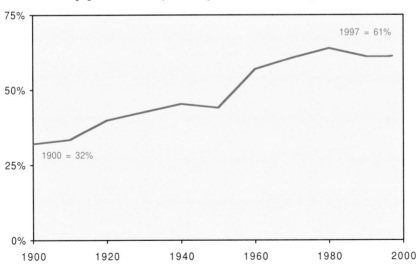

1997 = 61%

1900 = 32%

American homes were extensively mechanized.

The typical American home of 1900 did not use much more mechanical energy than the home of 1800 or even 1700. The occupants cooked and heated with iron stoves instead of open fireplaces. They read by the light of kerosene mantles or gas jets rather than candles or whale oil lamps. They used foot-powered sewing machines, which augmented the handheld needle and thread. The domestic lives of most Americans had changed very little by 1900.

In their landmark study of Middletown (Muncie, Indiana), a community whose residents enjoyed better-than-average household amenities, Robert and Helen Lynd noted that in 1890, "only about one family in six or eight had even the crudest running water—a hydrant in the yard or a faucet at the iron kitchen sink.... By 1890, there were not two dozen complete bathrooms in the city." Central heating was virtually unknown.

Between 1900 and 1950, however, a variety of conveniences brought spectacular improvements to the nation's private homes. During this time, the occupants of nearly all private homes acquired electrical service, complete bathrooms, refrigerators, central heating, and washing machines, along with vacuum cleaners, toasters, phonographs, telephones, and radios. Mechanization continued apace during the second half of the century as water heaters, color televisions, microwave ovens, and clothes dryers became standard household equipment. Tens of millions of families installed swimming pools, home freezers, personal computers, water softeners, whirlpool baths, and other technologically advanced conveniences. Air conditioning became standard, particularly in the South and Southwest, where it fostered both population and economic growth. Among its many effects, domestic mechanization greatly lightened the routines of housework, thereby enabling married women to seek work outside of their homes (see page 38).

Mechanization of the American Home
Percentage of occupied housing units with each item

Electricity
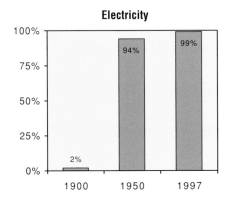

Flush Toilets
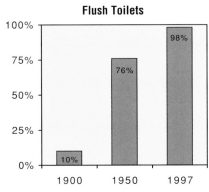

Central Heating
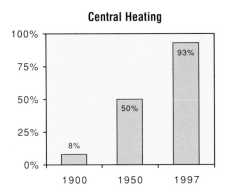

Refrigerators
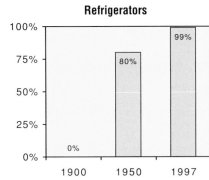

Washing Machines
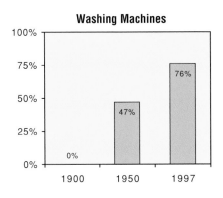

Air Conditioning
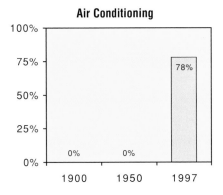

The automobile and television, introduced fifty years apart, diffused with extraordinary speed and affected virtually every aspect of American life.

Eight thousand passenger cars were registered in 1900, half a million in 1910, and nearly 10 million in 1920. No previous invention anywhere had ever spread so quickly. The first real automobile did not appear in the Lynds' Middletown until 1900; just twenty-two years later, there were two cars for every three Middletown families. Driven an average of more than five thousand miles a year in the 1920s, these automobiles had a major impact on work, leisure, religion, and sexual behavior.

By 1950, the basic open car of 1900 had evolved into a wide array of motor vehicles: sedans, coupes, station wagons, pickup trucks, delivery vans, large trucks, and buses. Further development led to the hotrod, the eighteen-wheel truck, the minivan, the sport-utility vehicle, and other variations. By the end of the century, some Americans made their homes in recreational vehicles as large as city buses, migrating seasonally between warm and cool sections of the country.

As the upper chart shows, the rise in motor vehicles per thousand population seldom flagged. The brief halt in car production during World War II was made up as soon as the war ended. Multiple vehicle ownership was not common until the 1950s, but by the end of the century, nearly half of car-owning families had two or more vehicles. More than 90 percent of American households had at least one. Nine of every ten journeys to work were made in private automobiles.

The spread of television was even more rapid. There were 8,000 television sets in the entire country in 1946. Eight years later, 26 million sets reached more than half the population. At the end of the century, 98 percent of American homes had television sets and most homes had at least two.

As the lower chart indicates, television viewing rose to a very high level by 1970 and remained at about the same level through the end of the century. In the average household, at least one set was on for more than seven hours a day, and the average person actually watched the screen for about four hours. Divining the alleged consequences of extensive television watching became an industry in itself. The list of putative effects included increased juvenile violence, the fading of regional accents, the commercialization of college sports, the growth of evangelical denominations, the decline of school homework, the commercialization of elections, and a global audience for scandal.

Automobiles, Buses, and Trucks
Per thousand population

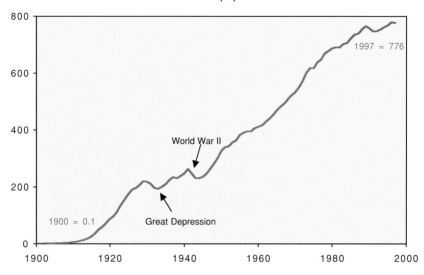

1997 = 776

World War II

1900 = 0.1   Great Depression

Households with at Least One Television Set
Percentage of all households

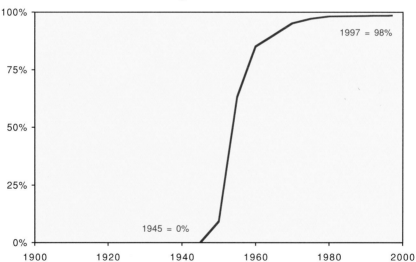

1997 = 98%

1945 = 0%

Residential mobility declined, while migration between states increased moderately.

The U.S. population at the end of the century was not conspicuously mobile. *Residential mobility*—the movement of individuals and families from one dwelling to another, whether across the street or across the country—declined during the century. As the upper chart shows, the proportion of people changing addresses from one year to the next declined from one of five in 1948, the earliest year for which national data are available, to one of six in 1999. Studies of residential mobility in several localities strongly suggest that the proportion of annual movers began to decline before 1900.

The principal factor affecting the rate of residential mobility is home ownership. Owners are much less inclined to change dwellings than are renters. Thus, as home ownership increased, residential mobility declined. A related factor is the rising average age of the population. Young adults move the most, but their share of the population was declining as the average age of the population increased.

In 1997, two of every three movers remained in the same county. Five of six movers found new homes in the same state. About 3 percent of the population made out-of-state moves in any given year. These numbers did not change appreciably throughout the second half of the century.

Migration—the movement of individuals and families between states—increased moderately during the century, as the lower chart indicates. In 1900, 79 percent of the native population lived in the state where they were born. By 1990, only 62 percent of the native population lived in their state of birth.

Residential Mobility
Percentage of population moving each year

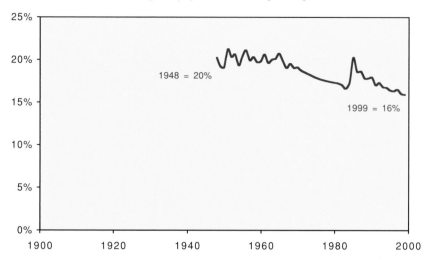

1948 = 20%

1999 = 16%

Geographic Migration
Percentage of population living in state of birth

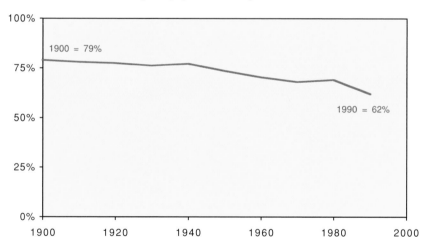

1900 = 79%

1990 = 62%

Chapter 6
Religion

Mission room with service in progress. Over the years, Americans reported higher levels of church attendance than any other developed nation. Photograph circa 1890. Courtesy of Bettmann/Corbis.

Membership in churches and other religious organizations increased slowly but steadily.

More than 150 years ago, in his *Democracy in America*, Alexis de Tocqueville wrote, "America is still the place where the Christian religion has kept the greatest real power over men's souls." That might still be said at the close of the twentieth century. Tocqueville attributed this phenomenon to the multiplicity of independent sects in the United States, unmatched anywhere else in the world, and to the equally unusual separation of organized religion from the state.

The official count of denominations increased from 186 in 1906 to 256 in 1936, when the Census Bureau stopped counting them. Although the number of denominations at the end of the century is not known, it included about eighty denominations with more than 60,000 members each. Seventy percent of the U.S. population belonged to a religious organization in 1998, up from 41 percent in the early years of the century.

At the end of the century, eight of every ten Americans were Christian, one adhered to another religion, and one had no religious preference. The non-Christians included Jews, Buddhists, and a rapidly growing number of Muslims (see page 112).

The separation of church and state became more contentious in some respects after 1960, as federal and state courts were called upon to adjudicate a wide range of issues related to religion, from the use of peyote by American Indian cults to the display of Christmas decorations on government property. The 1980s and 1990s saw the active involvement of religious groups in political campaigns, along with the presidential candidacies of two Protestant ministers, Jesse Jackson and Pat Robertson.

Membership in Religious Organizations
Percentage of population

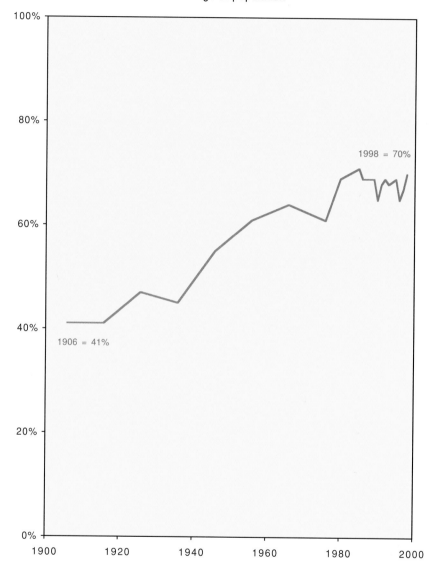

Conservative Protestant denominations grew, while mainstream Protestant denominations declined.

The chart shows the relative membership growth of the two largest Protestant denominations, the United Methodists and the Southern Baptists. Although both are large, disparate groups, the Southern Baptists are generally more evangelical and fundamentalist than the more mainstream United Methodists. While Methodist membership declined from 5.5 percent of the population in 1900 to 3.1 percent in 1998, Southern Baptist membership more than doubled during that period, from 2.2 percent of the population to 5.9 percent.

The Methodists were traditionally dominant in "the North of the South and the South of the North," while the Southern Baptist province occupied nearly the whole area below the 37th parallel (near the line between Virginia and North Carolina) from the Atlantic Ocean to the Rocky Mountains.

The decline of other mainstream Protestant denominations—Presbyterian, Lutheran, Episcopal, and the United Church of Christ—mirrored that of the Methodists. All of them had fewer members in 1998 than in 1965. Lutheran membership declined steeply and the others more moderately.

Similarly, the rapid membership growth of other churches on the right of the Protestant spectrum—Pentecostal, Evangelical, Nazarene, the several Gospel fellowships, and the smaller Baptist groups—matched that of the Southern Baptists.

Statistics on church membership take no account of the emergence of the "electronic church"—the millions of viewers of televised religious programs supported mainly by voluntary contributions. The rise of the televised church was part of the shift away from mainline denominations with increasingly liberal views on political and social issues, and toward evangelical churches that emphasized the born-again experience, a more literal interpretation of the Bible, and a "pro-life" position on abortion.

The liberal tendencies in mainline churches, combined with the conservative countercurrent among evangelicals and fundamentalists, produced a marked increase in political participation by churches and church-related organizations. It appears that the liberal positions of mainline churches were less acceptable to their members than the conservative positions of evangelical and fundamentalist groups were to theirs.

Largest Protestant Denominations
Membership as percentage of U.S. population

Methodist

1998 = 5.9%

1900 = 5.5%

Southern Baptist

1998 = 3.1%

1900 = 2.2%

The Roman Catholic share of the national population nearly doubled.

Apart from its natural increase, the growth of the Roman Catholic population was sustained by large-scale Polish and Italian immigration early in the century and large-scale immigration from Latin America in the latter decades of the century. As a result, the Catholic share of the U.S. population increased from 13 percent in 1900 to 23 percent by 1998. Unlike some other denominations, the Roman Catholic Church counts as members all persons baptized in that faith, without regard to their current religious activity.

While the Catholic proportion of the population was growing, American Catholics also experienced steep upward mobility. In 1900, American Protestants were more likely to attend college, and had higher average incomes and occupational statuses than Catholics. By 1965, American Catholics had reversed the Protestant advantage on each of these measures.

Catholic religious activity declined rather sharply between 1960 and 1975, when the proportion of Catholics attending weekly mass fell from about 75 percent to about 55 percent, the level at which it appears to have stabilized during the last quarter of the century. This decline was commonly attributed to reforms introduced by the Vatican II Council of 1962–1965, which did away with the old Latin liturgy and weakened other traditional practices such as confession and fasting. In *The Catholic Myth,* Andrew Greeley used survey evidence to show that the decline was attributable to the church's continuing prohibition of contraceptive practices, which most American Catholics do not obey.

Other signs of organizational stress in the Catholic Church included sharp reductions in the number of Catholic elementary and secondary schools, as well as the number of students they enrolled (see page 60). As recently as 1960, the great majority of teachers in these schools belonged to religious orders of nuns or monks. By the end of the century, nine out of ten teachers in Catholic schools were laypersons. At the same time, the Catholic priesthood faced a severe recruitment problem. This shortage of priests was addressed in part by enlisting laypersons as parish administrators.

Roman Catholics in the United States
Percentage of total population

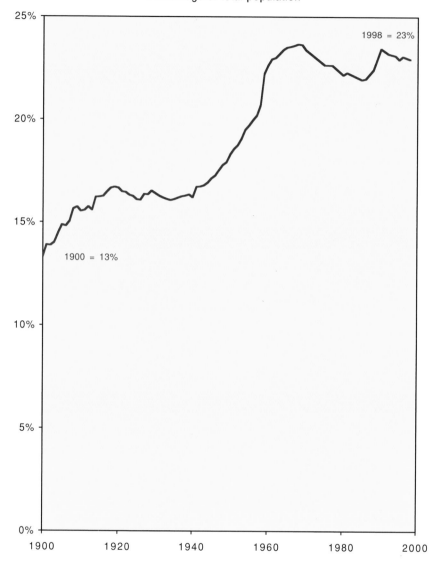

1998 = 23%

1900 = 13%

Organized religion became much more diverse as a result of the rapid expansion of Christian denominations that are neither Protestant nor Catholic and the simultaneous growth of non-Christian faiths.

The several Eastern Orthodox denominations (Greek, Russian, Serbian, Bulgarian) and The Church of Jesus Christ of Latter-day Saints, commonly known as Mormon, are Christian but distinctive in ritual and practice. As a result of immigration from Eastern European countries, membership in Eastern Orthodox denominations increased from about 400,000 at the beginning of the century to more than 4 million in 1998. During the same period, Mormon membership grew from about 200,000 to 5 million, partly because of substantially higher-than-average fertility rates, but also as the result of a vigorous missionary effort.

The three major Jewish denominations—Orthodox, Conservative, and Reform—combine their membership into a single total that is presented in estimated round numbers. Membership in the three Jewish denominations more than tripled during the century, from 1.5 million in 1900 to 5.5 million in 1998. Buddhists and Muslims registered the most spectacular growth, especially toward the end of the century. Although much of this growth can be traced to immigration, some non-Asians converted to Buddhism through New Age movements and to Islam through Black Muslim organizations. From 1950 to 1998, the number of Buddhists increased tenfold. Muslims were too few to count in 1950, but by 1998 their numbers exceeded 3 million and mosques were being erected throughout the nation.

The charts omit several Christian denominations that are not technically Protestant but seem to fall within the same religious tradition: Unitarian-Universalists, Seventh Day Adventists, and Jehovah's Witnesses. These denominations also grew rapidly during the century.

Other Religions
Membership in millions

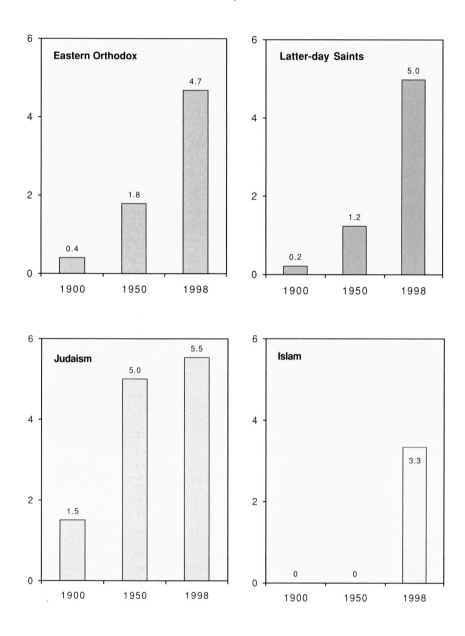

Eastern Orthodox

1900	1950	1998
0.4	1.8	4.7

Latter-day Saints

1900	1950	1998
0.2	1.2	5.0

Judaism

1900	1950	1998
1.5	5.0	5.5

Islam

1900	1950	1998
0	0	3.3

Church attendance remained fairly level in the latter decades of the century.

Little reliable information on attendance at religious services in the early part of the century is available. Beginning in 1939, however, national surveys repeatedly asked a cross-section of American adults, "Did you, yourself, happen to attend church or synagogue in the last seven days, or not?" As the chart shows, approximately 40 percent of adults answered in the affirmative, but the responses fluctuated over the years, with no discernible trend.

Responses to survey questions about religious beliefs and private devotions revealed that the overwhelming majority of Americans are religious. The percentage professing to believe in God ranged between 94 percent and 99 percent during the second half of the century. Nine out of ten respondents reported that they prayed privately, most of them daily, and similar numbers believed in an afterlife. At the end of the century, religious support groups numbered in the hundreds of thousands.

Women reported more church attendance than men, and attendance for both men and women increased with age. There was more churchgoing in the Midwest than the West, in rural areas than in cities, among blacks than among whites. But income and education were poor predictors of church attendance. In most surveys, people who went to college reported slightly higher church attendance than those who did not, although the college-educated tended to be more skeptical in their beliefs.

Weekly Attendance at Religious Services
Percentage of all adults

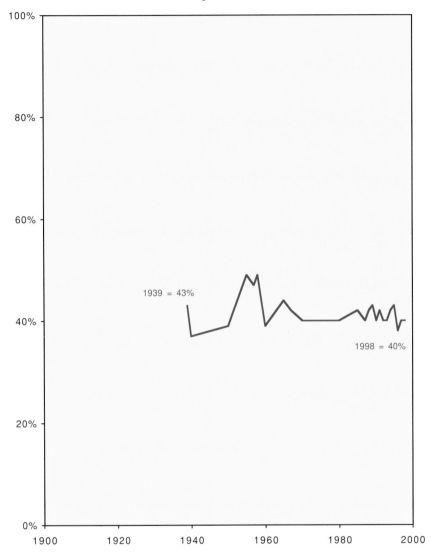

1939 = 43%

1998 = 40%

While levels of religious belief and practice remained relatively stable, the character of religion in the United States changed in important ways.

Religious ethnocentrism declined significantly during the century. As the upper chart shows, 91 percent of the Middletown high school students surveyed in 1924 were comfortable with the statement, "Christianity is the one true religion and all peoples should be converted to it." When the same questionnaire was administered to Middletown high school students in 1977, only 38 percent agreed. When it was administered again in Middletown high schools in 1999, 42 percent agreed, a statistically insignificant difference from 1977.

The majority view that one's own creed held a monopoly of religious truth gave way to a majority opinion that all religions were equally good—a view that 62 percent of Protestants and 74 percent of Catholics held in a 1996 Princeton survey.

The lower chart, which displays attitudes toward attending movies on Sunday, helps to clarify the implications of this shift in opinion. As recently as the 1920s, church membership was routinely inherited and implied obedience to a set of behavioral rules. Over the years, church membership became elective and behavioral rules lost their importance.

American religion lost much of its authoritative character. The mainline Protestant churches no longer applied their traditional sanctions against fornication, illegitimacy, divorce, homosexuality, suicide, and blasphemy. The majority of Catholics favored and practiced birth control, contrary to church doctrine.

The growth of evangelical denominations committed to biblical literalism can be interpreted as a reaction against this general trend, as the 1999 figures in the two charts suggest (see page 108). But even in that conservative sector of the religious spectrum, some old prohibitions—including those against fornication, illegitimacy, drinking, dancing, gambling, homosexuality, abortion, and illegal drug use—often appeared less enforceable by the end of the century.

Religious Attitudes
Percentage of Middletown high school students agreeing with the
following statements:

"Christianity is the one true religion and all peoples should be converted to it."

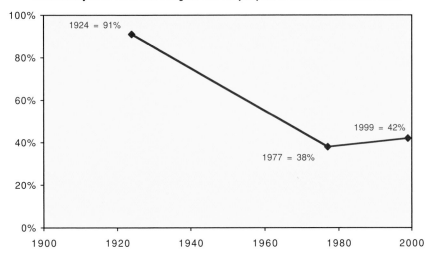

"It is wrong to go to the movies on Sunday."

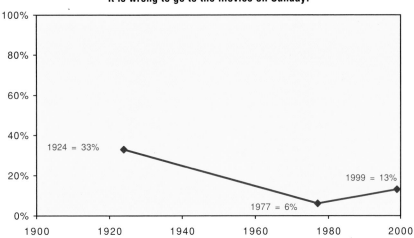

Chapter 7
Active Leisure

College students dance away their spring break in Fort Lauderdale, Florida. Photograph taken on March 20, 1962, by Ron Kuntz. Courtesy of UPI/Corbis-Bettmann.

The major professional sports of baseball, football, basketball, and ice hockey achieved extraordinary growth in the last two decades of the century.

Baseball was the dominant spectator sport during the first half of the century. The National Football League was founded in the 1920s but did not attract a significant following until after World War II. Professional basketball and ice hockey first acquired mass audiences in the 1950s.

Baseball continued to draw the largest total attendance in the latter decades of the century, but football and basketball had larger per-game shares of the television audience. According to the NFL, eight of the ten most watched television programs ever were Super Bowl games. Professional football's television revenues exceeded $1.2 billion in 1998, compared with about $600 million for basketball and about $300 million for baseball.

The rising income from television commercials and steeply rising ticket prices enriched the players. As late as the 1960s, ordinary players in professional sports were not paid much more than ordinary blue-collar workers. After 1980, however, their pay climbed rapidly. The stars in professional sports, whose large salaries were supplemented by huge fees from product endorsements, had some of the highest incomes in the nation, albeit usually for a relatively brief period of time. Many team owners benefited similarly. The Washington Redskins franchise was sold in 1999, after a particularly dismal season, for more than half a billion dollars.

Black players were barred from professional sports until 1947, when the Brooklyn Dodgers signed Jackie Robinson. At the end of the century, blacks held a majority of playing positions in basketball and large shares of the football and baseball rosters.

Other minority groups also achieved greater representation in professional sports. Among major league baseball players, for example, the proportion of Hispanics more than doubled in a decade, from 8 percent in 1987 to 17 percent by 1997.

Major Professional Sports
Attendance in millions

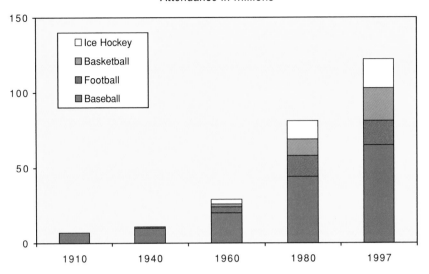

Players' average salaries in millions of 1999 dollars

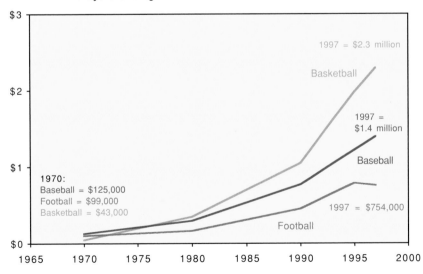

Track and field performance improved significantly.

The charts show the American records from 1900 to 1998 in four men's track and field events: the high jump, the long jump, the pole vault, and the mile run. Improvement in each of these events was intermittent. Some records went unmatched for decades; others were overturned within days.

From 1900 to 1998, the record high jump increased by 22 percent, the record long jump by 21 percent, and the record pole vault by 66 percent. The time of the record mile decreased by 11 percent. The extraordinary increase in the pole vault record was caused by technological advances that led to lighter and springier poles.

In 1900, the American records in all four of these events were also world records. As late as 1970, the American records in three of the four events were world records. In 1998, the long jump was the only one of these events in which an American held the world record. The high jump champion was a Cuban, the pole vault champion was a Ukrainian, and the fastest miler was an Algerian. But in the totality of men's events, the United States held as many records as the next four countries combined. The United States was much less dominant in women's track and field competition.

Men's Track and Field Records

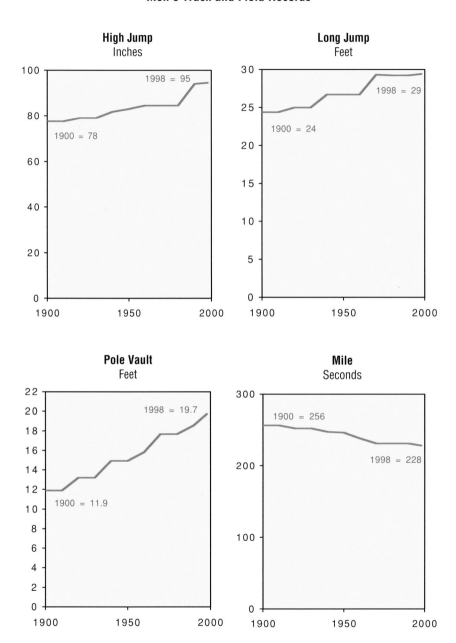

High Jump
Inches

100
1998 = 95
80
1900 = 78
60
40
20
0
1900   1950   2000

Long Jump
Feet

30
1998 = 29
25
1900 = 24
20
15
10
5
0
1900   1950   2000

Pole Vault
Feet

22
20   1998 = 19.7
18
16
14
12
1900 = 11.9
10
8
6
4
2
0
1900   1950   2000

Mile
Seconds

300
1900 = 256
1998 = 228
200
100
0
1900   1950   2000

The growth of leisure activities that followed World War II included significantly increased usage of the National Park System.

Yellowstone National Park—established by an act of Congress in 1872 in the territories of Montana and Wyoming "as a public park or pleasuring ground for the benefit and enjoyment of the people"—was the first national park anywhere in the world. It launched a movement that sparked the creation of national parks in more than a hundred countries, as well as a complex network of facilities in the United States. In 1998, the National Park System included 77 million acres, up from just 3 million acres in 1900.

In addition to large national parks such as Yellowstone, the National Park System includes national battlefields and battlefield parks and sites, national military parks, national historical parks, national historic sites, national lakeshores and seashores, the national memorial at Mount Rushmore, national monuments, national parkways, national preserves, national recreation areas, national rivers, the national capital parks, national wild and scenic rivers, national scenic trails, and national wilderness areas—altogether some four hundred sites occupying about 3 percent of the nation's land area.

In 1998, Yellowstone attracted 3.1 million visitors, primarily during the warmer months. Although this represented an increase of more than 50 percent since 1980, it was not sufficient to earn Yellowstone a place among the twenty most visited sites in the National Park System. Sixteenth-ranked Grand Canyon National Park, accessible all year round, attracted 4.6 million visitors, nearly 50 percent more than Yellowstone. The Great Smoky Mountains National Park, the third most visited site in the system, drew 10 million visitors, more than twice as many as the Grand Canyon. Still, the trend in visitor traffic at Yellowstone, shown in the chart, does reflect the trend for the National Park System as a whole.

Visitors to Yellowstone National Park
Millions per year

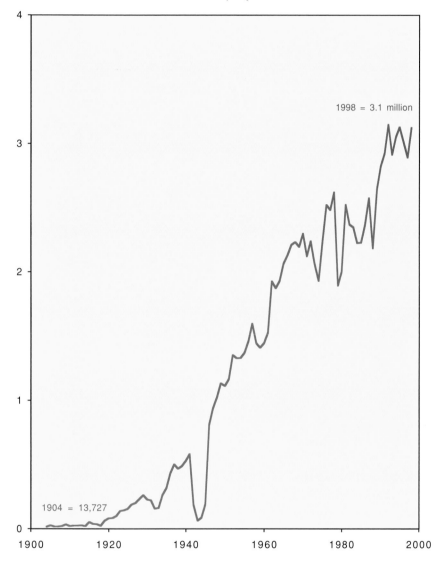

1998 = 3.1 million

1904 = 13,727

The steady increase in membership in the Boy Scouts of America peaked in the early 1970s and then fluctuated during the last quarter of the century.

The Boy Scout movement was founded in Great Britain in 1908 by Sir Robert Baden-Powell and exported to the United States in 1910, where it absorbed two organizations for boys that combined pioneer and outdoor skills with character-building exercises. These forerunner organizations were Daniel Beard's Sons of Daniel Boone and Ernest Thompson Seton's Woodcraft Indians. All three founders remained active in the Boy Scouts organization for many years and contributed to its considerable success.

Scouting was originally intended for boys aged twelve to fifteen, but over the course of time, membership was extended to younger boys through the Cub Scouts and to older boys through the Explorers and Sea Scouts. Scouts at each level progressed through a hierarchy of rank that is based on specific accomplishments, signified by merit badges and other insignia. The participation of adult volunteers was always very high. At the end of the century, there were about four adult leaders for every ten scouts.

The Golden Jamboree of Scouting held at Colorado Springs in 1960 attracted scouts from all over the world and perhaps marked the apogee of the movement. Membership peaked at 6.5 million in 1972 and then declined sharply; it increased through much of the 1980s and then declined again. In 1998, the Boy Scouts had 4.8 million members, down 26 percent from the organization's 1972 peak. In 1972, about 31 percent of the 19 million boys aged ten through nineteen were in Scouting. In 1998, about 25 percent of the 20 million boys in that age group were Boy Scouts.

Membership in Boy Scouts of America
Millions per year
(Includes Cub Scouts, Sea Scouts, Explorers, and adult volunteers)

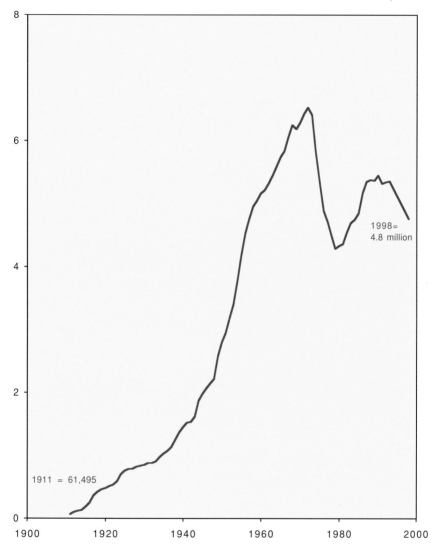

1998=
4.8 million

1911 = 61,495

The world record for land speed, not subject to any particular human limitation, increased throughout the century.

This was not a purely American record because several of the drivers, including the 1997 record holder, were British. But only the United States had the Utah salt flats and Nevada desert to provide the flat, open, hard, unpaved terrain on which massive automobiles could safely run a measured mile.

The chart shows a fairly constant rate of improvement from Henry Ford's 100 miles per hour in a seventy-two-horsepower Ford Arrow at Lake St. Clair, Michigan, in 1904 to Andy Green's 763 miles per hour in a Thrust SSC at Black Rock Desert, Nevada, in 1997. Early record-breaking cars were similar to production vehicles, with one or more internal combustion engines. By 1960, such a car was pushed to 400 miles per hour. Further advances became possible after the introduction of jet engines. At the end of the century, record-breaking vehicles resembled jet fighter planes without wings. Indeed, the 1997 record-holding driver was a British Royal Air Force pilot.

These steady improvements stood in sharp contrast to auto races on oval tracks, where the physical limitations inherent in the shape of the track and the actions of competitors imposed much tighter constraints on speed. Eddie Cheever averaged 145 miles per hour to win the Indianapolis 500 in 1998, which was nearly twice as fast as Roy Marroun's average speed of 74 miles per hour in 1911 but a little slower than A. J. Foyt's winning speed of 147 miles an hour for the same distance in 1964. The record for the Indy 500 was 186 miles an hour, set by Arie Luyendyk in a Lola–Chevy Indy in 1990.

Land Speed Record
Miles per hour

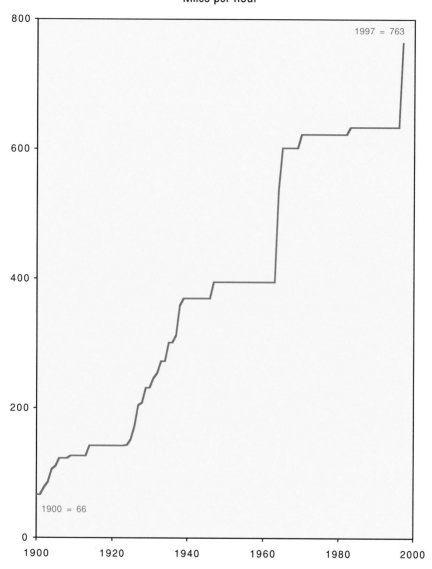

1997 = 763

1900 = 66

Overseas travel by Americans greatly increased during the latter part of the century, but the number of foreign visitors to the United States increased even more.

For most of the century, the number of Americans who went abroad for business or pleasure exceeded the number of foreigners who came to the United States. During World War II, international travel for business or pleasure almost disappeared.

In the 1950s, the jet airplane ushered in a new era of international travel. The number of foreigners visiting the United States and other tourist destinations grew rapidly. Indeed, in the last half of the century, the number of foreign visitors to the United States increased one hundredfold, while the number of American visitors abroad grew more than thirtyfold. In 1980, for the first time, foreign travelers to the United States outnumbered American travelers abroad. Although this pattern did not hold from 1982 through 1990, foreign visitors to the United States again outnumbered American visitors abroad for much of the last decade of the century. Japan, the United Kingdom, and Germany provided the largest contingents of visitors. Their favorite destinations were New York, Los Angeles, Miami, San Francisco, Orlando, Oahu, and Las Vegas.

Europe was still the preferred destination for American travelers, but the Far East was close behind. Within Europe, the leading tourist destinations were London, Paris, and Rome, as well as classic attractions such as Florence, Venice, the Swiss Alps, and the French Riviera. Business destinations were more widely distributed.

The chart does not cover travel to or from Canada and Mexico. Figures on international travel within North America are difficult to interpret because so many people made multiple or even daily border crossings. It appears that the volume of traffic between the United States and its close neighbors grew at least as much as the volume of overseas travel.

Overseas Travel
Millions of travelers per year

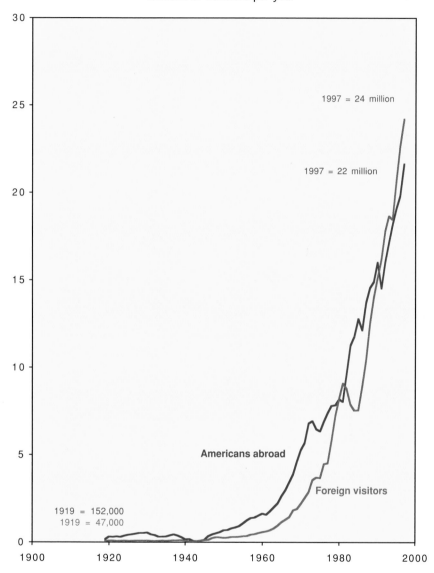

1997 = 24 million

1997 = 22 million

Americans abroad

Foreign visitors

1919 = 152,000
1919 = 47,000

BABIES DIE

When Mother is a Drunkard.

Out of Every 100 Children
24 die when mother is sober
33 to 72 die when mother drinks.

Drinking Exhausts Mother
Surviving Children are Predisposed to
Neuroses - Alcoholic and Drug Habits
Criminal Tendencies.

444 Children of Drunken Mothers
show the following death rate

	Cases	Per cent born dead	Per Cent dying before 3yrs.	Total
1st Births	80	6.2	27.5	33.7
2nd "	80	11.2	40.8	50.
3rd "	80	7.6	45.	52.6
4th to 5th Birth	111	10.8	54.9	65.7
6th - 10th "	93	17.2	54.8	72.

Chapter 8
Health

The health of children showed spectacular improvement.

Infant mortality, the ratio of deaths to live births in the first year of life, was very high in 1900, as the upper chart shows. About one of every six infants died before the first birthday. By the end of the century, only one of every 141 infants died before the first birthday (see page 4).

Much of this improvement predated the introduction of antibiotics and sophisticated obstetric methods. The most important factors in the decline of infant mortality included better nutrition and housing, central heating, pure drinking water, the shift of births from home to hospital, and the availability of feeding supplements. During the second half of the century, antibiotics, immunization, and new techniques for keeping premature infants alive drove infant mortality still lower.

Diphtheria, measles, and pertussis (whooping cough) were the leading killers of children early in the century. In 1920, more than 30,000 children died from one or the other. More than 200,000 cases of diphtheria were reported in 1921, almost 300,000 cases of pertussis in 1934, and 900,000 cases of measles in 1941. Many more cases probably went unreported.

By 1960, as the lower chart shows, the death rates for all three diseases had been reduced to zero. Diphtheria was becoming rare; measles and pertussis were still common but no longer lethal. By 1995, the incidence of measles and pertussis had fallen significantly, and not a single case of diphtheria was reported in the continental United States that year.

Other communicable childhood diseases—rubella (German measles), scarlet fever, and mumps, for example—followed similar trajectories, first becoming less dangerous and then all but disappearing. The outbreaks of acute poliomyelitis that frightened parents throughout the country every summer ended abruptly when an effective vaccine was developed in the 1950s.

Infant Mortality
Infant deaths in first year of life per thousand births

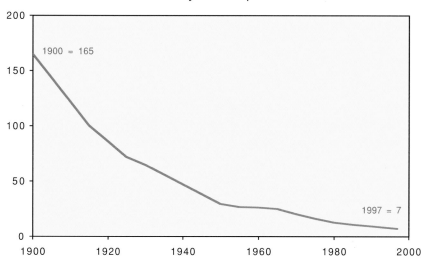

1900 = 165

1997 = 7

Common Childhood Diseases
Deaths per 100,000 population per year

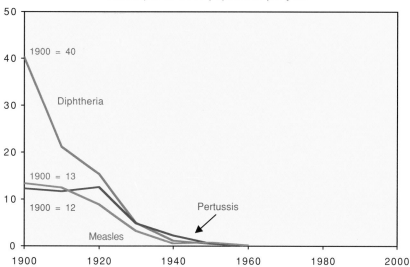

1900 = 40

Diphtheria

1900 = 13

1900 = 12

Pertussis

Measles

The infectious diseases that killed great numbers of adults in the early part of the century were largely brought under control. Cancer and cardiovascular diseases became the major killers of adults.

In 1900, tuberculosis caused more deaths than cancer. Equally lethal were the diseases known collectively as "influenza/pneumonia." Typhoid fever took thousands of lives every year. Children were by no means immune from these infections, but the majority of victims were adults. As happened with the common diseases of childhood, these diseases became much less lethal during the early part of the century, and typhoid fever, like diphtheria, was nearly eliminated by 1960.

Although the death rate from tuberculosis was close to zero, the number of new cases reported every year did not change much after 1960. New strains of the tuberculosis bacterium that are resistant to the usual antibiotics appeared in the 1990s.

Influenza/pneumonia—a catchall category rather than a single, reportable disease—included the three main types of viral influenza and several types of viral, bacterial, and fungal infections that cause pneumonia. Influenza epidemics are not uncommon; the worldwide influenza epidemic of 1918 was one of the most destructive in history. Approximately 20 million people died, including about half a million Americans. Separate death rates for influenza and pneumonia are available for the 1990s, but not for earlier years. These data indicate that pneumonia in the 1990s was about one hundred times more life threatening than influenza.

As the toll of infectious diseases diminished, the majority of Americans at the end of the century lived long enough to die of the degenerative conditions common in older individuals, such as cardiovascular diseases (heart disease, stroke, and high blood pressure) and cancer. Progress in the treatment of these conditions was necessarily slower. Cardiac therapies, both surgical and chemical, made impressive advances. Cancer therapies improved more slowly.

Major Infectious Diseases
Number of deaths per 100,000 population per year

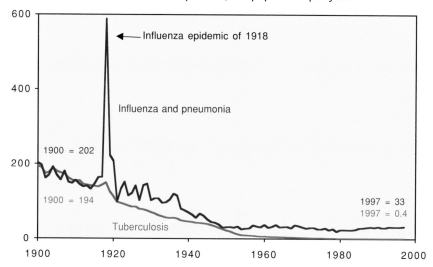

Influenza epidemic of 1918

Influenza and pneumonia

1900 = 202

1900 = 194

1997 = 33
1997 = 0.4

Tuberculosis

Major Degenerative Diseases
Number of deaths per 100,000 population per year

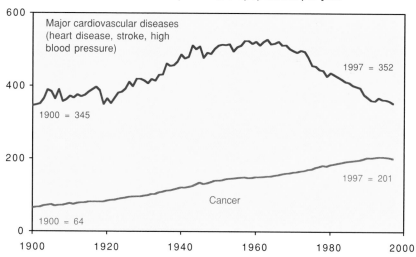

Major cardiovascular diseases
(heart disease, stroke, high
blood pressure)

1900 = 345

1997 = 352

1997 = 201

Cancer

1900 = 64

The incidence of sexually transmitted infections did not decline as much as that of other infectious diseases. In the last two decades of the century, the AIDS epidemic took a heavy toll of lives.

As the upper chart shows, the incidence of syphilis increased sharply from 1920 to 1943, when the number of reported cases per hundred thousand people reached an all-time high, presumably because of the proliferation of commercial sexual activity around military bases. Penicillin and other antibiotics brought a steady decline in the incidence of syphilis per hundred thousand people from its peak of 447 cases in 1943 to 18 cases in 1997. The 1997 rate, the latest available at this writing, was the lowest on record for this country.

The incidence of gonorrhea followed a different trend. Its incidence, like that of syphilis, reached a peak during World War II and then declined. In the 1960s, the rate began to climb again, apparently because of the increase in premarital sexual activity. The incidence of gonorrhea per hundred thousand people peaked at 441 cases in 1980 and declined steadily to 121 cases in 1997.

The most severe of the sexually transmitted diseases—indeed one of the most severe diseases known to history—is AIDS. It was first recognized in 1981, although it is believed that the first victims were infected around 1950. Homosexual intercourse was the mode of transmission for about half of the cases. Needle-sharing by drug addicts accounted for another fourth. The remaining patients were infected by contaminated blood, in utero, by heterosexual contact, or by other routes. Eighteen percent of the patients diagnosed from 1981 through 1997 were women.

Until the last few years of the century, as the lower chart shows, a diagnosis of AIDS had been a death sentence without much hope of reprieve. Of the 641,000 Americans diagnosed with AIDS through December 1997, only 256,000 were still alive at the end of that year. Perhaps a million other Americans were infected with HIV. The number of new AIDS cases began to fall in 1994 and then declined quite sharply in 1996, presumably because more of the people at risk took preventive measures. At about the same time, new medications helped in the treatment of HIV and AIDS, and the number of deaths began to decline.

Sexually Transmitted Infections
Per 100,000 population per year

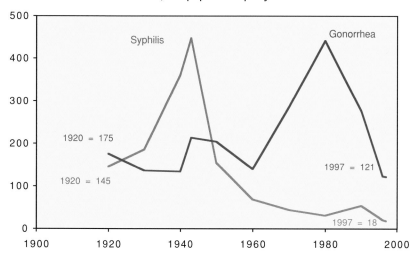

The AIDS Epidemic
Number of new cases and deaths per year

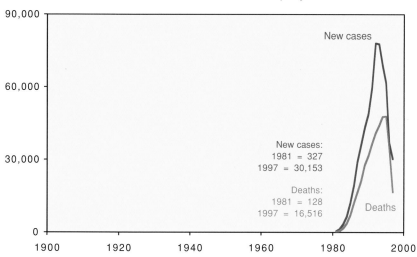

The suicide rate fluctuated with economic conditions during the first half of the century and then leveled off in the second half. Every year, more Americans killed themselves than were killed by others.

As the chart shows, the suicide rate fluctuated sharply in the early part of the century, rising during recessions and dropping during economic expansions. The suicide rate reached a high of 17.4 per 100,000 people in the depths of the Depression. After 1945, it averaged 11.5 per 100,000 people, with little annual variation.

The number of suicides exceeded the number of homicide victims by nearly 60 percent. In 1997, there were 29,700 suicides and 18,800 homicide victims. (See page 214.)

The incidence of suicide was highest among whites and males. The suicide rate for whites was about twice as high as the rate for blacks, regardless of gender or age. This disparity was greater in the early years than the later years of the century. Male suicides were four times more numerous than female suicides. The gender disparity was also greater in the early years of the century. After age sixty-five, the propensity for suicide increased dramatically for men but declined slightly for women. Older white men have a suicide probability about 500 times higher than older black women.

The periodic surges in adolescent suicide reported in the media seem to be local phenomena. Although the adolescent suicide rate increased 11 percent from 1980 to 1997, it remained below the rate for any adult age group. Suicide attempts, however, were more frequent among adolescents. One authority estimated that 98 percent of adolescent suicide attempts were unsuccessful.

Guns were the preferred means of suicide for both sexes, although by a lesser margin for women, who preferred poison until about 1970. There is considerable regional variation in suicide, with the highest rates in the Mountain and Pacific states and the lowest in the Mid-Atlantic and New England states.

Suicides
Per 100,000 population per year

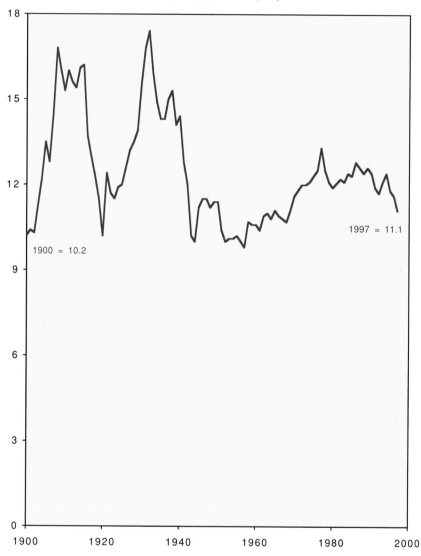

1900 = 10.2

1997 = 11.1

The per capita consumption of alcoholic beverages fluctuated.

No one knows exactly how much illegal alcohol was consumed from 1919 to 1933 when national prohibition was in force. The decline in the consumption of legal alcohol after 1980, the peak year for alcohol consumption in the United States, is well documented, however. Between 1980 and 1997, hard liquor consumption declined by about a third. Beer consumption (equivalent in 1997 to a twelve-ounce beer every day for every person in the country) declined slightly. Wine consumption remained roughly steady.

The decrease in per capita consumption of alcohol has been plausibly attributed to the aging of the adult population, the increase in the legal drinking age from eighteen to twenty-one, the campaign against drunk driving, and growing concern about alcohol's health effects. Between 1972 and 1996, the proportion of young adults of both sexes who had some experience with alcohol rose from 82 percent to 90 percent, but heavy drinking seemed to decline.

Alcohol was an important element in American rituals of sociability. The great majority of American adults and a large minority of adolescents drank on frequent occasions in the company of friends and relatives. Five to 10 percent became physiologically addicted to alcohol, typically with conspicuous damage to their health, their work, and their relationships. About the same percentages engaged in antisocial actions such as drunk driving and impulsive assault. A study by the National Institute on Alcohol Abuse and Alcoholism estimated that 107,400 Americans died in 1992 from the effects of alcohol, about a third from drinking-related injuries, and the remainder from alcohol-related diseases. A large proportion of the injuries involved sober persons who got in the way of a drunk driver or someone on a binge.

Alcohol Consumed
Gallons of each beverage per adult per year

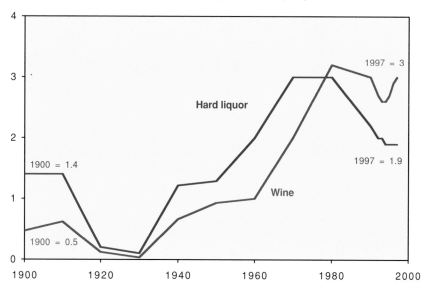

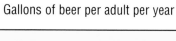

Gallons of beer per adult per year

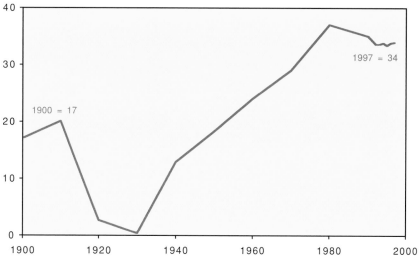

Cigarette consumption increased enormously during the first half of the century but declined when the health effects became known.

The cigarette habit spread from a small circle of urban men in 1900 to about half of the adult population in 1950. The per capita consumption of cigarettes in 1950 was sixty-six times greater than in 1900. Among twenty-five- to forty-four-year-olds in 1955, seven of ten men and four of ten women were smokers. Among other factors, this reflects the adoption of smoking by women; the substitution by men of cigarettes for cigars, chewing tobacco, and snuff; and the impetus given to smoking by the free distribution of brand-name cigarettes to members of the armed forces during World War II.

The consumption of cigarettes staggers the imagination. The 48 million smokers in the United States in 1997—about 25 percent of the adult population—consumed an average of about twenty-seven cigarettes per day. By coincidence, there were also 48 million smokers in the United States in 1970—37 percent of the adult population at that time—and they averaged about thirty cigarettes per day.

As research evidence of the harmful effects of smoking emerged, it became clear that cigarettes were far more dangerous to their users than any other legal consumer product. By the end of the century, about 430,000 deaths were attributed to smoking annually. Lung cancer, other pulmonary diseases, and cardiovascular diseases caused most of these deaths. Various studies reported that the life expectancy of nonsmokers exceeded that of smokers by six to nine years. One study found that lifelong nonsmokers lived eighteen years longer than lifelong smokers.

After the first Surgeon General's warning in 1964, smoking came under increasing regulatory pressure. Cigarette advertising was dropped from television and radio in 1971. Smokers began to be segregated in restaurants and hotels, and on common carriers around 1983. By 1990, smoking was barred altogether on commercial aircraft and soon afterward in most offices, stores, and schools. The U.S. military, which had distributed free cigarettes for decades, became a virtually smoke-free organization.

As smoking slowly declined in response to this pressure, it developed an inverse correlation with income and education. On average, smokers at the end of the century had lower incomes and much less education than nonsmokers.

Cigarette Consumption
Number of cigarettes per capita per year

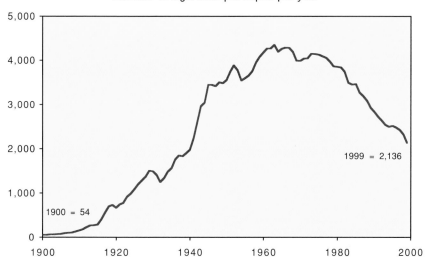

1999 = 2,136

1900 = 54

Smokers
Percentage of adults

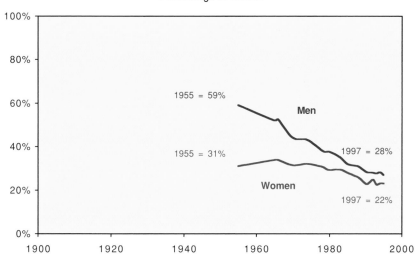

1955 = 59%

Men

1955 = 31%

1997 = 28%

Women

1997 = 22%

The popularity of psychotropic substances fluctuated.

Although marijuana was never unknown in the United States, it was not widely popular until the 1960s, when it became symbolic of the counterculture. As the chart shows, the number of first-time marijuana users grew dramatically in the 1960s and early 1970s, then declined to a somewhat lower level until the early 1990s, when it turned sharply upward again.

After a flurry of popularity at the turn of the century, cocaine all but disappeared from the American drug scene until the late 1960s, when it reappeared in the form of a white powder to be inhaled. A smokable form of cocaine known as crack began to spread through the country in the 1980s. The growth of a mass market for cocaine is suggested by the rise in federal seizures of the drug—from 45 pounds in 1967 to 263,998 pounds in 1998.

Although precise figures are lacking, estimates indicate that there were relatively more opiate addicts in the United States in 1900 than there were at the end of the century. Most were older white women habituated to "tonics" that contained generous amounts of laudanum (tincture of opium). The self-administration of opiates was entirely legal at the time, and many doctors and nurses were addicted to morphine.

Heroin, a derivative of the opium poppy, is most often injected but can be inhaled or smoked. Heroin use remained localized in big cities, especially New York, until the 1960s, when the heroin habit spread to other parts of the country. The number of new users reached a peak in 1972 and then remained fairly stable until the early 1990s, when the number of first-time users rose to its highest recorded level, before beginning a descent in 1997.

The chart also shows the number of first-time users of two classes of illegal drugs: hallucinogens such as LSD, PCP, mescaline, psilocybin, and MDMA; and inhalants, such as amyl nitrite, toluene, ether, nitrous oxide, and various spray-can products. By 1997, new users of hallucinogens outnumbered new users of cocaine and heroin combined; the number of new users of inhalants came close.

The number of new users is an excellent measure of the spread and decline of various illegal drugs. Statistics on the number of people who currently use or have ever used a particular drug are also useful. For most illegal drugs, people who have ever tried the drug outnumbered current users by about ten to one. In 1997, there were 5 million current users of marijuana—by far the most commonly used illegal drug—but 33 million people had used marijuana at some point in their lives. For less common drugs, the ratio of current users to ever-users was higher. In 1997, 700,000 people reported current usage of cocaine, but 10.5 million people reported having used it at some other time in their lives.

Illegal Drug Use
Millions of new users per year

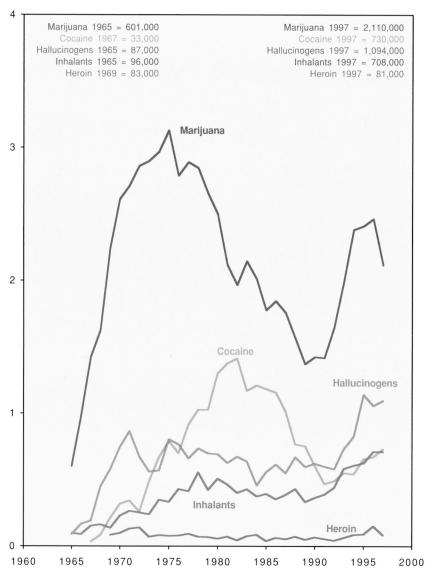

Marijuana 1965 = 601,000
Cocaine 1967 = 33,000
Hallucinogens 1965 = 87,000
Inhalants 1965 = 96,000
Heroin 1969 = 83,000

Marijuana 1997 = 2,110,000
Cocaine 1997 = 730,000
Hallucinogens 1997 = 1,094,000
Inhalants 1997 = 708,000
Heroin 1997 = 81,000

Life in America became much safer.

The death rate for nonvehicular accidents declined steadily from 94 per 100,000 people in 1907 to 19 in 1997. (See page 236 for a discussion of the decline in the motor vehicle accident rate and page 28 for a discussion of the decline in fatal accidents in dangerous occupations.)

As the chart shows, deaths from all of the most common types of home, street, and work accidents declined fairly steadily throughout the century. Accidental falls, for example, killed fifteen of every 100,000 Americans in 1910, ten in 1965, and only five in 1990. This is somewhat surprising because older people, who were proportionately about three times as numerous in 1990 as in 1910, are the most likely to suffer such falls.

Aside from vehicular accidents, falls were the leading cause of accidental death during the century. Other significant causes were drowning, fire, poisoning, and the accidental discharge of firearms. With the exception of poisoning, which shows no clear trend, accidents from all these causes declined significantly. Between 1950 and 1995, the rate of accidental drowning decreased by more than half and gun accidents by more than two-thirds, despite major growth in water sports and gun ownership.

The causes of declining accident rates have not been fully analyzed. Much of the credit must go to a better-educated population using better-engineered devices. Some credit must also go to more effective treatment of potentially lethal injuries, and to the safety-consciousness stimulated by government efforts and the litigation boom. The better-educated population using better-engineered devices presumably played the leading role, however, because most of the reduction in accidents occurred before recent advances in trauma therapy, prior to the creation of the Occupational Safety and Health Administration, and before the litigation boom.

Nonvehicular Accidental Deaths
Per 100,000 population per year

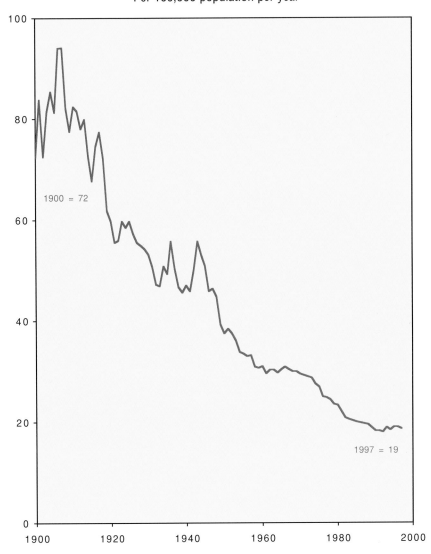

1900 = 72

1997 = 19

The use of general hospitals increased steadily from the beginning of the century to about 1980, when usage began to decline.

The hospitals that are the subject of this discussion are known variously as general or community or short-term hospitals, under either public or private management. The category excludes institutions for the long-term treatment of mental disorders, special hospitals for tuberculosis and other chronic diseases, hospices that care for terminally ill patients, and the network of hospitals run by the Veterans Administration.

In 1900, most Americans were born at home and died in their own beds. By 1930, nearly all births and a large proportion of deaths took place in hospitals, as was the case at the end of the century. During the fifty years that followed, the capacity of hospitals, measured by the number of beds, continued to grow a little faster than the population, while average occupancy rose from 63 percent of capacity in 1930 to 78 percent in 1980. Thereafter, the number of hospital patients began to decline, while community hospitals, stimulated by federal construction subsidies, continued to add new capacity. In the mid-1980s, declining occupancy forced many hospitals to close or consolidate, but not fast enough to match decreasing demand. By 1997, the occupancy rate had returned to the 1930 level and was still falling.

Several interlocking factors account for the ongoing decline in general hospital usage. The ever-rising cost of hospital care encouraged health care managers to shorten hospital stays whenever possible and to rely increasingly on outpatient visits for various types of treatment, including surgery. From 1980 to 1995, the ratio of hospital admissions to population declined by a fourth, the average hospital stay shortened from 7.6 days to 6.5 days, the proportion of hospital surgical procedures performed on outpatients increased from 16 percent to 58 percent, and the ratio of outpatient visits to hospital admissions more than doubled.

Average Daily Census of Hospital Patients
Number of patients per million population

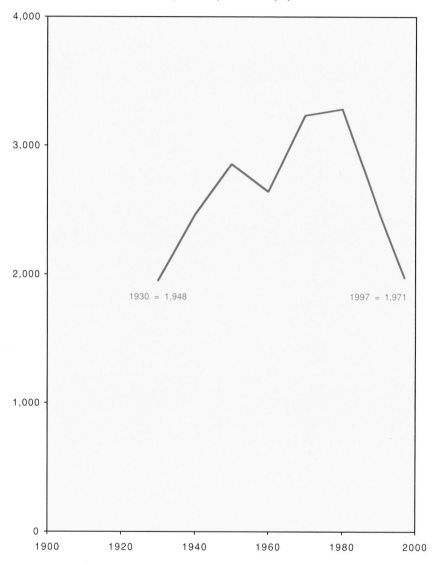

1930 = 1,948

1997 = 1,971

Health care expenditures increased sharply toward the end of the century.

When national health care expenditures were first calculated in 1929, they amounted to 3.5 percent of the Gross Domestic Product. Nearly all health care costs were borne by patients or private institutions.

By 1960, health care expenditures had risen moderately to 5.1 percent of GDP or $20 billion. A third of this total—$6.6 billion—was borne by the federal government, primarily for medical and hospital treatment of World War II veterans.

The introduction of Medicare and Medicaid in 1966 began a period of sharper growth. Per capita health care costs nearly tripled between 1970 and 1997. The cost of Medicare benefits for the elderly was borne by the federal government. The cost of Medicaid benefits for the poor and disabled was divided between the federal government and the states.

This substantial infusion of public money was one factor that stimulated price increases throughout the health care sector. During the subsequent thirty years, the annual inflation of medical, hospital, and pharmaceutical prices significantly exceeded the general rate of inflation. Total health expenditures as a percentage of GDP rose to 13.5 percent in 1997, up from 7.9 percent in 1980. Meanwhile, the share borne by the federal and state governments rose to nearly half of the total.

At the end of the century, hospital charges were the largest single component in the trillion-dollar price of health care in the United States, accounting for about half of all third-party health care payments by government agencies and private insurers. Less than 5 percent of hospital patients paid all or most of their own charges, although copayments were often substantial. Between 1950 and 1995, the average cost per patient-day in general hospitals, excluding the effect of inflation, increased by more than 1,000 percent.

Before World War II, hospital charges were billed directly to patients. As late as 1939, only 6 percent of Americans were covered by any form of hospital or surgical insurance. That percentage increased to 51 percent in 1950 and 86 percent by 1970, approximately the same level it was at the end of the century.

Among the major causes of the increase in hospital costs were improvements in medical technology, advanced diagnostic equipment, and expensive procedures such as burn victim recovery, coronary bypass surgery, organ transplants, and the care of premature infants.

Health Care Expenditures
1999 dollars per capita per year

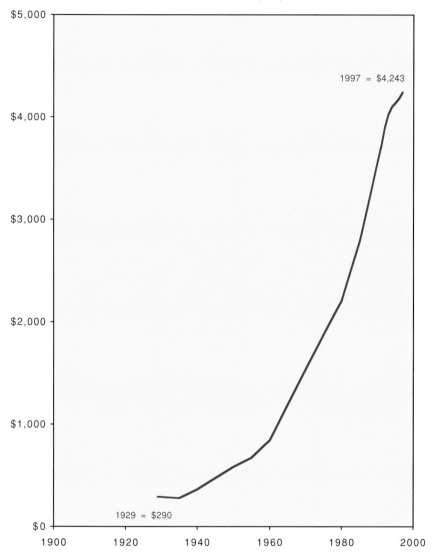

1997 = $4,243

1929 = $290

The population institutionalized for mental disorders increased from early in the century to the 1950s and then declined sharply. The number of people institutionalized for mental retardation, however, continued to grow throughout the century.

During the first half of the century, an increasing number of people with severe mental disorders were confined involuntarily for long or permanent stays in certain state and county hospitals, popularly known as insane asylums. Lacking effective methods of treatment, the behavior of inmates was controlled by straitjackets, ice baths, beatings, and isolation.

The advent of phenothiazine tranquilizers in the late 1950s, followed by other reliable chemical therapies, coincided with a shift in attitudes toward mental illness and revulsion against the inhumane conditions of the typical asylum. A new psychiatric consensus held that most mental patients could be safely accommodated in community facilities with follow-up care. As the upper chart indicates, the asylums began to empty out, but community facilities were often inadequate or absent, and many de-institutionalized mental patients were soon homeless or in prison.

In the early years of the century, most people with mental retardation lived at home in the care of their families. Only a handful of residential facilities provided care for the "feeble-minded." In 1931, the earliest year in which people with mental retardation were counted, they constituted only a small fraction of the institutionalized population. Their numbers grew steadily in the decades thereafter.

As the availability of health insurance and third-party payments for care increased, so too did the number of patients in private facilities. As shown in the lower chart, many patients with mental illness and mental retardation moved from decaying public institutions into private institutions of generally higher quality.

Patients in Mental Institutions
Thousands of patients by diagnosis

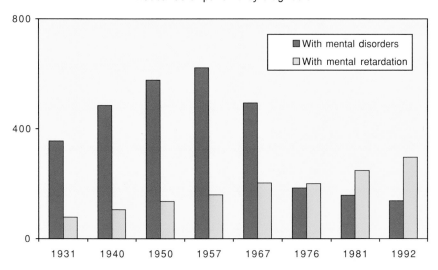

Thousands of patients by type of institution

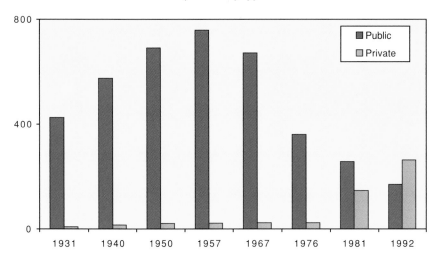

Fewer blind people received public assistance at the end of the century than in 1950. At the same time, the number of public assistance recipients with other types of disabilities increased fortyfold.

The upper chart indicates that the incidence of blindness in the American population declined during the second half of the century. There were 64 blind people receiving public assistance per 100,000 population in 1950 and only 30 per 100,000 population in 1997. These public assistance recipients, moreover, constituted a large share of all blind people.

This striking improvement was largely attributable to a decrease in industrial accidents, enormous progress in cataract surgery and the repair of detached retinas, and advances in controlling glaucoma and other diseases of the eye.

But the lower chart seems to indicate that the incidence of total disability from other causes increased substantially during the same period. The number of people with disabilities that received public assistance rose from 46 per 100,000 population in 1950 to 1,886 per 100,000 population in 1997. This increase is puzzling because it occurred at a time of declining industrial (and household) accident rates and impressive progress in the medical treatment of genetic anomalies, traumas, and mental disorders.

The most likely explanation appears to be that the criteria for classifying public assistance applicants as disabled were progressively liberalized, while the criteria for classifying applicants as blind remained essentially unchanged. (See page 196 for a discussion of government payments to individuals.)

Blind Persons Receiving Public Assistance
Number of blind persons per 100,000 population

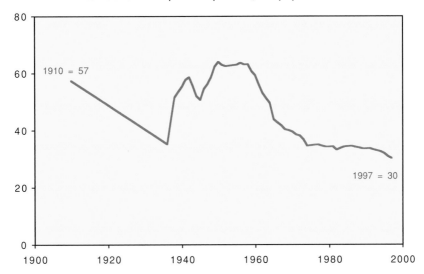

1910 = 57

1997 = 30

Disabled Persons Receiving Public Assistance
Number of disabled persons per 100,000 population

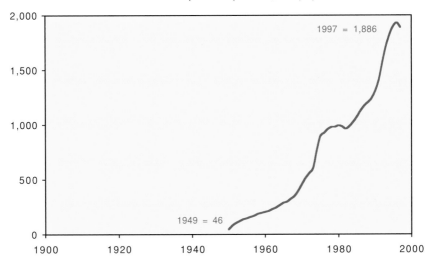

1997 = 1,886

1949 = 46

Chapter 9
Money

A woman stands before a bank teller as she prepares to make a deposit in 1929. During the Depression, 40 percent of the nation's commercial banks failed, and depositors lost more than $140 billion (in 1999 dollars). Courtesy of Corbis/Bettmann-UPI.

The real earnings of American workers improved steadily during the first three quarters of the century, but economists disagree about what happened during the last quarter.

The hourly earnings of manufacturing workers, measured in 1999 dollars, quadrupled from early in the century through the mid-1970s. As the upper chart indicates, the wages for these workers, who were somewhat better paid than hourly workers in general, rose from $3.80 per hour in 1909 to $15.38 in 1973. In the last quarter of the century, however, earnings declined by about 10 percent, to $13.90 in 1999. The chart is based on data for manufacturing "production workers" because this is the only wage series that extends back to the early years of the century.

The steady improvement of wages from the early part of the century until the mid-1970s is undisputed, but economists disagree about the trend after that time. In *The Illustrated Guide to the American Economy*, Herbert Stein and Murray Foss present a chart similar to this one, showing a decline in real earnings from 1978 to 1998, and four additional charts using alternate measures that show increases in real earnings during that period. Other economists claim to see a steep decline in those decades.

There are two aspects to this puzzle: a shift from wages to other forms of compensation and significant flaws in the way the Consumer Price Index attempts to capture "real" wages. Wages may not have increased much after the mid-1970s, but the total compensation package received by employees improved significantly, as shown in the lower chart. The difference is made up by a growing array of fringe benefits that became increasingly valuable. Benefits such as employer-provided health insurance, bonuses, stock options, child care, tuition assistance, and vision and dental benefits expanded dramatically.

To complicate matters further, experts are divided about whether the Consumer Price Index measures inflation accurately (see page 176 for a discussion of how the CPI is constructed). If the CPI significantly overstates inflation, then real earnings may actually have increased somewhat since the mid-1970s.

Real Earnings in Manufacturing
Average hourly pay of production workers in 1999 dollars

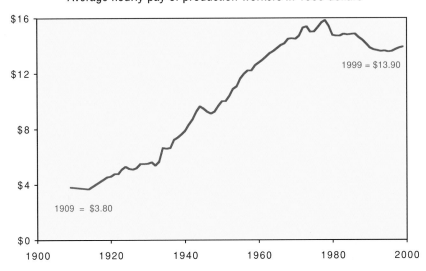

1999 = $13.90

1909 = $3.80

Employment Cost Index
Total compensation package adjusted for inflation

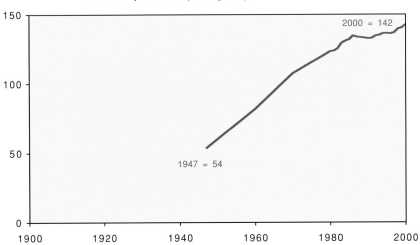

2000 = 142

1947 = 54

Although the equalization of women's and men's earnings proceeded slowly, the process accelerated after 1980. The gap between the average earnings of white male workers and black male workers also narrowed.

The ratio of female to male earnings moved upward during most of the century, except for a moderate downturn from 1955 to 1980, when women were entering the labor force in large numbers. After 1980, however, the equalization of women's and men's earnings accelerated. Legislation mandating equal employment criteria and promotion opportunities, equal pay for equal work, and equal access to occupational training, especially in privileged occupations, was instrumental in this change.

In 1997, the earnings of women working full-time year-round were equal to only 74 percent of the earnings of male full-time, year-round workers. This comparison, however, ignored large differences between the average qualifications of men and women in the labor force. When women were compared with men of equivalent education and work experience, much of this difference in earnings disappeared. Among Americans aged twenty-seven to thirty-three, for example, women who never had a child earned an average of 98 percent of men's earnings.

Data on earnings by race for the early years of the century are not available, but anecdotal evidence suggests that by 1940 the earnings gap between black and white males had narrowed considerably. From 1940 to 1980, the ratio of black male earnings to white male earnings increased substantially. There was a brief decline around 1990, but by 1997, the earnings of black men working full-time, year-round had climbed to 76 percent of the earnings of their white counterparts.

Some of the difference between the earnings of black and white males can be traced to their levels of education. Although the difference in educational achievement between black and white males was much smaller at the end of the century than at midcentury, the education gap remained substantial. In 1998, 27 percent of white males, but only 14 percent of black males, had completed at least four years of college.

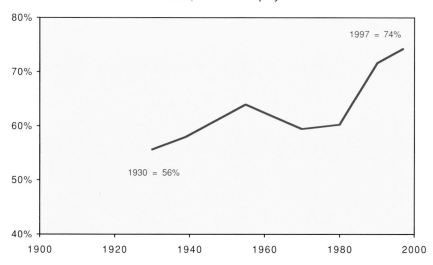

Women's Earnings as Percentage of Men's Earnings
Year-round, full-time employment

1997 = 74%

1930 = 56%

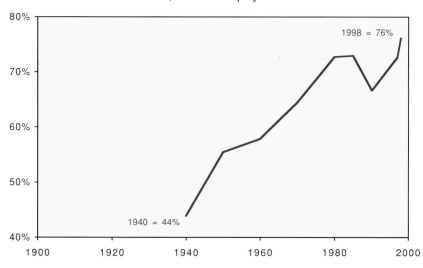

Black Earnings as Percentage of White Earnings
Year-round, full-time employment of men

1998 = 76%

1940 = 44%

The real incomes of middle-income families at the end of the century were five times greater than those of middle-income families in 1900.

Middle-income families—those in the middle fifth of the aggregate income distribution—saw their average annual incomes, measured in constant dollars, increase from more than $15,000 in 1929 to more than $47,000 in 1998. National data on family or household income were not available before 1929. Fairly reliable estimates of per capita Gross National Product, however, show a rise of about 65 percent from 1900 to 1929, indicating that the mean income of middle-income families had registered significant improvement even before 1929.

The only major dip in this upward trend occurred during the Depression of the 1930s, but income levels recovered by the end of that decade. Wartime shortages and price controls kept the trend relatively flat during the 1940s. In the almost unbroken prosperity of the 1950s and 1960s, the real incomes of middle-income families nearly doubled. After 1972, they continued to rise, but at a slower rate.

These calculations do not take into account a variety of factors that affect real income, such as taxes, social services, fringe benefits attached to employment, and the costs of working. If each of these could be accurately calculated, the trend in real income would shift in one direction or another. On the one hand, the tax burdens of middle-income households were distinctly heavier at the end of the century than in earlier years, and the costs of working were much greater for the dual-earner families of the 1990s than for the sole breadwinners of the 1950s. On the other hand, most middle-income families at the close of the century benefited not only from government subsidies (guaranteed mortgages, Social Security payments, Medicare, student loans) that were not available earlier in the century, but also from the fringe benefits attached to full-time jobs, which were far more extensive and valuable than they had been in the past.

Nor is the quality of available goods factored into calculations of real income. Many of the goods and services that middle-income families purchased at the end of the century, such as cameras or heart surgery, were incomparably superior to those available at the beginning or middle of the century. Others, such as cellular telephones and in vitro fertilization, did not exist until the last decade of the century. When all these criteria are assessed, the vast improvement in the material circumstances of middle-income families during the century is unmistakable.

Average Income of Middle-Income Households
1999 dollars per year

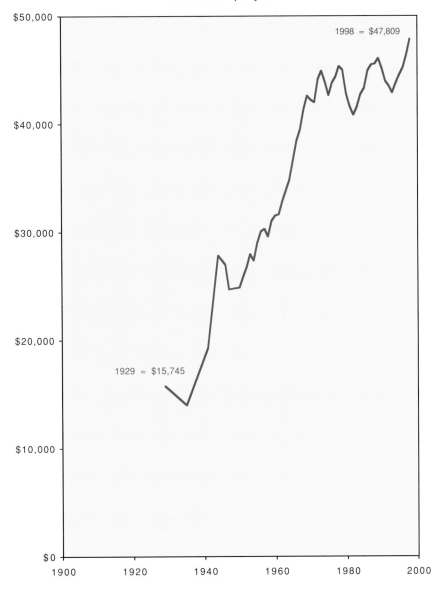

As real incomes increased during the century, Americans spent smaller shares of their incomes on food and clothing, but larger shares on medical care and transportation.

Engel's Law, proposed in the 1857 by German economist Ernst Engel after he studied the budgets of Belgian families, states that the lower a family's income, the higher the proportion spent on food, and vice versa.

As the charts show, Engel's Law remains valid. The families surveyed in 1901 spent nearly half of their incomes on food. As family income grew, that proportion declined steadily until 1997, when food accounted for only a sixth of personal consumption expenditures. The share of income spent on clothing also declined regularly. The share devoted to transportation increased sixfold from 1901 to 1950 and remained at that level through the end of the century.

The share of expenses dedicated to having and maintaining a home remained remarkably constant over the century, while the average residential space per person soared upward (see page 94). Household operations include light, heat, gas, electricity, and telephone bills, together with furniture, appliances, and cleaning materials.

Medical care costs were so small in 1901 that they were included in the "sundries" category in questionnaires. The share of personal consumption expenditures devoted to health care doubled from 1929 to 1970 and then doubled again from 1970 to 1997. The residual category is of particular interest. It includes a wide variety of elective expenditures, from life insurance premiums to football tickets, church collections, and foreign travel. These discretionary expenditures probably have a greater effect on satisfaction with one's economic situation than the absolute level of income.

Personal Consumption Expenditures
Percentage spent on each category

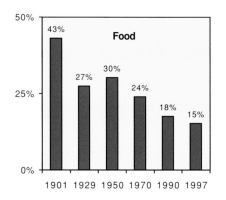

Food

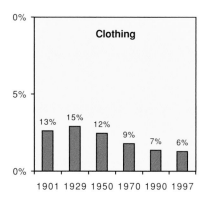

Clothing

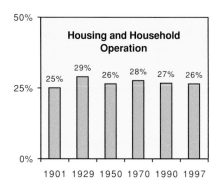

Housing and Household Operation

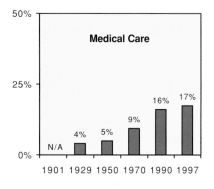

Medical Care

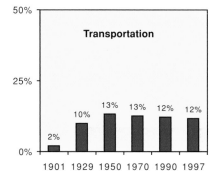

Transportation

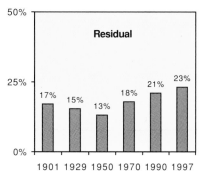

Residual

Private philanthropy increased more than fivefold in the last half of the century.

The enormous expansion of government funding for education, health, research, welfare, and the arts did not dampen private funding.

A surprising trend in private philanthropy, shown in the chart at left, is the predominance of gifts by living donors, which greatly exceeded the combined total of charitable bequests, corporate gifts, and foundation grants. The major increase in private fortunes after 1980 made it possible for individuals to make gifts of unprecedented scale. In the capital campaigns that were conducted almost continuously by major universities, a contribution of $1 million was not unusual.

Corporate philanthropy was almost unknown before 1950. Indeed, it was often considered an illegitimate misuse of money belonging to stockholders. But during the second half of the century it became almost obligatory for large business enterprises to display a list of good works that were not necessarily restricted to their own employees or the local community.

In 1950, the combined worth of all U.S. foundations was less than $3 billion; only four had more than $100 million in assets. In 1995, their combined worth totaled $227 billion, and about 300 foundations had assets of more than $100 million each.

The principal beneficiaries of private donors were churches and other religious organizations. The largest share of corporate gifts and foundation grants went to educational institutions, followed by human service agencies, hospitals and health research, art and culture. Although the bulk of philanthropic contributions in every category went to well-established organizations, some new activities were funded as well.

Philanthropic Donations
Billions of 1999 dollars per year by type of donor

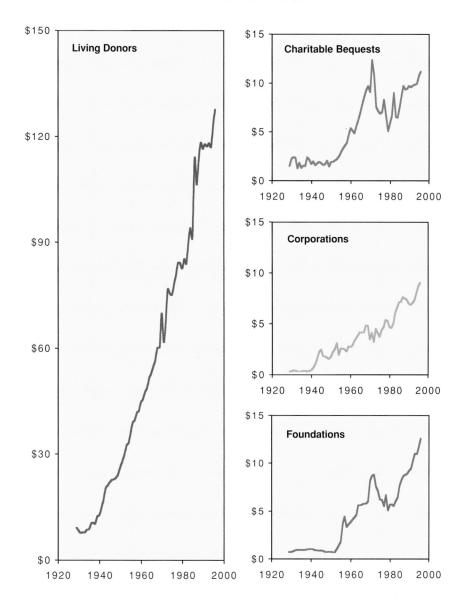

The ratio of personal debt to personal income reached a peak in the 1990s. The bankruptcy rate climbed slowly after World War II and more rapidly during the last two decades of the century.

The ratio of the aggregate debt owed by individuals to the aggregate income received by individuals was relatively low in the early part of the century. It rose to a then-unprecedented level of .52 at the depth of the Depression in 1933, and then declined until 1945. By 1960, the ratio exceeded that of 1933, and in the last two decades of the century, it rose to record levels.

The 1998 ratio of 0.9 signifies that the total debts owed by individuals were close to their total annual incomes. At more than $7 trillion, personal debt exceeded the federal debt by a considerable margin.

Approximately three-quarters of this personal debt represented residential mortgages, most of them long-term and borrowed at moderate interest rates. The effective interest rate was even lower because mortgage interest is deductible from taxable income.

The remainder of the debt burden was composed of short-term consumer credit and home equity loans. Earlier in the century, retail merchants and service suppliers carried consumer credit accounts and installment purchase loans at nominal or no interest. In the last two decades of the century, most credit of this type was offered through credit card companies. Home equity loans, an innovation of the 1980s, represented a small but growing fraction of consumer debt, at rates substantially lower than those charged by credit card companies.

The lower chart shows all bankruptcies—municipal, corporate, farm, nonprofit, and individual—but most bankruptcies were individual. The quadrupling of bankruptcies in the last two decades of the century is partly attributable to the liberalization of the law under the Bankruptcy Reform Act of 1978 on the one hand, and to credit card debt, medical costs for catastrophic conditions, and legalized gambling on the other. Beginning in the 1980s, credit card lenders abandoned traditional measures of creditworthiness in exchange for high interest rates on revolving card balances. During the same period, legalized gambling became available throughout the United States. Both of these developments encouraged some consumers to accumulate debts they could not repay, and bankruptcy offered them a fresh start. At the same time, a booming economy led to more business startups, some of which failed and went to bankruptcy court (see page 246).

Ratio of Personal Debt to Personal Income

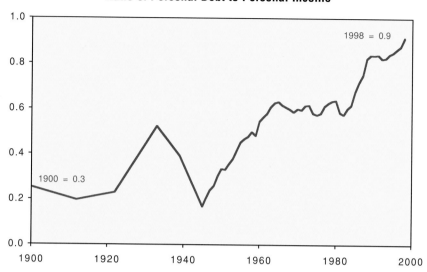

1998 = 0.9

1900 = 0.3

Bankruptcy Rate
Bankruptcies per thousand population per year

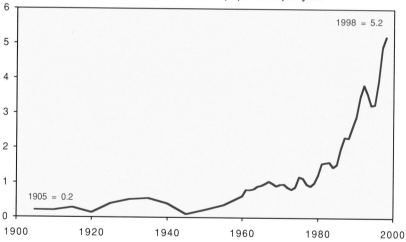

1998 = 5.2

1905 = 0.2

Income inequality decreased throughout much of the century, increased from 1980 to 1995, and then leveled off.

The upper chart compares the mean income, in 1999 dollars, of families in the upper 5 percent of the national income distribution with the mean income of families in the lower 40 percent of the distribution. Both groups experienced substantial increases in their incomes after 1929, and both suffered a slight loss of income during the 1970s and into the recession of 1982. But after 1982, the two groups diverged markedly.

The average income of families in the lower 40 percent of the national income distribution increased 12 percent between 1982 and 1998, from $19,243 to $21,520. The picture is quite different for families in the upper 5 percent of the national distribution, however. Between 1982 and 1998, the average income of these affluent families rose 77 percent, from $143,052 to $252,582.

The lower chart tells this story in a different way. It compares the share of the total income of all American families that went to the affluent families in the upper 5 percent of the income distribution with the share that went to the nonaffluent families in the lower 40 percent of the distribution. In 1929, the aggregate income of the affluent 5 percent was more than twice the aggregate income of the nonaffluent 40 percent. This difference declined and then disappeared until 1985, when the affluent share began to rise again. But in the 1990s, the affluent share stabilized at 21 percent and the nonaffluent share leveled off at 14 percent.

This development can be plausibly attributed to several factors, including changing family structure, tax policy, global trade, technology, immigration, and the decline of labor unions, but it is exceedingly difficult to determine the relative weights of each factor. Neither chart takes account of noncash income such as health benefits.

Average Incomes of Affluent and Nonaffluent Families
Average income of each group in 1999 dollars, logarithmic scale

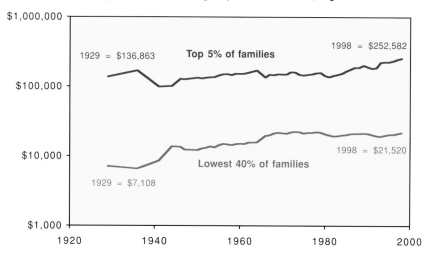

Income Shares of Affluent and Nonaffluent Families
Percentage of total national income going to each group

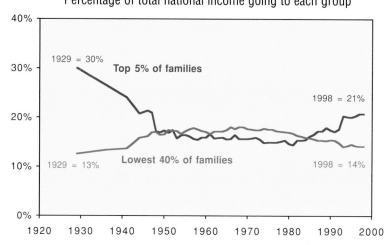

Poverty decreased significantly from 1959, when official measurements began, until 1973, when it increased moderately and remained at a slightly elevated level during the subsequent two decades. Between 1993 and 1999, however, the incidence of poverty declined by more than a fifth.

The federal government's poverty threshold is determined by calculating the annual cost of a basic list of groceries for a reference family of four (two adults and two children) and then multiplying that number by three. Families whose annual incomes are less than this amount are considered "below the poverty line." The amount of income is adjusted for the number and ages of the people living in the household, along with other factors. The chart shows the proportion of the population living in households that were below the poverty line.

In the United States, the incidence of poverty was related to race and ethnicity, location, family composition, age, and education. The incidence of poverty was more than twice as high among blacks and Hispanics than among whites. The central districts of metropolitan cities had the most poverty. The suburbs of the same cities had the least, while small towns and rural areas had poverty rates that fell between those of the inner cities and their suburbs. Far fewer married than unmarried people were poor. People living alone were more likely to be poor than people in families, and women were more likely to be poor than men. Children and young adults aged eighteen to twenty-four were more likely to be poor than any other age group. People who did not complete high school were more likely to be poor than those who attended college. These effects were cumulative so that, for example, a black unmarried mother under age twenty-four was likely to be poor, while a married white college graduate between the ages of forty-five and fifty-four was almost certain not to be.

In 1999, the incidence of poverty fell to its lowest level in two decades. It declined among every racial and ethnic group, falling to a record low among blacks and matching historic lows among Hispanics. The poverty rate was the lowest since 1979 among children, and the lowest on record for Americans aged sixty-five and older. The incidence of poverty fell to record lows for married-couple families as well as families headed by women with no husband present. Much of this significant decline in poverty occurred among residents of central cities.

Poverty, as defined by the government's monthly income threshold, was a permanent or semi-permanent condition for some Americans, but a transient experience for many others. During 1993 and 1994, the latest years for which these data are available, 30 percent of the population was poor for at least two consecutive months. However, only 5 percent of the population was poor for the entire twenty-four months.

The government's measure of poverty is simple but rather crude. Its most basic flaw is the measure of income, rather than expenditure or standard of living. Households "below the poverty line" actually spend considerably more money than they take in: they draw down assets, borrow money, and avail themselves of nonincome benefits such as food stamps and Medicaid.

Incidence of Poverty
Percentage of each group below poverty income threshold

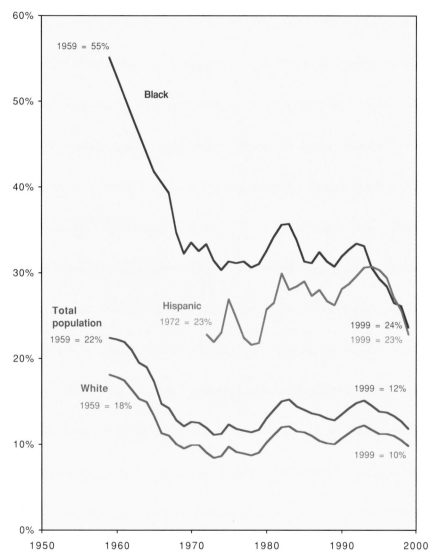

Inflation alternated with deflation and periods of price stability from 1900 to 1955. Every year thereafter witnessed some inflation, although at substantially reduced levels toward the end of the century.

The century's most extreme increases in consumer prices were registered before, during, and immediately after American participation in World War I. Serious deflation was associated with the Panic of 1907, the recession of 1921–22, and the first part of the Depression of the 1930s. After 1955, consumer prices rose every year, but the amount of the increase varied from a minimum of eight tenths of 1 percent in 1959 to a maximum of 13.5 percent in 1980. The amplitude of these variations subsided in the 1980s and 1990s.

The chart shows the year-to-year change in the Consumer Price Index, commonly known as the inflation rate. The CPI is constructed by combining the price indices of eight classes of goods and services that are components of the budget of nearly all consumer units: food and beverages; housing; clothing; transportation; medical care; recreation; education and communication; and "other goods and services." The latter category is composed primarily of personal expenses. The eight broad categories are broken down into smaller categories. Every month, prices for approximately 71,000 goods and services are collected from 22,000 outlets in 44 geographic areas to construct the price index.

The eight categories that are combined in the CPI do not necessarily move in tandem. Between 1980 and 1998, for example, the CPI rose by 98 percent, while the price of medical care rose by 223 percent and the price of clothing increased by 46 percent. Nor do the prices of individual items within each category move in tandem. Between 1980 and 1998, the price of tomatoes increased 192 percent, while the price of eggs went up 53 percent.

The prices of rare objects of all kinds, from baseball cards to Old Master paintings, frequently exhibited inflation rates much higher than those of the CPI, in some cases hundreds of times higher. Similarly, the prices of rare services, from the stud fees of winning racehorses to the hourly rates of corporate lawyers, often exceeded the prices of ordinary commodities by wide margins.

Inflation Rate
Annual percent change in Consumer Price Index

1999 = 2.2%

Price stability

Chapter 10
Politics

A staffer from Dr. George Gallup's Institute
of Public Opinion takes notes during an inter-
view. Gallup did not invent scientific sampling, but he was the first to report results
publicly and regularly through his syndicated
newspaper column "America Speaks."
Courtesy of the Gallup Organization.

Democrats and Republicans shared presidential election victories almost equally. Voter participation declined from 1900 to 1912 and then fluctuated during the rest of the century with no clear trend.

The twenty-five presidential elections of the twentieth century produced twelve Democratic and thirteen Republican presidents (see upper chart). In seven of these elections, the winning margin in the popular vote was 5 percent or less. In the 1960 and 1968 elections, with Richard M. Nixon as the Republican candidate in both, the winning margin was less than 1 percent. In two elections, the tally was so close that the ultimate losers, Charles Evans Hughes in 1916 and Thomas E. Dewey in 1948, were announced as the winners on the morning after the election.

American voters seemed to prefer a two-party system and were often reluctant to cast their votes for third parties. Nevertheless, third-party candidates had considerable influence in four of the century's twenty-five presidential elections. Theodore Roosevelt won nearly 30 percent of the popular vote in 1912. Robert La Follette captured 17 percent of the vote in 1924. George Wallace garnered 14 percent of the vote in 1968. Ross Perot won 19 percent of the vote in 1992. In three of these elections—1912, 1968, and 1992—the winning candidates garnered a plurality, rather than a majority, of the votes cast.

The American system is unique among industrial democracies. It is characterized not only by the long-term balance between the two major parties and resistance to third-party candidates, but also by an electoral college system that maintains the "winner-take-all" principle in every state.

Voter participation—the ratio of actual voters to the total number of eligible voters—is difficult to calculate. Ballot-box stuffing and miscounts cause errors in the count of actual voters, but these problems are trivial compared with the difficulty of estimating the number of eligible voters. Early in the century, each state decided independently who was qualified to vote in national elections. A number of states gave the vote to resident aliens and a few to women. Residence, age, and literacy requirements varied from state to state, as did the administrative practices that in some states excluded blacks, American Indians, and Asian Americans from the voting population.

Amendments to the Constitution, federal legislation, and a series of federal court decisions that struck down literacy and residency requirements eliminated much of the discretion the states had enjoyed. But substantial differences among states remained. In 2000, for example, fourteen states denied the vote to convicted felons.

For every presidential election since 1916, several official estimates of voter participation are available. The lower chart shows the maximum and minimum estimates of participation in each election. Both series indicate that voter participation was exceptionally low in 1920, 1924, 1948, and 1996, and exceptionally high in 1952 and 1960.

Popular Vote in Presidential Elections
Percentage of votes cast

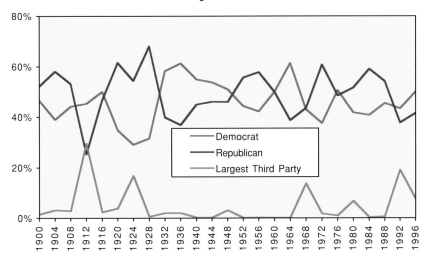

- Democrat
- Republican
- Largest Third Party

Voter Participation in Presidential Elections
Percentage of eligible voters

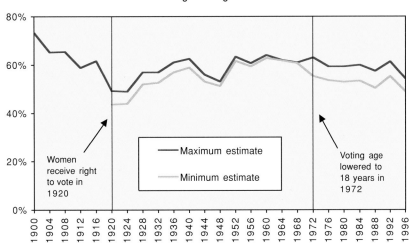

Women receive right to vote in 1920

- Maximum estimate
- Minimum estimate

Voting age lowered to 18 years in 1972

Control of the U.S. House of Representatives and the U.S. Senate oscillated between the two major parties.

In thirty-two of the fifty Congresses elected from 1900 to 1998, Democrats held a majority of seats in the U.S. House of Representatives, elected the Speaker, and dominated the committees. The Democrats held their largest majority in the Seventy-fifth Congress (1937–38), with 333 Democrats to 89 Republicans and 13 third-party members. The Democrats ruled the House of Representatives without a break from 1955 to 1995.

The periods of Republican advantage occurred earlier in the century, from 1901 to 1911 and from 1917 to 1933. The latter period began and ended with majorities of fewer than ten seats. The Republicans held their largest majority, 300 to 132, in 1921.

Dramatic turnarounds occurred in 1920, when the Republicans gained 64 seats, and in 1932, when the Republicans lost 99 seats. In the postwar election of 1946, the Democrats lost 55 seats, but in the following election, they gained 75. The "Republican Revolution" of 1994 was comparable in scale. The GOP gained 54 seats to take control of the House for the first time in thirty years, and then maintained control in the 1996 and 1998 elections.

The Democrats held a majority of U.S. Senate seats in twenty-nine of the fifty Congresses elected during the century. As in the House, the largest Democratic majority was achieved in the Seventy-fifth Congress (1937–39), with 75 Democrats to 17 Republicans and 4 third-party Senators. The longest period of Democratic control lasted from 1955 until 1980.

The Constitution requires a two-thirds vote in the Senate to ratify a treaty, and the rules of the Senate require a supermajority to close off debate. In more than 80 percent of the century's Congresses (forty-two of fifty), neither party had a two-thirds majority in the Senate. In eighteen of those Congresses, the majority party had a margin of no more than ten seats. The Senate, by its structure, is more inclined to bipartisan compromise than the House.

The House elects its own Speaker, but the vice president of the United States presides over the Senate and casts the deciding vote in the case of a tie. In fifteen of the century's fifty Congresses, the vice president did not belong to the same party as the Senate majority.

U.S. Senate
Seats held by each party

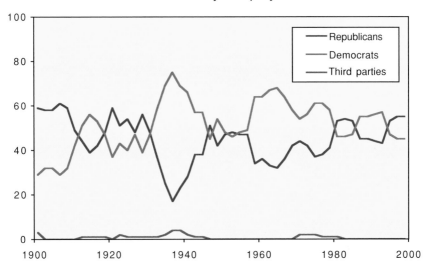

U.S. House of Representatives
Seats held by each party

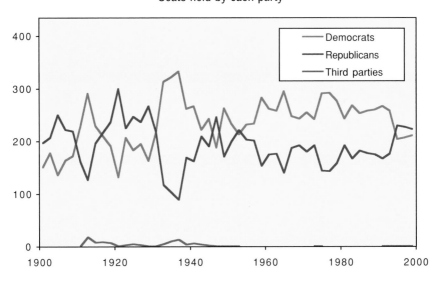

After women first entered Congress early in the century, their numbers increased slowly and then rose rapidly.

The first woman member of Congress, Jeannette Rankin of Montana, was elected in 1916. That was four years before the adoption of the Nineteenth Amendment to the Constitution enfranchised women nationally, but Montana and some other states had already done so.

Congresswoman Rankin served one term when first elected and another when she was elected again in 1940. In her first term, she was the only woman in the House. In 1941, she had eight female colleagues, and together they held less than 2 percent of the seats in the House. By 1991, women held 28 seats. In 1999, they held 56 House seats—13 percent of the total.

Once elected, congresswomen won reelection as easily as their male colleagues. Forty-one of the 103 women elected to the House between 1916 and 1986 remained for five or more terms. The longest-serving incumbent, Frances Bolton of Ohio, held office for thirty years.

The first female senator, Rebecca Felton of Georgia, was appointed to fill an unexpired term in 1922. Hattie Caraway of Arkansas, the first woman senator to be regularly elected, served from 1931 to 1945. Only one other female senator, Margaret Chase Smith of Maine, was elected and reelected more than once. Twelve of the 27 women who entered the Senate during the century were appointed to fill out unexpired terms, an honor often bestowed on the widows of deceased senators. Until 1992, there had never been more than three female senators serving at the same time. Nine women held Senate seats in 1999, just under 10 percent of the total.

Congresswomen
Number of women in the House of Representatives and the Senate

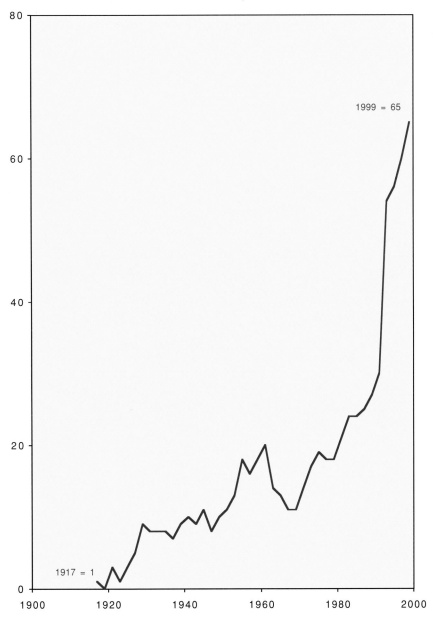

1999 = 65

1917 = 1

The number of black elected officials increased greatly after 1970.

From 1867 to 1877, following the Civil War, blacks had voting rights in the former Confederate states. Numerous black officials won election to Congress during that period. With the demise of Reconstruction, however, a combination of legal and illegal devices effectively canceled black suffrage throughout most of the South, where the black population was concentrated. Thereafter, a handful of blacks held minor offices in communities with large black populations, but none was elected to national or state offices.

This situation persisted throughout the first half of the century and into the second half. It did not change very much until the civil rights movement gathered momentum in the 1960s. In 1966, Edward Brooke, Republican of Massachusetts, was elected as the first black U.S. senator in eighty-eight years. In 1967, Carl B. Stokes was elected as mayor of Cleveland and Richard G. Hatcher as mayor of Gary, Indiana. In 1968, Shirley Chisholm, Democrat of New York, became the first black woman ever elected to Congress. The trend in appointive offices was similar. Thurgood Marshall took his seat on the Supreme Court in 1967.

In the last three decades of the century, the number of black elected officials increased sixfold, from 1,469 in 1970 to 8,868 in 1998. During that time, blacks gradually achieved an impressive share of certain high public offices. Most of the country's largest cities elected one or more black mayors. In 1999, the 37 House seats that black representatives held accounted for about 9 percent of all seats in the U.S. House of Representatives.

But only one black governor and two black senators were elected in the century. At the lower levels of elected government—school boards, sheriffs, and county tax assessors, for example—blacks were also significantly underrepresented. At the end of the century, only about 2 percent of all elected officials were black.

Black Elected Officials
Total number of blacks holding elected office at all levels of government

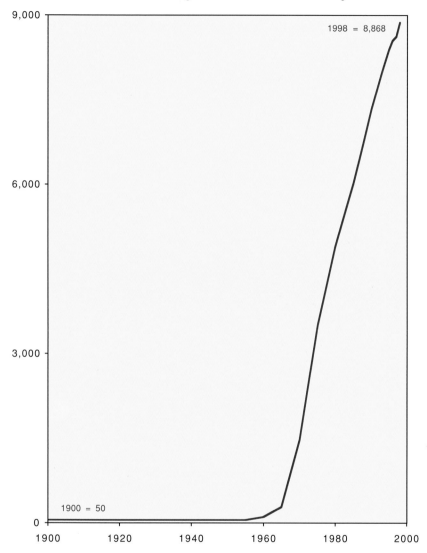

1998 = 8,868

1900 = 50

The attitudes of Middletown adolescents toward social issues did not vary dramatically between 1924 and 1999.

The 1924 survey of Middletown high school students by Robert and Helen Lynd included items designed to elicit their attitudes toward two basic social issues: the Protestant Ethic of unlimited personal responsibility, and economic inequality in the United States. Students were asked whether they agreed or disagreed with the following statements:

"It is entirely the fault of a man himself if he does not succeed."

"The fact that some people have so much more money than others shows that there is an unjust condition in this country that ought to be changed."

These items were repeated without change in the 1977 and 1999 replications of these surveys. As the chart shows, the percentage of Middletown adolescents agreeing with the Protestant Ethic remained level from 1924 to 1977 but increased from 1977 to 1999, while the proportion agreeing with action against economic inequality increased in each of the three surveys from 1924 to 1999.

Social Attitudes of Middletown Adolescents

"It is entirely the fault of a man himself if he does not succeed."

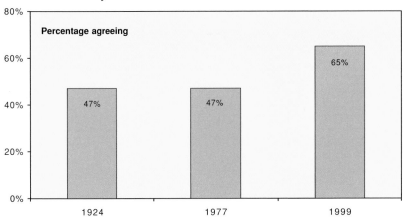

"The fact that some people have so much more money than others shows that there is an unjust condition in this country that ought to be changed."

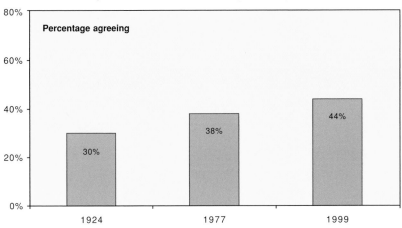

Chapter 11
Government

Federal, state, and local governments expanded their activities.

In 1900 and for three decades thereafter, the federal government was a remote presence in the lives of most Americans, except during wartime. In peacetime, their primary contact with the federal government occurred at the post office.

Federal spending first peaked during World War I. Between 1930 and 1940, annual federal expenditures more than doubled. During World War II they quadrupled, reaching 44 percent of the Gross Domestic Product by the end of the war. Federal expenditures plummeted after the war, but not to prewar levels. During the last four decades of the century, federal expenditures held at about 20 percent of GDP.

A great expansion in federal activity occurred in the first Roosevelt administration (1933–1937) with the creation of the Social Security retirement system, unemployment insurance, government guarantees of bank deposits and home mortgages, income support for families with dependent children, low-rent public housing, direct subsidies to farmers, work relief projects, and regional development programs. Another wave of expansion occurred during the Johnson and Nixon administrations (1963–1974) with the introduction of Medicare and Medicaid, and the growing involvement of the federal government in education, urban development, environmental protection, occupational safety, emergency food distribution, and dozens of other functions.

More than 60,000 state and local governments have taxing power in the United States: fifty states, about 3,000 counties, 20,000 municipalities, 17,000 townships, 14,000 independent school districts, and more than 10,000 special districts. Before World War II, state and local governments combined spent a good deal more than the federal government during peacetime. From 1942 through the last decade of the century, however, Washington's annual expenditures exceeded those of all state and local governments.

Government Expenditures
Percentage of Gross Domestic Product

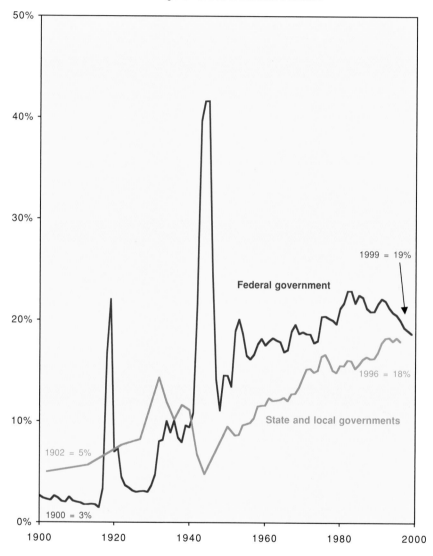

1999 = 19%

Federal government

1996 = 18%

State and local governments

1902 = 5%

1900 = 3%

Federal government employees were a smaller component of the labor force at the end of the century than at any time since 1940.

As the chart indicates, in 1997, state and local governments employed six times more people than the federal government. This may seem counterintuitive, given the fact that all state and local governments combined spend somewhat less each year than the federal government.

These employment trends can be easily explained, however. First, the federal government makes much greater use of contractors to perform governmental functions than do state and local governments. Federal agencies routinely outsource research and development, strategic planning, employee training and evaluation, computer installation, system and standards design, transportation, printing and even some national security and intelligence operations. Second, more than half of the federal budget consists of payments to, or on behalf of, individual beneficiaries—Social Security, Medicare, Medicaid, food stamps, welfare, veterans' benefits, civil service and military retirement, housing subsidies, student aid, and so forth. Other substantial chunks go to the armed services, debt service, and grants to the states, leaving only about a fifth of the federal budget for the civilian payroll. The principal reductions of federal employees in the last decade of the century were among civilians working at the Department of Defense.

Government Civilian Employees
Percentage of the civilian labor force

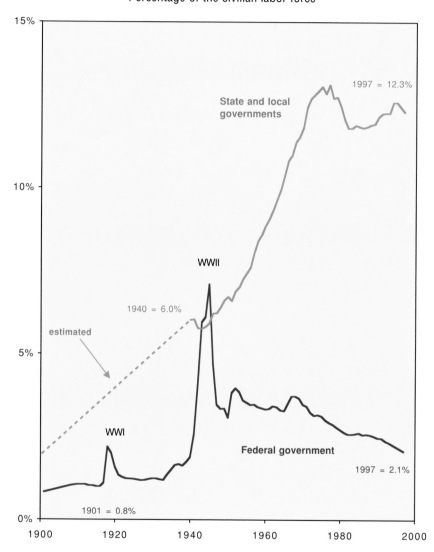

State and local governments

1997 = 12.3%

WWII

1940 = 6.0%

estimated

WWI

Federal government

1997 = 2.1%

1901 = 0.8%

Government payments to, or on behalf of, individual citizens increased during the second half of the century.

In 1900, the only people receiving direct payments from Washington were war veterans and their dependents. In any given year at the end of the century, the majority of American families received direct benefits from the U.S. Treasury under one or more entitlement programs.

Entitlements are automatic government payments to, or on behalf of, individuals or organizations that fall into some category defined by law, such as all college students or all homeowners in disaster-stricken counties. The largest entitlement is Social Security—more precisely, Old Age, Survivors, and Disability Insurance—the system of federal pensions for retired workers and their dependents, disabled workers and their dependents, and survivors of deceased workers. The next largest is Medicare, which pays some, but not all, of the medical and hospital expenses of people over age sixty-five, followed by Medicaid, a system of health insurance for low-income and needy people. The chart shows only the federal contribution to Medicaid; the cost of this expensive and rapidly growing program is shared by the states.

The other programs shown on the chart are less costly. Veterans' benefits actually declined after 1975. Direct subsidies to the poor—welfare grants and food stamps—increased, but their combined cost remained far less than the cost of Medicaid.

The chart shows only the largest and most conspicuous of the federal entitlements. It does not include dozens of others, including the military and civil service retirement systems, unemployment insurance, income programs for the blind and disabled, school breakfasts and lunches, housing subsidies, child care support, nutrition for the elderly, vocational training, disaster relief, flood insurance, farm subsidies, and various special benefits for handicapped persons, American Indians, pregnant women, displaced defense workers, tobacco farmers, and graduate students.

Growth of Federal Entitlements
Billions of 1999 dollars

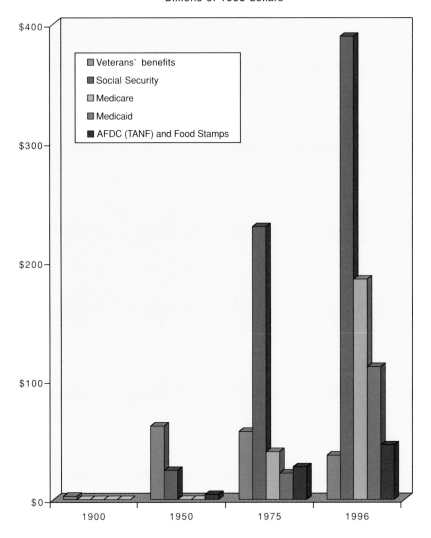

In the last three decades of the century, the judicial branch of the federal government grew at a much faster rate than the executive and legislative branches.

From 1970 to 1998, the number of federal employees in the judicial branch quadrupled from 6,887 to 31,742 (see upper chart). In the same period, the number of federal employees in the legislative branch remained almost exactly the same: 30,715 in 1970 and 30,747 in 1998. The number of employees in the much larger executive branch actually declined slightly from 2.8 million to 2.7 million, including postal workers.

The growth of the judicial branch followed a sharp increase in the number of civil cases commenced in federal district courts after 1960 (see lower chart). In the 1940s, about half of all new cases were criminal cases, but the proportion of criminal cases declined to less than a fifth by the end of the century. The largest categories of civil cases were prisoner petitions, civil rights complaints, and product liability claims—all of which were rare or nonexistent in the federal courts before the 1960s. In one three-year period alone, 1993 to 1996, prisoner petitions increased by 32 percent, civil rights complaints by 53 percent, and product liability claims by 82 percent.

Despite the rapid expansion of judicial branch personnel, the district courts would have collapsed under this tidal wave of litigation if the proportion of cases going to trial had remained about the same. The fact is that fewer cases went to trial at the end of the century than in 1970. In 1997, only 3 percent of cases went to trial, usually a bench trial without a jury. Most cases were withdrawn by the plaintiffs, dismissed by the court, or settled at an early stage of the proceedings. Indeed, many were filed in the expectation of a quick cash settlement.

Federal Judiciary
Thousands of employees

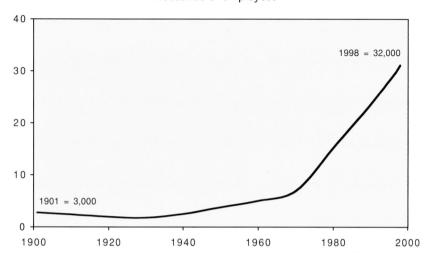

1998 = 32,000

1901 = 3,000

Thousands of cases commenced each year

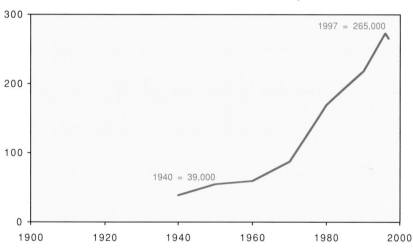

1997 = 265,000

1940 = 39,000

U.S. armed forces expanded rapidly for each major conflict during the century. During the Cold War, the nation maintained a large permanent force for the first time in its history.

The Founding Fathers regarded standing armies as inimical to constitutional government. Throughout the nineteenth and much of the twentieth century, the United States had a much smaller military establishment in peacetime than any other great power and made no peacetime use of conscription.

With the outbreak of each war, the armed forces were expanded with extraordinary speed, from 179,000 active personnel in 1916 to almost 3 million in 1918, and from less than half a million in 1940 to more than 12 million in 1945. The contraction in the number of personnel was equally rapid. The number of military personnel on active duty declined by 88 percent between 1918 and 1920, and by exactly the same percentage between 1945 and 1948.

The Cold War, which was neither war nor peace, altered this pattern. From 1948 until the collapse of the Soviet Union in 1991, the armed services remained at historically high numbers, peaking at 3.6 million during the Korean War and 3.5 million during the Vietnam War. After 1987, the size of the armed forces declined slowly from year to year.

The conversion to an all-volunteer force in 1972 and the subsequent increase in military pay to the level of market wages had dramatic effects on the military community. At the end of the century, enlisted soldiers and sailors were older, better educated, and more highly trained than their predecessors. The majority were married and lived with their spouses when serving at domestic stations. The harsher forms of military discipline were largely replaced by job incentives. Courts-martial were rare by the end of the century; the usual penalty for a serious military offense was dismissal from the service.

Armed Forces Personnel on Active Duty
Millions each year

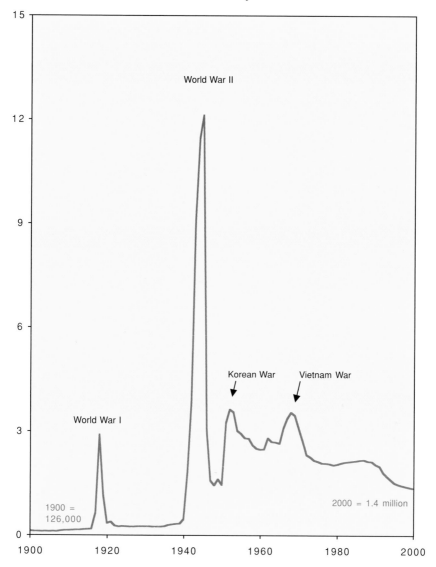

World War II

World War I

Korean War

Vietnam War

1900 = 126,000

2000 = 1.4 million

15

12

9

6

3

0

1900   1920   1940   1960   1980   2000

The armed services, rigidly segregated by race during the first part of the century, became a model of successful integration.

Black soldiers enlisted in every American war prior to World War II, beginning with the American Revolution, but they were always placed in segregated units under the command of white officers, commonly assigned to manual labor, and usually discharged when the war ended. Nearly 400,000 black enlisted men and a few black officers served in World War I, mostly in noncombat assignments.

The Selective Service Act of 1940 allowed qualified persons to volunteer or be drafted regardless of race or color. Black soldiers soon made up 11 percent of the Army's strength. They were all placed in segregated units, and with a few important exceptions, segregation remained in full effect throughout World War II. The Army adopted full integration as a planning goal in 1951 and was able to announce in 1954 that its last segregated unit had been abolished. Many issues, such as segregation in officers clubs and military cemeteries, remained to be worked out, but after the Army became an all-volunteer force in 1972, it came as close to being color-blind as any segment of American society. By 1996, blacks made up a proportionate share of the Army's officers (12 percent) and 30 percent of the Army's enlisted strength.

In 1900, blacks could serve only as stewards or stokers in the Navy. The Navy entered World War II with about 4,000 black enlisted men and no black officers. All but six of the enlisted men were on mess duty. By 1943, their numbers had risen to 27,000. Two-thirds of them were still assigned to the stewards' branch. The war was nearly over when the Navy conducted some experiments with mixed ships' crews, but in February 1946, the Navy announced, "Effective immediately, all restrictions governing types of assignments for which Negro naval personnel are eligible are hereby lifted."

The Marine Corps had been an all-white organization since 1798. Forced to accept black draftees during World War II, the Corps adopted a policy of rigid segregation that continued until the Korean War, when the exigencies of battle led to rapid integration.

When the Air Force became a separate branch of the armed forces in 1947, it shared the Army's tradition of segregated units, enlistment quotas, and the axiomatic beliefs that white soldiers would not take orders from black officers or live peaceably in mixed units. But by 1949, the Air Force was officially and effectively integrated.

Blacks in the Armed Services

Percentage of officers and enlisted personnel in each service

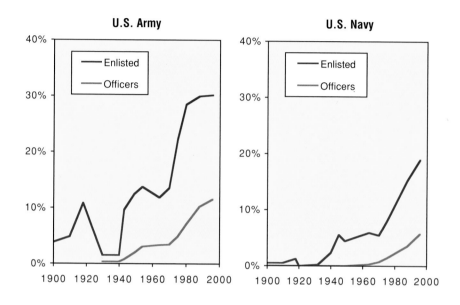

U.S. Army

- Enlisted
- Officers

U.S. Navy

- Enlisted
- Officers

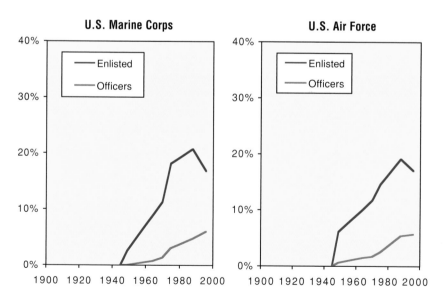

U.S. Marine Corps

- Enlisted
- Officers

U.S. Air Force

- Enlisted
- Officers

The proportion of women in the armed forces rose rapidly in the last third of the century.

In the Civil War, as in earlier wars, a few women disguised themselves as men and joined combat units; soldiers' wives and other women accompanied campaigning armies, and many women on both sides nursed the wounded. But military rank and status continued to be male prerogatives. The Army Nurse Corps, founded in 1901, was the first official female military organization, but its members were technically civilians.

In World War I, the Navy and the Marine Corps authorized female enlistments for yeoman, radio operator, and other support positions, and more than 10,000 Army nurses served overseas. In 1920, in recognition of their wartime services, the nurses were granted "relative rank," from second lieutenant through major, and were permitted to wear military uniforms and insignia.

The Women's Auxiliary Army Corps was established in 1942 as a quasi-military organization, without formal enlistment or military benefits. But a year later, it was incorporated into the Army as the Women's Army Corps. The Navy, Marines, and Coast Guard soon followed suit. By 1945, 265,000 women were in uniform, all of them volunteers.

The separate status of women in the armed forces continued until the early 1970s, when the anticipated passage of the Equal Rights Amendment and a series of federal court decisions on gender discrimination persuaded the armed services to abolish their female branches by separate and piecemeal measures. Women were put on the same footing as men with respect to training, rank, pay, and promotion. As the chart indicates, between 1975 and 1998, the female share of officers and enlisted personnel tripled to about 14 percent of the armed services. By the end of the century, women were allowed to serve in some front-line positions and on combat ships. As integration proceeded, little notice was taken when women sometimes commanded men in U.S. military operations.

Women in the Armed Forces
Percentage of officers and enlisted personnel

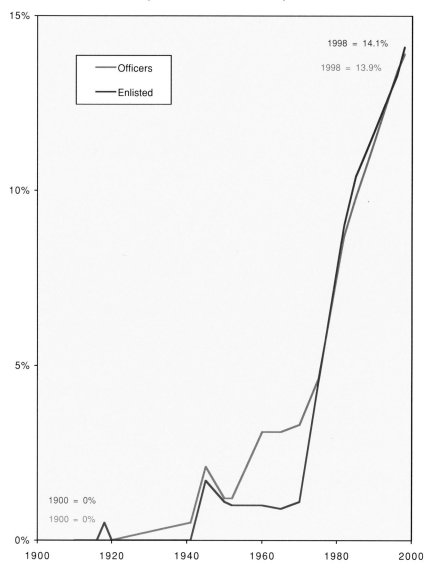

In the five major conflicts in which the United States engaged during the century, American losses were highest in World War II.

A total of 440,000 U.S. military personnel were killed in action in the wars of the twentieth century, two-thirds of them during World War II. The battle death rate ranged from 3.1 percent of the Marines in World War I to 0.006 percent of naval personnel in the Persian Gulf War. In all five conflicts—World Wars I and II, the Korean and Vietnam wars, and the Persian Gulf War—Marines and Army ground units bore the brunt of the losses. But none of the services approached the 6.1 percent rate of battle deaths recorded by the Union forces in the Civil War.

These tragic losses were much lighter in number than those borne by our allies and adversaries. Worldwide, more than 100 million soldiers and civilians were killed in the wars of the twentieth century. Besides the human costs, most of the nations involved in these wars suffered vast physical destruction. Because of its geographic location, the United States was exempt from the civilian casualties, property damage, and most of the domestic disruption suffered by other nations.

Aside from the risks of combat, wartime military service became progressively less hazardous during the century. In every war the United States fought before this century, deaths of military personnel from disease and accidents greatly outnumbered battle deaths. As late as World War I, nonbattle deaths were somewhat more numerous than battle deaths, but thereafter the balance shifted. In the Korean and Vietnam conflicts, for example, battle deaths outnumbered nonbattle deaths by almost 5 to 1.

Battle death rates declined because of America's increasing technological advantage in military equipment and improved treatment of battle wounds. U.S. weapons, vehicles, and defensive measures were superior to those of most of its adversaries. American casualties were quickly evacuated to hospitals, saving thousands of lives.

War Deaths of Armed Forces Personnel
Thousands

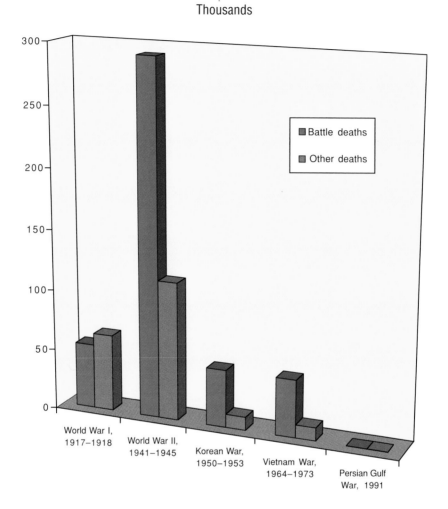

Veterans made up a large part of the civilian male population during the second half of the century.

By 1900, most of the Union veterans of the Civil War were dead. The government did not count Confederate veterans, but most of them were deceased as well. The forces engaged in the Spanish-American War were quite small. By 1910, only one of twenty-five American men had seen military service, the lowest proportion since the founding of the Republic.

That changed in 1917. Five million men served in World War I. In the course of World War II, more than 16 million men, mostly young, were inducted into the armed forces. Five million men served during the Korean War. By 1960, 40 percent of American men over age eighteen—and a much higher proportion of those in their thirties and forties—had served in the military. As World War I veterans died, Vietnam veterans took their place. Almost 9 million Americans served in the armed forces during the Vietnam era.

The median age of veterans oscillated with the incidence of war and passage of time. It declined from sixty-seven years in 1910 to twenty-seven years in 1920 and then rose from thirty-two years in 1950 to sixty-one years in 1998. In the last decade of the century, many World War II veterans reached their eighties, and the veteran population diminished from year to year.

Generous veterans' benefits had important consequences. Employers in both the public and private sectors gave hiring preferences to veterans, which helped to maintain support for the armed forces throughout the long Cold War. The G.I. Bill sent millions of men back to school for advanced education and permanently enlarged American colleges and universities. Mortgages guaranteed by the Veterans Administration made home ownership possible for families with relatively low incomes and strongly encouraged suburban growth.

Veterans in Civilian Life
Millions

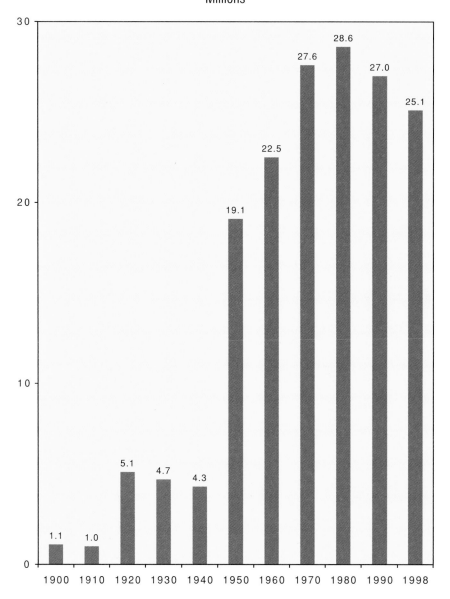

Patriotic attitudes of Middletown adolescents declined between 1924 and 1999, especially among females.

The charts show male and female responses to four items from the 1924 Middletown High School Survey. The statements were repeated in the 1977 and 1999 replications of that survey.

Students were asked to agree or disagree with the following statements:

"The United States is unquestionably the best country in the world."

"The United States was entirely right and England was entirely wrong in the American Revolution."

"A pacifist or a conscientious objector in wartime is a 'slacker' who doesn't do his share and should be prosecuted by the government."

"Every good citizen should act according to the following statement: 'My country—right or wrong!'"

In 1924, more than nine of ten students agreed that the United States was the best country in the world; in 1977, more than seven of ten agreed; and in 1999, about six of ten. The proportions favoring the slogan "My country—right or wrong" declined in each survey, as did the percentage in favor of prosecuting conscientious objectors in wartime. The overall trend in responses to the statement about the American Revolution was inconclusive.

The differences in the responses of male and female students changed markedly over time. In 1924, girls were more strongly patriotic than boys on all four items. In 1977, boys were more patriotic than girls, and by 1999 the difference between them had widened further. In 1999, for example, only 51 percent of girls, compared with 68 percent of boys, agreed that the United States was the best country in the world. The most extreme change in the difference between male and female attitudes concerned the statement about the American Revolution. In 1924, the proportion of girls who believed the United States was entirely right in that conflict was 10 percentage points higher than that of boys; in 1999, it was 17 percentage points lower.

Patriotic Attitudes of Middletown Adolescents
Percentage agreeing with each statement

My country—right or wrong

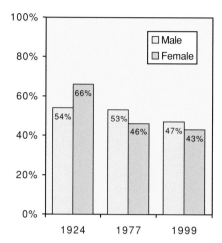

Conscientious objectors should be prosecuted

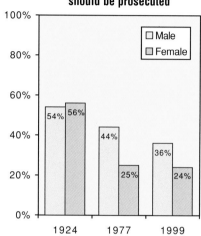

England was entirely wrong in the American Revolution

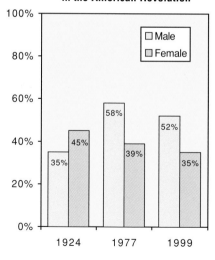

The U.S. is unquestionably the best country in the world

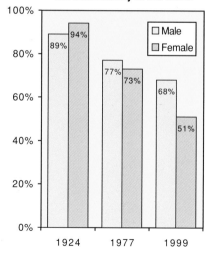

Chapter 12
Crime

Spectators watch as a policeman sits beside a homicide victim and takes notes. Photograph taken on September 20, 1952, by Bob Wendlinger. Courtesy of UPI/Corbis-Bettmann.

Homicides increased sharply during the first third of the century and then declined to a lower level during the second third. The homicide rate escalated to new peaks during the final third and then declined sharply in the last decade of the century.

The best single indicator of the incidence of violent crime in the nation is the annual homicide rate (murders and non-negligent manslaughters per 100,000 population. Unlike other crimes, which often go unreported, nearly all homicides are known to the police and counted in the statistics. For the same reason, a great deal was known about the perpetrators and victims of homicides.

Homicide was more common in metropolitan areas than in small cities and rural areas, but the rate varied enormously among cities, states, and regions of the country. In 1997, for example, the homicide rate ranged from 1.4 per 100,000 in South Dakota to 15.7 per 100,000 in Louisiana. Two-thirds of all homicides were committed with firearms, and most of the rest with knives or clubs.

Homicide rates were heavily influenced by age, race, and gender. The prime age group for both victims and perpetrators was eighteen to twenty-four. Blacks were about eight times more likely than whites to be involved in homicides, both as victims and perpetrators. Males were about four times more likely than females to be homicide victims and ten times more likely to be homicide perpetrators.

Killer and victim were acquainted in about three out of four homicides. Indeed, the probability of being killed by a close relative or lover was higher than the probability of being killed by a stranger. But strangers did murder strangers in robberies, drug deals, psychopathic episodes, and barroom brawls.

These characteristics of homicides and their perpetrators and victims remained fairly stable from year to year.

Homicides
Per 100,000 population per year

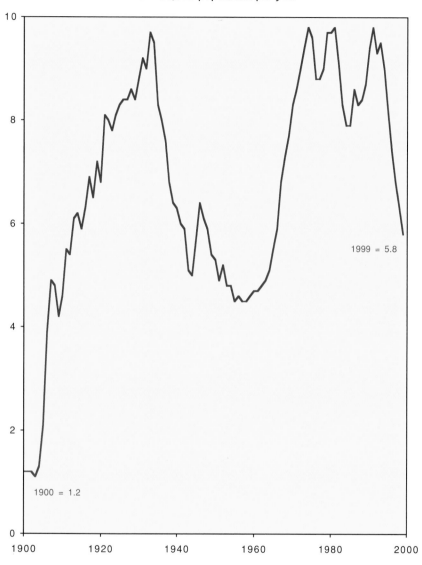

1999 = 5.8

1900 = 1.2

Robberies increased rapidly from the early 1960s to the mid-1970s and remained at a high level until the last decade of the century, when a sharp downturn ensued.

The incidence of robbery is considered the best overall indicator of a population's exposure to criminal risk. Unlike homicides or rapes, nearly all robberies are committed by strangers. Unlike thefts or assaults, most robberies are reported. And only robbery is both a violent crime and a property crime.

Unfortunately, the trend data for robbery are incomplete. Data from the FBI's *Uniform Crime Reports* go back only to 1957, as shown in the chart. A series based on the *National Criminal Victimization Survey* goes back no further than 1972. No information is available about the nationwide incidence of robbery before 1957, and data from the two official sources do not agree for the period they both cover.

What is clear from the data is that the incidence of robbery tripled between 1965 and 1975 and then remained at a high level, peaking in 1991. The incidence of robbery dropped sharply during the remainder of the century, declining 44 percent between 1991 and 1999.

Criminologists disagree about the reasons for the abrupt surge in robbery and other serious crimes during the 1960s, as well as the causes of the decline in the 1990s. The original rise has been blamed on the social unrest of the 1960s, the spread of illegal drugs, court-imposed restrictions on police practices, demographic and ethnic shifts, the expansion of street gangs, and youth unemployment. The subsequent decline has been attributed variously to a huge increase in incarceration, new policing strategies, the maturation of the illegal drug market, a sharp decline in youth unemployment, the substitution of credit cards for cash, and enhanced security measures in stores and other public places.

None of these factors, taken alone, seems to explain much about the trend in robberies during the last four decades of the century. Presumably these factors worked in some as yet unknown combination to produce the trend described here.

Robberies
Per 100,000 population per year

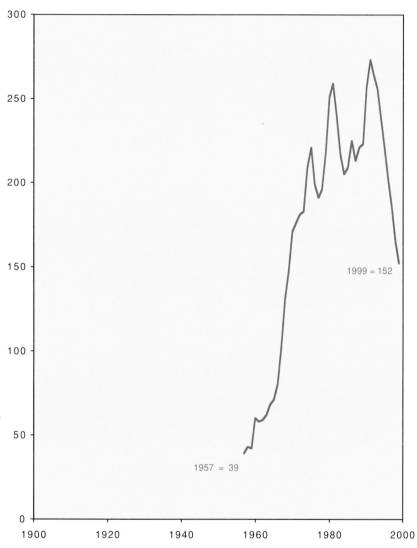

1999 = 152

1957 = 39

Capital punishment increased during the first four decades of the century and then declined sharply in the subsequent three decades. The practice was abolished and then restored during the 1970s, and its use increased in the last two decades of the century.

By 1972, the United States was almost alone among developed nations in retaining capital punishment, but fourteen states had abolished it, and half a dozen other states had effectively abandoned its use. In that year, in *Furman v. Georgia,* the Supreme Court preempted the issue by ruling that the death penalty as then applied was "cruel and unusual punishment" and therefore prohibited under the Constitution. The decision overturned more than 600 death sentences, but it provoked a backlash as states enacted new legislation to meet the Supreme Court's objections. After a five-year interval, executions resumed slowly and increased through the end of the century.

Before *Furman,* executions for rape were not uncommon, and some executions for treason, espionage, and kidnapping also occurred. After *Furman,* murder was the only crime that warranted a penalty of death.

The states vary greatly in their use of the death penalty. Thirty-eight states had capital statutes in 1998, while twelve states and the District of Columbia did not. In 1997, thirty-three states held no executions and sixteen of these had no one on death row. Texas, Florida, and Virginia accounted for most of the executions carried out in the last two decades of the century. Few women were sentenced to death during the century and even fewer were executed.

By the 1980s, capital punishment had become something of a paradox, as one set of courts handed down death sentences freely and another set of courts prevented most of them from being carried out. As a result, the normal time between sentencing and execution was prolonged from months to years and eventually to decades. At the same time, the number of prisoners on death row grew rapidly, increasing fivefold between 1980 and 1998. In 1997, 256 newcomers arrived on death row, while only 74—2 percent—of the 3,335 prisoners awaiting execution on January 1, 1997, were executed that year.

Executions under Civil Authority
Number during time period by type of conviction

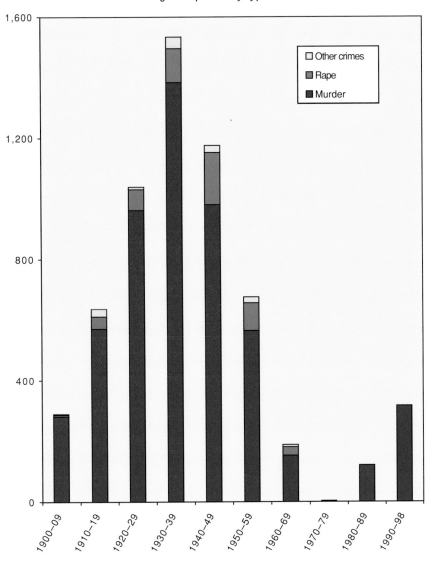

The cost and complexity of maintaining order increased sharply in the second half of the century.

Policing became a much more complex and expensive activity than it was in the past. As the chart indicates, per capita spending on police protection increased more than fivefold between 1950 and 1996. In part, this trend reflects technological improvements, such as the development of computer data banks and the adoption of more sophisticated weaponry and communications, and in part, it reflects the diversification of police functions.

The federal government, for example, employed sworn gun-carrying law enforcement officers in more than a score of civilian agencies, including the Federal Bureau of Investigation; the Bureau of Alcohol, Tobacco, and Firearms; the Secret Service; the U.S. Customs Service; the Bureau of Indian Affairs; and other less well-known agencies. Most local communities in the United States were actively policed by more than one official force: state troopers, city and county police, sheriff's deputies, town constables, and campus police, for example.

The most consequential growth in policing costs, however, occurred not among official police but among private police and correctional officers. The Census Bureau does not distinguish clearly between armed private police, guards armed with nonlethal weapons, and unarmed guards, but all of these categories expanded rapidly and steadily after 1970. Private police of various types numbered more than 1 million in 1998, exceeding the number of official police (764,000). Retail stores, hotels, casinos, office buildings, residential developments, industrial plants, and even private individuals ceased to rely on the official police for routine protection and hired their own protective forces. The number of correctional officers increased even more rapidly. Between 1983 and 1998, their numbers doubled, from 146,000 to 299,000.

Spending on Police Protection
1999 dollars per capita per year

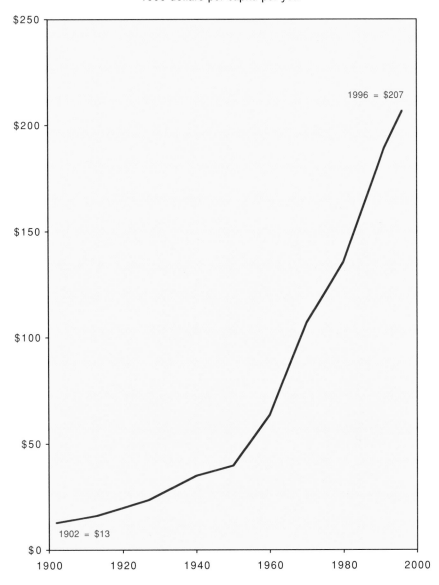

1996 = $207

1902 = $13

The inmate population of state and federal prisons increased significantly after 1980.

Before the 1990s, imprisonment rates of more than 400 inmates per 100,000 population had never been approached in the United States or any other developed nation. As the chart shows, the U.S. inmate population more than tripled in the last two decades of the century, reaching 462 per 100,000 population in 1999.

The ethnic, gender, and age distributions of prison inmates differed greatly from those of the general population. At the end of 1997, according to a Bureau of Justice Statistics estimate, 48 percent of state and federal prisoners were white, 49 percent were black, 2 percent were American Indian, and 1 percent were other races. Hispanics, who may be of any race, constituted 18 percent of state and federal prisoners. Women composed about 6 percent of the prisoner population, twice the female share of inmates in the early years of the century. The overwhelming majority of prisoners were between the ages of eighteen and fifty-four, with a concentration around age thirty.

These inmate characteristics produced enormous variations in the imprisonment rates of subgroups of the population. In 1996, for example, the imprisonment rate among eighteen- to fifty-four-year-olds ranged from 59 per 100,000 white women to 6,286 per 100,000 black men.

At the end of 1998, 123,041 inmates were in the federal prison system, and 1,178,978 inmates were in state prisons. In addition, almost 600,000 were confined in local jails, where they were awaiting trial, serving short sentences, or waiting for prison space.

Among the factors contributing to the increase in the inmate population were the enhanced prosecution of drug offenses, longer sentences for common crimes, and reduced access to parole and probation.

State and Federal Prisoners
Per 100,000 population

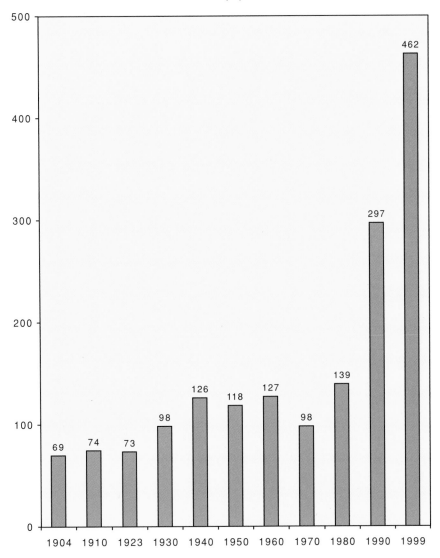

Toward the end of the century, the proportion of new state and federal prisoners committed for property crimes declined, while the proportion committed for drug crimes increased.

Among felons committed to state and federal prisons for terms of more than a year, relatively few were sentenced for a violent crime—about one of every four new prisoners in 1910 and about one of four in 1996. The most frequent offense among perpetrators of violent crime was aggravated assault, which may or may not have involved injury to the victim. The presence of a weapon in an assault classified it as aggravated in most jurisdictions. Murderers, robbers, and rapists together made up about 7 percent of new inmates.

For most of the century, the majority of new prisoners were convicted of property offenses, divided almost evenly among burglary, larceny, and fraud. At the end of the century, little more than a quarter of incoming prisoners were sentenced for property offenses, although the incidence of those crimes did not decline dramatically. The burglary rate was slightly lower in 1996 than in 1970, but rates of larceny and fraud were significantly higher. The diminishing representation of property offenders among new prisoners is attributable in part to the growth of the absolute size of the prison population and in part to a tendency for the criminal justice system to treat property crimes more leniently than in the past. In 1996, only one of three property offenders went to prison after a felony conviction; a greater number received probation, while some were sentenced to short terms in local jails.

In the last decade of the century, the biggest change in the offenses of new prisoners was an increase in the proportion sentenced for drug offenses. Some were sentenced for trafficking and some for possession, with most of the latter group serving after a plea bargain from a trafficking offense.

The "other crimes" category includes a wide variety of offenses such as espionage, counterfeiting, violations of securities law, the harboring of fugitives, evasion of customs duties, illegal possession of firearms and explosives, immigration fraud, bribery of officials, and abuse of office. Additional offenses in this category—perjury, obstruction of justice, and jury tampering—arise from within the justice system itself.

The chart covers only civilian prisoners. The population of the federal government's separate prison system for military personnel did not grow at all after 1970. With about 2,000 inmates, the military system operated at less than 50 percent of capacity at the end of the century.

Offenses of Prisoners Received in State and Federal Prisons
Percentage of all offenses

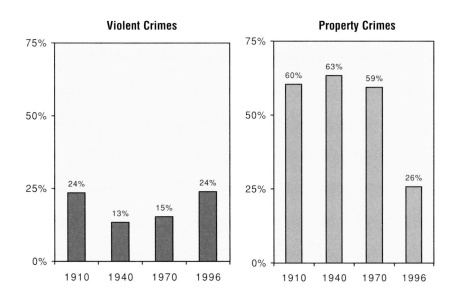

Violent Crimes

Year	Percentage
1910	24%
1940	13%
1970	15%
1996	24%

Property Crimes

Year	Percentage
1910	60%
1940	63%
1970	59%
1996	26%

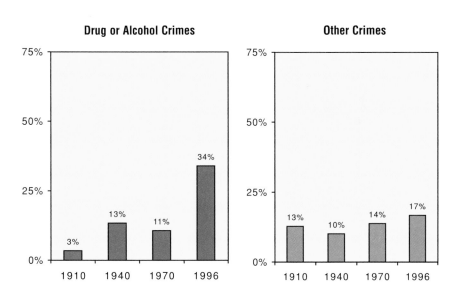

Drug or Alcohol Crimes

Year	Percentage
1910	3%
1940	13%
1970	11%
1996	34%

Other Crimes

Year	Percentage
1910	13%
1940	10%
1970	14%
1996	17%

Juveniles became more heavily involved in serious crime during the second half of the century.

The Federal Bureau of Investigation tracks four major violent "index crimes": murder, rape, robbery, and aggravated assault. The FBI also tracks serious property crimes, which comprise burglary, larceny, and auto theft. (Arson is also an index crime, but its frequency is so low compared with the others that it is omitted from many analyses.)

In 1947, the first year for which reliable figures on juvenile participation in serious crime were available, 4 percent of the people arrested for violent crimes and 13 percent of those arrested for property crimes were under the age of eighteen. Assault and larceny were the most common juvenile offenses.

It is impossible to determine whether the 1947 figures represented an increase or decrease from earlier years, but the enormous rise in juvenile criminality that occurred during the subsequent two decades is unmistakable. By 1968, the juvenile share of arrests had climbed to 22 percent for serious violent crimes and 55 percent for serious property crimes. In other words, more juveniles than adults were arrested for serious property crimes that year.

Juveniles were responsible for a smaller share of serious crimes at the end of the century than in the 1960s and 1970s. Persons under age eighteen were involved in 17 percent of arrests for serious violent crimes and 33 percent of arrests for serious property crimes in 1998.

Juvenile Share of Serious Crimes
Juvenile arrests as percentage of all arrests

Property Crimes

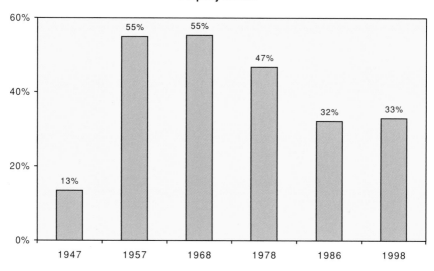

Violent Crimes

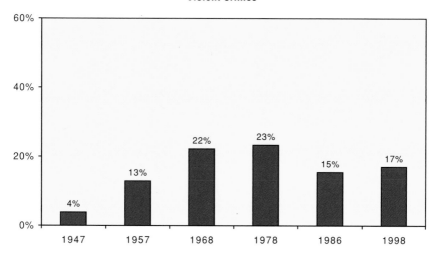

Chapter 13
Transportation

Oklahoma migrants stalled on a New Mexico highway in May 1937. In that year, there were twenty-four registered vehicles per mile of surfaced road; sixty years later, there were fifty-seven. Photograph by Dorothea Lange. Courtesy of Library of Congress.

Travel within the United States increased enormously, while the modes of travel changed.

Passenger traffic on American railroads grew steadily from the late 1800s until the 1920s, when the bulk of intercity travel shifted to the private automobile and rail travel began a decline that continued until World War II. When wartime gasoline rationing and the suspension of auto production made cars less available, the railroads were pressed back into service to accommodate the great volume of travel by soldiers and war workers. Intercity bus lines, whose operations had been very limited before 1940, expanded to carry part of the load.

After the war, the decline of rail passenger services resumed. Most rail companies abandoned passenger service altogether. Many passenger stations were razed or abandoned, and most railroad cars were taken out of service. In an effort to salvage the vestiges of the rail passenger network, Congress created Amtrak in 1970. After taking control of rail passenger service from the private rail companies the following year, Amtrak continued to operate with federal subsidies and carried about half of the remaining rail passenger volume. Commuter lines accounted for the rest.

Less than a decade after taking control of the nation's passenger railroads, the federal government deregulated the nation's airlines. The great expansion in air travel that began after midcentury is projected to continue indefinitely, putting constant pressure on air transit facilities but offering speedy and safe transportation.

Bus travel provided a low-cost alternative for travelers who could not afford the price of a seat on an airplane or a train. Bus travel retained a small but relatively stable niche.

Intercity Common Carriers: Passengers
Billions of passenger-miles per year

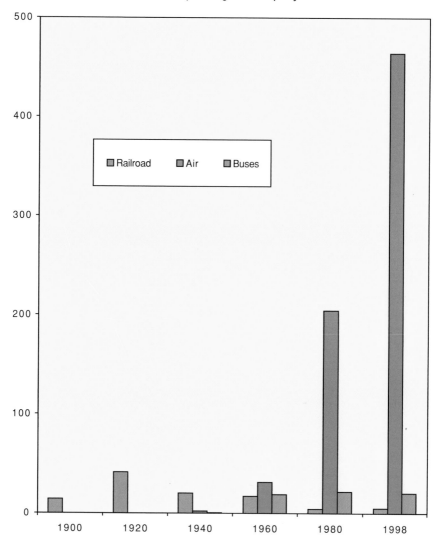

The tonnage of domestic freight carried by rail increased throughout the century, while the tonnage carried by trucks, waterways, and pipelines began to increase around 1930. Trucks ranked behind other carriers in the tonnage they transported but ahead of all other carriers in the value of their shipments.

Unlike rail passenger traffic, rail freight traffic continued to grow with the national economy. More tonnage was carried by rail than by truck. And the combined tonnage carried by less visible modes of transportation—inland waterways and oil pipelines—exceeded the tonnage carried by truck.

But the value of truck shipments was much higher than the value of rail, waterway, and pipeline shipments. Railroads, waterways, and pipelines tended to carry bulk cargoes, while trucks typically carried finished goods. In 1997, trucks carried less than half of the total ton-miles of freight, but almost 90 percent of the total value.

The great expansion of truck traffic after 1950 coincided with the construction of the interstate highway system. The increasing use of heavy trucks for shipping time-valued goods of all kinds was a major factor in the growth of the suburbs, commercial strip development, industrial relocation, and other centrifugal trends that reshaped American communities.

Despite the growing importance of air express and air package services, air freight does not appear on the chart. Only a fraction of 1 percent of intercity freight tonnage—and only 3 percent of intercity freight measured by value—moved by air. But air freight occupied a critical niche for time-sensitive items such as cut flowers, fresh seafood, and zoo animals.

Air freight statistics do not include packages shipped by the postal service and its competitors. The U.S. Postal Service alone shipped 1.2 million tons of mail by air in 1998. The United Parcel Service estimated that the packages it shipped in 1998 were worth about 6 percent of the Gross Domestic Product. The advent of Internet shopping also accelerated the growth of package delivery to consumers. Many of these packages moved by air at some point in their journey.

Intercity Common Carriers: Freight
Billions of ton-miles per year

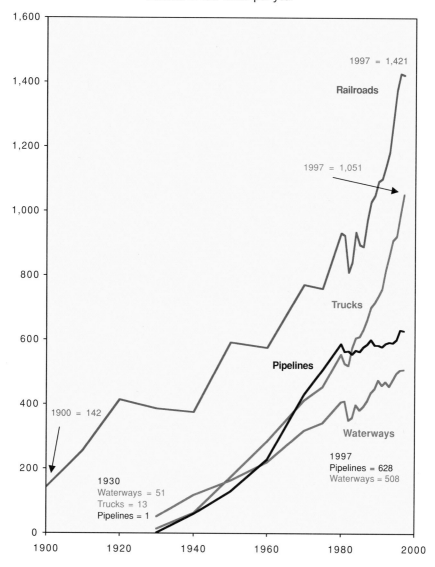

1997 = 1,421

Railroads

1997 = 1,051

Trucks

Pipelines

1900 = 142

Waterways

1930
Waterways = 51
Trucks = 13
Pipelines = 1

1997
Pipelines = 628
Waterways = 508

The number of motor vehicles exceeded road capacity.

In an effort to define the scope of the nation's road system and the distances Americans travel on it, the U.S. Department of Transportation reported in 1997 that "the sheer physical size of the transportation network is difficult to comprehend. Its 4 million miles of roads would circle the globe more than 157 times or go to the moon and back more than 8 times. In 1995, cars and light trucks—the vast majority of them personal vehicles—were driven 2.2 trillion miles in the United States. This is literally an astronomical distance, nearly one-tenth of the distance to the nearest star outside the solar system. A more down-to-earth measure: the distance traveled by the average car or light truck in the United States in 1995 equaled a journey nearly halfway around the earth."

The upper chart shows how the number of registered motor vehicles per mile of surfaced road (including city streets, county roads, state highways, and the interstate highway system) climbed from two in 1910 to fifty-seven in 1997. Because the chart is based on road mileage, it understates the effect of multiple lanes, which increase effective road capacity. On the other hand, it ignores the increased mileage of individual vehicles, which has an opposite and probably greater effect. The average daily travel per vehicle increased by 68 percent between 1980 and 1997, while miles of paved road increased by 14 percent.

As the lower chart shows, the number of miles traveled by motor vehicles in the United States increased steadily throughout the century. Individually owned passenger vehicles accounted for most of this travel. The overwhelming majority of employed persons got to their workplaces by private motor vehicle and most of them drove alone. Only 5 percent of commuters used public transportation. Many parents drove their children to school. Nearly all shoppers drove to the supermarket or the mall.

Traffic
Number of registered motor vehicles per mile of surfaced road

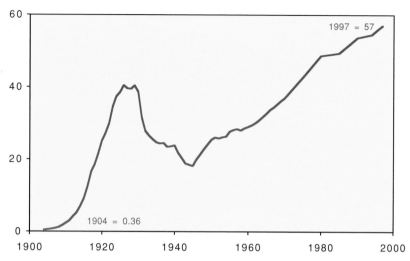

1997 = 57

1904 = 0.36

Total Travel by All Motor Vehicles
Billions of miles per year

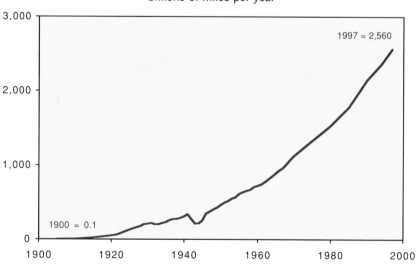

1997 = 2,560

1900 = 0.1

The annual traffic death rate fluctuated until about 1970, when it began to decline markedly. Deaths per vehicle-mile decreased throughout the century.

The motor vehicles that were so large a part of American life in the twentieth century took a heavy toll of casualties. Annual traffic deaths in 1970 (52,627) exceeded total American battle deaths during the Vietnam War (47,355). (See page 206). For every traffic death, there were about 100 traffic injuries. No other mode of transportation was associated with such large numbers of fatalities and injuries. In 1997, 92 percent of transportation-related deaths were occupants of passenger cars, light trucks, and motorcycles, or persons struck by one of these vehicles. The U.S. Department of Transportation logged more than 6 million highway crashes in 1998. In the same year, by contrast, U.S. airlines were involved in 48 crashes in which a total of one person died.

As the upper chart shows, the traffic death rate per 100,000 population in 1997 was almost exactly the same as it was in 1921, although it had been diminishing for nearly three decades.

The traffic death rate per mile traveled, shown in the lower chart as deaths per 100 billion vehicle-miles, declined steadily during the century. Between 1925 and 1997, this rate declined by 91 percent.

The seven-decade decline in the traffic death rate per mile traveled reflects the steady improvement of brakes, lights, steering gear, and tires; the introduction of safety equipment such as seatbelts, padded interiors, crumple zones, and airbags; improved highway design and signals; better driver education; and the slowing of traffic by increased congestion. The decline in the absolute number of fatal traffic accidents after 1990 can be attributed to a significant reduction in drunk driving.

Alcohol was said to be a factor in about two-thirds of fatal vehicle accidents around 1970. In 1985, the earliest year for which precise figures are available, 52 percent of fatal accidents involved drunk drivers; that figure was down to 41 percent by 1995.

The greatest number of fatal accidents involved a single vehicle, usually a passenger car, colliding with an immovable object or a pedestrian or cyclist. The most dangerous drivers were under age twenty-four and over age eighty. The wide-open highways of the Mountain States were the most dangerous per vehicle-mile. The crowded streets and country roads of New England were the safest.

Traffic Deaths
Per 100,000 population per year

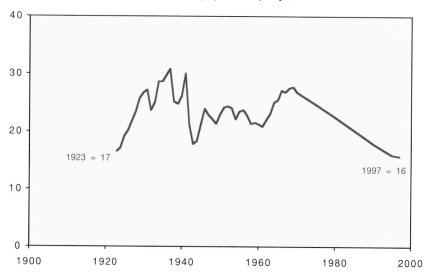

1923 = 17

1997 = 16

Deaths per 100 billion vehicle-miles per year

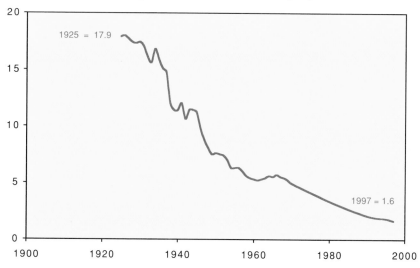

1925 = 17.9

1997 = 1.6

Bicycles, like horses and sailboats, did not disappear when they were superseded by motorized transportation.

As the chart shows, the annual production of bicycles declined after 1900 with the advent of the automobile, along with the construction of subways and elevated railroads in large cities and interurban streetcar lines in smaller cities. But the Depression of the 1930s forced many commuters back to bicycles, and gasoline rationing during World War II had the same effect.

In the prosperous 1950s, the bicycle ceased to be an important means of commuting to work but became a primary mode of transportation to school and places of recreation for many high school and college students. The annual production of bicycles more than doubled in the six years between 1954 and 1960, and then doubled again in the following decade. This upward trend persisted as students continued to depend on bicycles, and great numbers of adults took up bicycle riding for exercise and pleasure. In 1990, almost 11 million bicycles were added to an existing stock that probably exceeded 50 million.

Other archaic modes of transportation—horses, boats, and even balloons—that no longer had much practical utility, continued to thrive as well. At the end of the century, families kept more than 4 million horses for riding, driving, or companionship. Although the age of sail came to an end around 1920, Americans still used the force of the wind to propel innumerable watercraft, from windsurfers to ocean cruisers, on ponds, lakes, rivers, bays, estuaries, and the open ocean. The Wright brothers' invention of the airplane eclipsed hot-air balloon technology, but people continued to enjoy aerial sightseeing from the balloons.

Bicycles
Millions sold per year

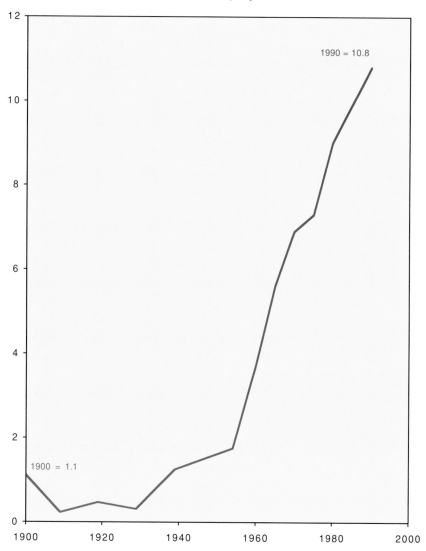

1990 = 10.8

1900 = 1.1

Chapter 14
Business

The trading floor of the New York Stock Exchange
during the 1929 stock market crash. By the year
2000, more than half of American households held
equity in stocks. Courtesy of Library of Congress.

The Gross Domestic Product per capita, in constant dollars, grew eightfold during the century.

The Gross Domestic Product attempts to measure the entire output of the American economy that is traded in the marketplace: every computer, every haircut, every car, every college course taken by a student, and so forth. The "real" GDP is the GDP adjusted for changes in prices. When the real GDP is divided by the number of people in the U.S. population, an approximate measure of the nation's standard of living is obtained. The United States enjoyed phenomenal economic growth in the twentieth century. The GDP per capita increased in every decade of the century. Even during the decade of the Depression, 1929–1939, the per capita GDP actually increased 2 percent, overcoming a sharp drop in the early years of the decade.

The extraordinary growth in GDP per capita was caused primarily by growth in inputs to the economy: more energy, more capital, better-educated workers, and research and development that produced better technologies. Some of the growth can also be traced to improved organization of productive activities.

Real Gross Domestic Product
1999 dollars per capita

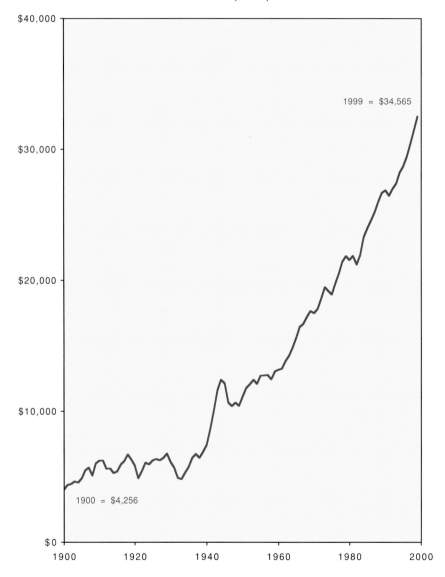

The economy became more stable.

In the first half of the century, large, year-to-year fluctuations in the real GDP indicated severe swings in the business cycle between expansion and contraction of the economy. In the second half of the century, as the chart shows, these fluctuations became much more moderate, while the economy continued to expand.

The moderation of the business cycle after midcentury has often been attributed to improved monetary policy and the effects of government programs. Better monetary policy prevented rapid, "unsustainable" expansion of the economy and also arrested contractions of the economy. Some government spending programs, such as unemployment insurance and farm subsidies, were deliberately designed to counterbalance economic swings. Federal insurance of bank deposits prevented economic contractions from causing liquidity crises. Government spending, which tends to be independent of the business cycle, represented a larger part of the economy in the second half of the century. Government transfer programs such as Social Security were also insulated from the business cycle.

Fluctuations in Real Gross Domestic Product
Annual percent change

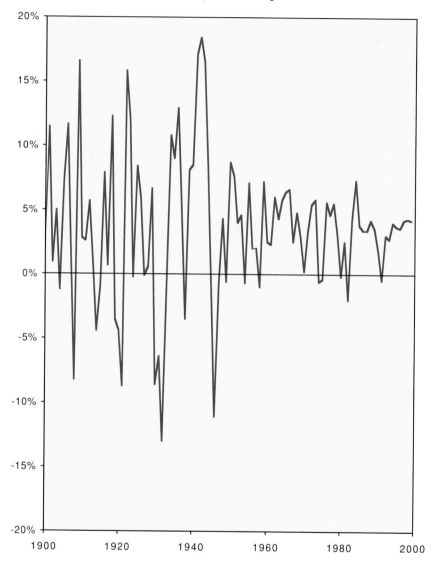

After 1939, business activity expanded enormously. The corporate share of business activity increased at the expense of proprietorships and partnerships.

The sheer size and growth of American business is difficult to comprehend. In 1939, American businesses had revenues of $2 trillion (in constant 1999 dollars). By 1996, these revenues had increased ninefold to $18 trillion, while the population had only doubled. As the chart indicates, between 1939 and 1996, the business revenues of corporations increased nearly tenfold, while those of partnerships and proprietorships grew sevenfold and threefold, respectively.

This remarkable growth in business revenues had three major components. Part of the increase represented a transfer of social activities to the business sector. Child care, for example, was almost completely noncommercial in 1939. By 1992, child care had become an $8 billion sector of private enterprise (see page 38). The largest component of the growth in business revenues, however, represented an increase in the quality and quantity of products and services. Most of the products available in 1939—automobiles, for example—were available at the end of the century, but in greater quantities and with much better quality. The final component of the increase in business revenues was the introduction of new products and services. Television shows, computer virus protection programs, and feng shui real estate consultations represented entirely new sources of business revenue.

Between 1939 and 1996, the proportion of business revenue that went to corporations increased from 78 percent to 89 percent. At the same time, the share that went to proprietorships decreased from 14 percent to 5 percent, while the proportion that went to partnerships declined from 8 percent to 6 percent.

The increase in the corporate share of business revenues was a natural outgrowth of the increasing size and scale of American business. As the overall economy expanded, many entrepreneurs with growing businesses that started as proprietorships or partnerships decided to incorporate. For growing businesses, incorporation often involved the sale of stock to the public, which allowed these entrepreneurs to raise capital for the business and receive cash for some share of the business.

Business Revenues
Trillions of 1999 dollars

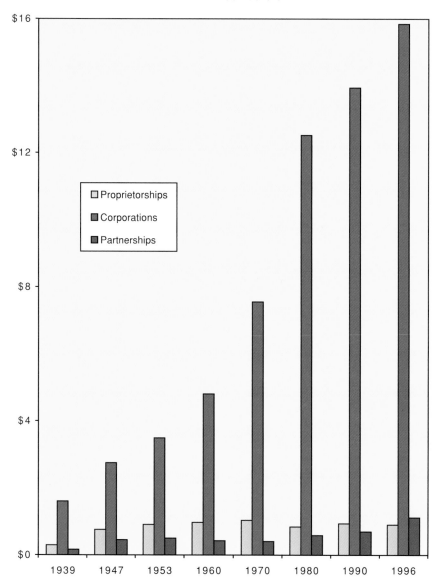

The volume of stock transactions expanded greatly after 1970.

Fluctuations in the volume of stock trading were much greater in the early years of the century when economic growth patterns were more volatile. A comparison of trading volume on the New York Stock Exchange during two consecutive five-year periods, for example, shows that annual trading volume decreased by 77 percent from 1909 to 1914 and then increased by 560 percent from 1914 to 1919. After 1960, trading volume increased almost every year. The number of shares traded on the least active day of 1999 greatly exceeded the number traded on the most active day of 1980.

Trading on the New York Stock Exchange does not tell the whole story, however. For most of the century, trading volume on the New York Stock Exchange constituted about 80 percent of the nation's total trading volume, which also included other stock exchanges (American, Chicago, Pacific, Philadelphia). A new factor emerged in the 1970s as "over-the-counter" trading evolved into the computerized NASDAQ system under the auspices of the National Association of Securities Dealers. In 1994, for the first time, the number of NASDAQ shares traded surpassed the number traded on the New York Stock Exchange. The gap continued to widen and by 1999, trading volume on the NASDAQ exceeded that of the New York Stock Exchange by more than a third.

Between the early 1970s and 1999, the aggregate value of NASDAQ shares traded increased from a small fraction of the value of shares traded on the New York Stock Exchange to approximate parity. By the end of the century, the number of companies whose shares were listed by NASDAQ exceeded the number listed by all of the other exchanges combined. NASDAQ-listed companies tended to be younger and were more likely to be in the newer sectors of the economy.

Annual Trading Volume of Corporate Stocks
Billions of shares traded per year, logarithmic scale

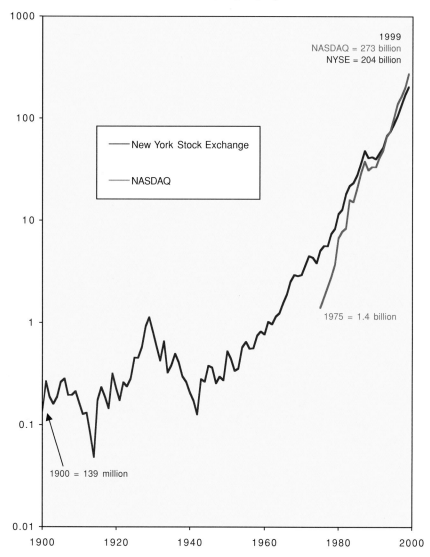

1999
NASDAQ = 273 billion
NYSE = 204 billion

New York Stock Exchange

NASDAQ

1975 = 1.4 billion

1900 = 139 million

In the first five decades of the century, the Dow Jones Industrial Average rose almost 250 percent. In the subsequent five decades, the average rose by more than 4,700 percent.

The Dow Jones Industrial Average, commonly known as "the Dow," is a weighted composite of the prices of the common shares of thirty large industrial corporations. Some corporations are added or deleted from time to time as corporate circumstances change (Microsoft and Intel made the list in 1999), but the number of stocks remains at thirty. These thirty stocks alone represent about a fifth of the value of all stocks in the United States.

Although there are many other indexes of stock prices, the Dow commands more attention in the news media than all of the other indexes combined. The investing public, moreover, typically accepts the Dow as the basic measure of all stock prices.

Nothing in the history of the American stock market compares with the Dow's elevenfold rise from 1982 to 1999. Accompanying this extraordinary growth were a decline in dividend yields and an increase in price-earnings ratios. The dividend yield of the Standard and Poor's 500 fell from 5.8 percent in 1982 to 1.3 percent in 1999. In the same period, the average price-earnings ratio increased from 8 to 32.

The rise in stock market volume and value was partly attributable to two forms of tax-sheltered savings authorized by Congress in the 1970s—Individual Retirement Accounts and 401(k) plans. The combined assets in these special accounts, measured in constant dollars, rose from $300 billion in 1985 to more than $2.5 trillion in 1997, with a large proportion invested in common stocks.

Another factor that stimulated the equities market was the rapid growth of mutual funds, which combine the contributions of individual investors into large funds with stated investment objectives. By 1998, there were more than 3,500 equity funds (principally invested in stocks) and a like number of income, bond, and money market funds. The equity funds alone held assets of more than $3 trillion. In addition to household investors, mutual fund investors also included nonprofit organizations, business corporations, labor unions, bank-administered trusts and estates, private pension funds, credit unions, and state and local governments.

Other factors probably contributed to this phenomenal rise in equity values. For example, the baby boomers—the largest birth cohort in American history—recently entered the period in life when people focus on asset accumulation.

The Dow Jones Industrial Average
Value at end of year, logarithmic scale

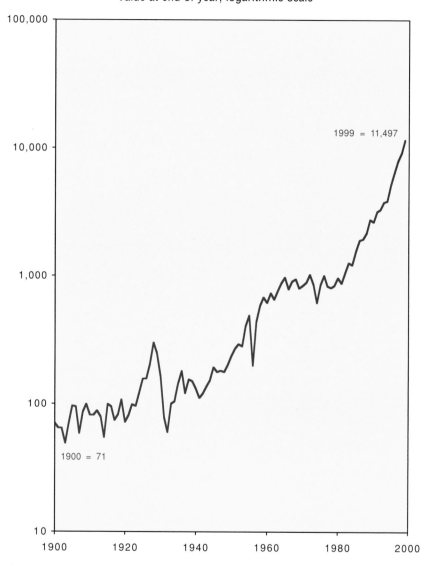

1999 = 11,497

1900 = 71

For much of the century, only a small fraction of the population owned stock, but from 1980 to 1998, the proportion of stockholders grew rapidly.

In 1998, 52 percent of Americans owned shares in public companies or equity mutual funds, either directly in their own accounts, or indirectly in retirement and trust accounts. This percentage was four times higher than in 1980, when only 13 percent of Americans owned stock. By the end of the century, more than half the population were capitalists in some sense.

Many factors contributed to the broadening of stock ownership. New pension laws shifted many employees' pensions to the new 401(k) plans, most of which are invested in stocks. Mutual funds made it easier and cheaper to start investing. Federal law deregulated brokerage commissions. On-line investing facilitated stock purchases by reducing both paperwork and commissions. Finally, after almost twenty years of unprecedented prosperity, many Americans had significant wealth with which to invest in equities.

Historically, according to Jeremy Siegel of the University of Pennsylvania, investments in equities have grown by 7 percent per year, after inflation. When compounded, such investments double in value every decade. At 7 percent compound interest, a twenty-two-year-old employee investing $2,000 a year with matching funds from his or her employer, would have $1.5 million at age seventy.

Stockholders
Percentage of population

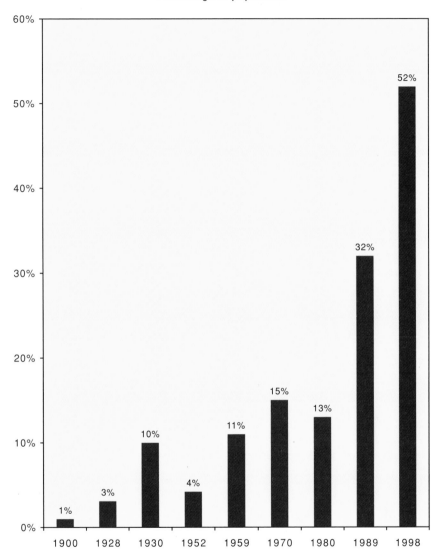

Coal was the principal fossil fuel of the nineteenth century. In the twentieth century, petroleum became the critical energy source. Unlike its adversaries in World War II, the United States was essentially self-supporting in petroleum. But thereafter, imports increased, reaching 20 percent of consumption in the early 1970s and exceeding half, for the first time, in 1994 (see upper chart). By 1998, imports constituted 58 percent of U.S. petroleum consumption.

In 1973, the Organization of Petroleum Exporting Countries (OPEC), led by Saudi Arabia and Iran, took advantage of U.S. (and European and Japanese) dependence on Persian Gulf oil to raise the price of crude oil from about $3 a barrel to more than $12. Later that year, some oil-exporting countries declared an embargo on oil shipments to the United States. The oil embargo and its effects temporarily disrupted daily life in the United States. Gasoline and heating oil became scarce. A national speed limit was imposed to save fuel. A scheme of odd-even days of gasoline buying was imposed. The U.S. government established a "Strategic Petroleum Reserve" to stockpile oil. Further OPEC price increases brought the price to $32 in 1980.

But the high price could not be sustained. In the 1980s, the elevated price of oil led to the discovery of new fields, as well as increased availability from fields in Mexico, Russia, Alaska, and the North Sea. High prices also brought sharp increases in energy efficiency, especially in automobiles. As the lower chart shows, U.S. consumption of petroleum, which peaked at 1,214 gallons per capita in 1980, declined to an annual average of 1,062 gallons per capita during the 1990s. Contrary to all expectations, the real price of oil in the 1990s dropped to near pre-OPEC levels. In 1999, however, the price began to rise again, exceeding $35 per barrel by September 2000.

Crude Oil Consumed
Billions of barrels per year

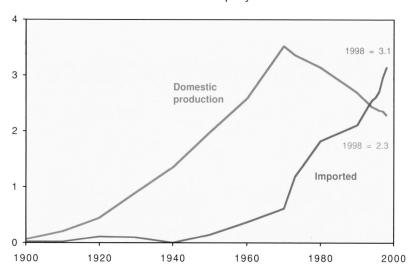

Domestic production

1998 = 3.1

1998 = 2.3

Imported

Petroleum Products Consumed
Gallons per capita per year

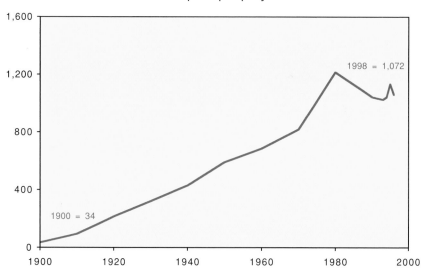

1998 = 1,072

1900 = 34

Material progress required large inputs of mechanical energy and greater efficiency in the use of that energy.

The enormous gulf between high-energy and low-energy societies was dramatized by Buckminster Fuller when he proposed the unit of an "energy-slave," based on the average output of a hard-working man doing 150,000 foot-pounds of work per day and working 250 days per year. In low-energy societies, the nonhuman energy slaves are typically horses, oxen, windmills, and riverboats. Using Fuller's unit, the average American at the end of the century had more than 8,000 energy-slaves at his or her disposal. Moreover, Fuller pointed out, "*energy-slaves*, although doing only the foot-pounds of humans, are enormously more effective because they can work under conditions intolerable to man, e.g., 5,000 °F, no sleep, ten-thousandths of an inch tolerance, one million times magnification, 400,000 pounds per square inch pressure, 186,000 miles per second alacrity and so forth."

By 1900, as shown in the upper chart, the United States already used a vast amount of energy, much of it in factories and commercial establishments. Per capita energy use grew substantially during the century, but the American standard of living increased even more. Between 1900 and 1997, per capita energy consumption nearly tripled, but the U.S. standard of living, measured as real GDP per capita, increased more than sevenfold (see page 242).

Technological advances led to greatly increased efficiency in the extraction of energy from fuel and in the application of energy to work. As the lower chart shows, the energy efficiency of the economy—the amount of goods and services the economy produces with a single barrel of oil or ton of coal—more than doubled during the century. This impressive rise in efficiency accelerated around 1973. In that year, per capita energy use reached 351 million British thermal units (Btu) per year. After 1973, energy use per capita barely changed. But economic output per capita grew by 51 percent without any increase in energy consumption per capita.

Energy Consumption Per Capita
Millions of Btu per year

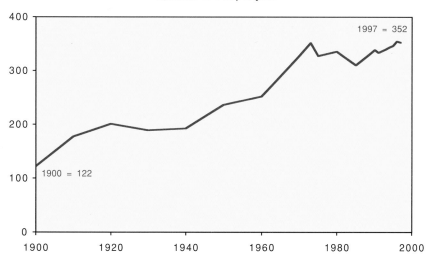

1997 = 352

1900 = 122

Energy Efficiency of the Economy
GDP per million Btu in 1999 dollars

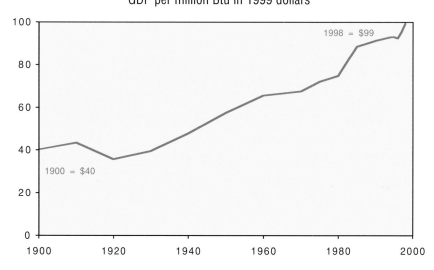

1998 = $99

1900 = $40

As the number of U.S. patents grew, fewer patents were issued to individuals and more were issued to corporations. The proportion of U.S. patents issued to foreigners increased.

Patents allow their owners to prohibit others from making, using, or selling the invention for a period of twenty years from the date of application for the patent. About 95 percent of all patents are issued for inventions, as distinct from the small number of patents issued for designs and botanical plants. Prior to 1986, the charts show only patents for inventions; starting in 1986, patents of all types are included.

The lone inventor whose Yankee ingenuity enables him to build and patent a better mousetrap is a stock American hero. In 1901, four out of five U.S. patents were issued to individuals. In 1999, more than four out of five were issued to corporations (see upper chart). Some of this change occurred as individuals incorporated their businesses (see page 246), but the trend toward larger-scale organization of technological innovation is clear.

In the early part of the century, nearly all U.S. patents were issued to Americans. The lower chart shows the steadily increasing share of foreign corporations receiving U.S. patents. The ten largest recipients of patents from 1977 through 1999 were evenly divided between U.S. and Japanese corporations: IBM, Canon, GE, Hitachi, Toshiba, Mitsubishi, Motorola, Eastman Kodak, U.S. Philips, and NEC. Foreign individuals also received about a quarter of the small number of patents issued to individuals. Counting corporations and individuals, the foreign share of U.S. patents issued in 1999 was 44 percent.

The trends shown in these charts are attributable primarily to two related factors: the rising cost of the patent process and globalization. As the patent archives grew, the process of searching and validating a patent claim became the domain of experts whose services could be formidably expensive. Moreover, because a U.S. patent provides no protection against imitations produced and sold abroad, and only partial protection against imitations produced abroad and imported into this country, significant inventions had to be patented worldwide. Unlike U.S. patents, many foreign patents require annual maintenance payments to remain in force. These procedures are far beyond the means of the typical individual inventor. Furthermore, nearly all corporate organizations, including universities and research centers, reserve the right to patent any invention made by an employee, often, but not always, with some financial reward for the inventor.

U.S. Patents Issued
Patents to individuals and corporations each year

150,000

1999
To corporations = 140,164
To individuals = 27,826

100,000

To corporations

1901
To individuals = 20,896
50,000 To corporations = 4,650

To individuals

0

1900   1920   1940   1960   1980   2000

U.S. patents per year to U.S. and foreign corporations

90,000

1999
U.S. corporations = 75,936
Foreign corporations = 64,228

60,000

To U.S. corporations

1901
U.S. corporations = 4,370
30,000 Foreign corporations = 280

To foreign corporations

0

1900   1920   1940   1960   1980   2000

In the last three decades of the century, U.S. imports and exports increased nearly fivefold, while the trade balance shifted.

In every year from 1900 to 1970, the value of the raw materials and manufactured products exported from the United States exceeded the value of imported goods. In 1971, for the first time in the century, the merchandise trade balance was negative—imports exceeded exports by $9.5 billion, measured in 1999 dollars. The balance was positive again in 1973 and 1975, but every year thereafter the balance was negative. In the last two decades of the century, U.S. merchandise trade, in 1999 dollars, increased 78 percent, while the excess of merchandise imports over exports widened from $52 billion in 1980 to $346 billion in 1999.

The initial shift from surplus to deficit in the merchandise trade balance was attributable to the oil shock of the early 1970s, which sharply raised the price of imported oil. Subsequent deficits were more strongly influenced by America's uneven trade relationships with Japan and other Asian countries.

Imports and exports of services increased as well, as shown in the lower chart. Services include airfares, film royalties, engineering consultations, and insurance premiums, for example. U.S. exports of services first exceeded imports of services in 1971, and the nation maintained this positive balance in services in subsequent decades. The excess of service exports over imports, measured in constant dollars, increased significantly during the last decade of the century, from $28 billion in 1990 to $81 billion in 1999. This positive balance in payments for services partly offsets the negative trade balance in merchandise.

The overall balance of international transactions also includes transfers of income and capital, government grants, and other intangible items. With everything factored in, the U.S. deficit in its exchanges with other countries was calculated as $46 billion in 1999. Most of the dollars retained by foreigners when these international accounts are settled come back to the United States for the purchase of income-producing assets in this country. Others remain in circulation indefinitely overseas because the U.S. dollar functions as the "reserve currency" for the world economy.

Imports and Exports of Goods
1999 dollars per capita, logarithmic scale

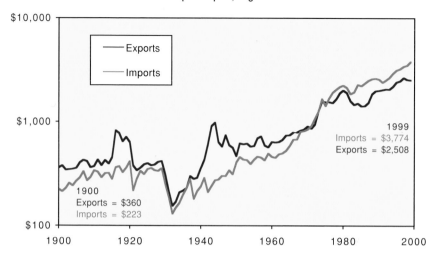

Exports
Imports

1999
Imports = $3,774
Exports = $2,508

1900
Exports = $360
Imports = $223

Imports and Exports of Services
1999 dollars per capita, logarithmic scale

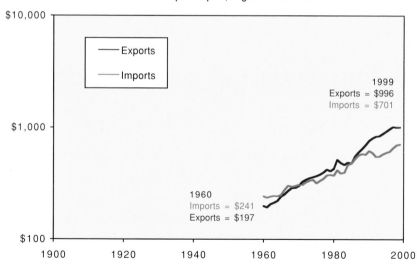

Exports
Imports

1999
Exports = $996
Imports = $701

1960
Imports = $241
Exports = $197

From colonial times until 1918, foreign, principally European, investments in the United States always exceeded American investments abroad. European capital helped to create the infrastructure of the new continent—canals and railroads, mines and mills. In World War I, European investments in the United States were consumed to pay for war materials, while new opportunities for American investors opened up abroad. The United States became a creditor nation and remained so for seventy-five years.

At first, these international investments were relatively modest and their effects were barely visible. As late as 1970, foreigners owned very few American enterprises outright, and U.S. investment abroad consisted largely of the foreign branches of large corporations.

This changed with the advent of globalization and the sharp increase in international transactions that occurred in the last two decades of the century. Between 1980 and 1999, the value of the foreign assets owned by Americans, corrected for inflation, increased sixfold. Ford and General Motors bought all or part of Isuzu, Mazda, Subaru, Jaguar, Saab, and Volvo. McDonald's Corporation opened restaurants in 118 foreign countries. As the chart indicates, U.S. investment abroad, on a per capita basis, increased from $5,406 per American in 1980 to $26,286 per American in 1999.

The value of the domestic assets owned by foreigners increased more than eightfold. On a per capita basis, foreign investment in the United States increased from $4,461 per American in 1980 to $31,688 per American in 1999. Foreign ownership and management of domestic enterprises—factories, farms, retail chains, commercial buildings, publishing companies, film studios—became commonplace. By 1999, foreign investments in this country exceeded U.S. investments abroad by more than a trillion dollars. Much of this increase was the result of the huge rise in U.S. stock prices, which raised the value of foreign investments here.

In *The Illustrated Guide to the American Economy*, Herbert Stein and Murray Foss pointed out that the consequences of the nation's international investment position are less serious than might be supposed, because the total wealth of Americans continued to increase, greatly exceeding American liabilities to the rest of the world.

International Investment Position of the United States
1999 dollars per capita (American population), logarithmic scale

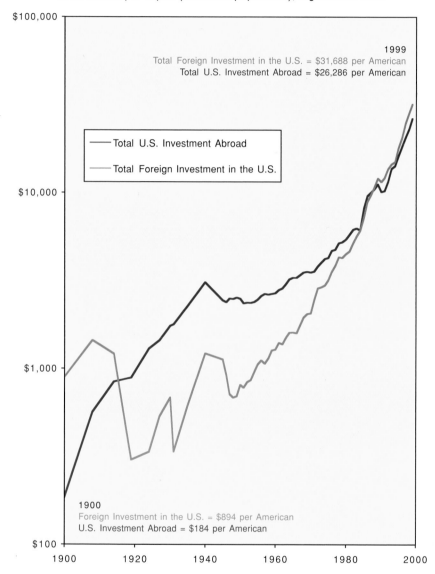

1999
Total Foreign Investment in the U.S. = $31,688 per American
Total U.S. Investment Abroad = $26,286 per American

Total U.S. Investment Abroad

Total Foreign Investment in the U.S.

1900
Foreign Investment in the U.S. = $894 per American
U.S. Investment Abroad = $184 per American

Chapter 15
Communications

The number of new books published in the United States remained fairly level during the first half of the century but surged upward thereafter.

The neglect of reading in favor of television has been regularly deplored since the advent of telecasting. A prominent academic, warning the nation about the spread of the "literate nonreader," wrote in 1970, "He reads no more than a book a year, hardcover or paperback, fiction or nonfiction. His medium of choice and greatest exposure for relaxation, entertainment, current events, and cultural uplift is television."

But in the previous decade—1960 to 1970—the number of new book titles more than doubled, the ratio of novels to nonfiction works declined, and book sales grew rapidly. Those trends continued, at a somewhat slower pace, in the last three decades of the century.

In 1935, Middletown (Muncie, Indiana) had no bookstores at all, and the public library was virtually the sole source of books for recreational reading or private study. Fifty years later, in the heyday of network television, Middletown had sixteen retail bookstores and innumerable outlets for paperbacks, but per capita circulation of library books remained about the same.

In 1997, American consumers spent upwards of $26 billion on purchases of more than 2 billion books. More than a third of these books were hardbound, and only a quarter of them were mass-market paperbacks. The Internet revolution was particularly important in the growth of book sales, with amazon.com leading the field.

The habit of reading books was largely a function of education and income: the higher their education and income, the more likely people were to read books. But women read more than men, the young more than the old, the married more than the single, and westerners more than residents of other regions.

New Books Published
Thousands per year

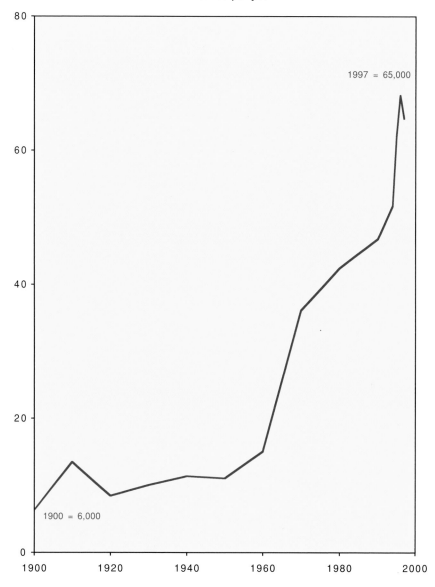

1997 = 65,000

1900 = 6,000

Per capita newspaper circulation increased during the first half of the century and declined during the second half.

Newspaper circulation proved resistant to the advent of national news magazines in the 1920s, but began to lose ground first to television news around 1950; then to all-news radio broadcast and cable television stations in the 1980s; and then to the Internet, with its innumerable news sources, in the 1990s. Competition from these other media had an enormous impact on newspaper circulation: after growing 56 percent from 1904 to 1947, daily newspaper circulation per thousand population dropped 44 percent between 1947 and 1998.

But newspapers remained a critical part of the nation's communications system. Despite the ever-increasing volume of information purveyed by competing media, the daily newspaper seemed to hold a place as the trusted recorder of local, national, and international events. Many newspapers became part of media conglomerates that also produced television programs, magazines, and huge Internet sites, which often recycled information first published in newspapers. The *Washington Post* alone spent $85 million on Internet operations in 1999.

While aggregate circulation increased throughout the first half of the century, the number of newspapers declined continuously. In 1900, most cities of moderate size had both morning and evening papers, and every major city had a rack of competing papers. Fewer than fifty cities had competing papers at the end of the century. As recently as 1980, evening papers outnumbered morning papers. In 1998, morning papers were four times as numerous as evening papers. This change was probably related to the greater impact of television news programs on the circulation of evening papers.

On the other hand, at the end of the century, two daily newspapers—*USA Today* and the *Wall Street Journal*—had achieved national readership. Another, the *New York Times,* was read far beyond its original domain.

In 1900, less than a fifth of daily newspapers had Sunday editions. By the end of the century, more than half of them did. Sunday papers—packed with comics, magazines, classified and display advertising, political commentary, style, sports, travel, entertainment, art, book, and business sections—had grown in another way as well: they weighed ten to twenty times as much as their modest precursors of 1900.

Newspaper Circulation
Number of newspapers circulated per thousand population

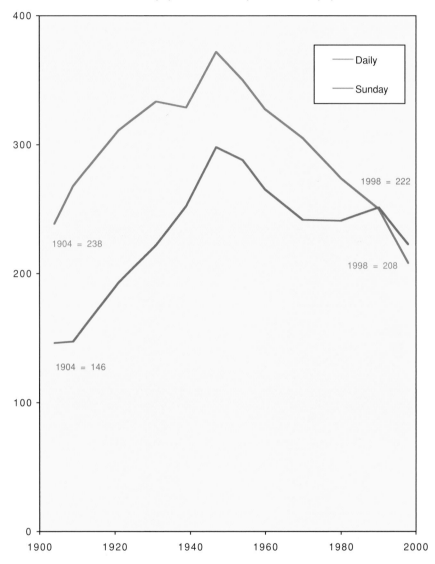

The importance of advertising in the national economy increased slowly during the first half of the century and rapidly during the second half.

A turning point occurred around 1950, with the advent of television. After mid-century, as the chart shows, per capita expenditures on advertising nearly tripled in constant dollars. In 1999, various enterprises targeted $759 of advertising to every American consumer.

Newspapers, television, and direct mail attracted similar shares of advertising expenditures. Together, they represented about 70 percent of the total. Newspapers specialized in retail promotions and classified advertising. Television was the dominant medium for marketing branded consumer products and political candidates. Direct mail catalogs offered a wide range of merchandise, especially clothing and luxury goods. Other important media were magazines, radio, the yellow pages of telephone directories, and increasingly, the Internet. A wide fringe of minor media included billboards, flyers, coupons, athletic sponsorships, and telephone solicitations.

By the end of the century, the share of newspaper space devoted to advertising had grown, and commercials cut more deeply into television program time. About three-fifths of all advertising dollars were spent on national campaigns, while the balance was spent locally.

The skepticism about the efficacy of advertising that once prevailed in many sectors of the economy almost completely disappeared by the end of the century. Enterprises that had no retail customers nevertheless advertised for good will. Pharmaceutical manufacturers promoted prescription products to the general public. Protest groups advertised for supporters. Charities advertised for contributions. Even colleges and hospitals learned how to market their services through the mass media.

Advertising Expenditures
1999 dollars per capita

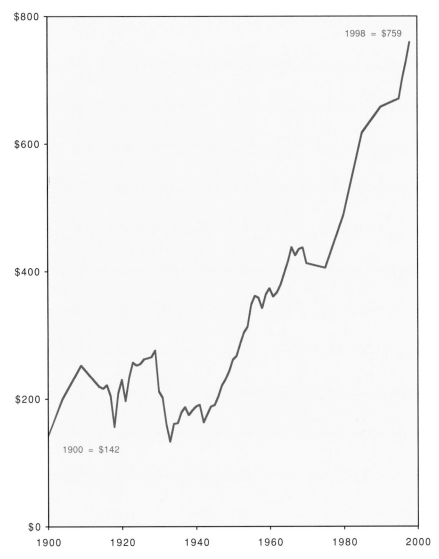

1998 = $759

1900 = $142

As communities grew, the number of post offices decreased, while the volume of mail increased substantially.

In 1900, the local post office was the only agency of the federal government that the average citizen encountered in everyday life. There was no Social Security, no Medicare or Medicaid, no income tax, no college loan program, no FBI or SEC, no NLRB or EPA, no interstate highway system.

The post office in every village, town, and city had been the principal link with the rest of the country since 1739. Benjamin Franklin, a postmaster general appointed by the British crown, was fired from his post in 1774 because of his revolutionary sympathies. The new postal system he organized for the Continental Congress was the predecessor of the U.S. Postal Service.

The number of post offices increased with clocklike regularity from 75 at the founding of the Republic to 77,000 in 1900, when the average post office served less than a thousand people and often gave a local community its name and its boundaries. Thereafter, to save expense, the number was reduced with almost equal regularity. By the end of the century, the number of post offices had declined by almost two-thirds. In 1998, each of the nation's 28,000 post offices served an average of ten times more customers than the post offices of 1900.

But the mail handled by the consolidated post offices rose in every decade except that of the Depression. The average person received 93 pieces of mail in 1900 and 729 pieces in 1998. The post office was not the only source of growth in paper messages, however. A substantial and growing volume of letters and other paper documents was handled every day by private express companies that compete with the U.S. Postal Service and offer guaranteed on-time delivery in return for premium charges.

Electronic services began to compete with the post office around 1850, with commercial telegraph service from New York to Philadelphia and Chicago. Commercial telephone service began in a modest way in 1876. By 1900, almost 8 million calls were made every day. Fax machines, long available to large enterprises, achieved widespread consumer use in the 1980s.

But all previous electronic competition pales next to e-mail, which did not become widely available until the 1990s. E-mail and other Internet messages reach the remotest parts of the world instantaneously and at negligible cost. In theory, these electronic innovations could erode the volume of hand-delivered paper communications. At the end of the century, however, they had not and there was no indication that they would.

Number of Post Offices
Thousands

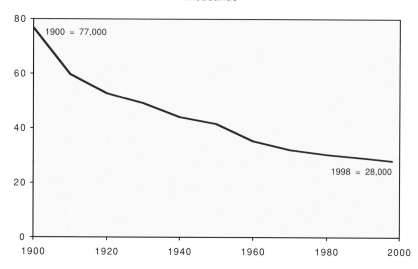

1900 = 77,000

1998 = 28,000

Mail Volume
Pieces of mail per capita per year

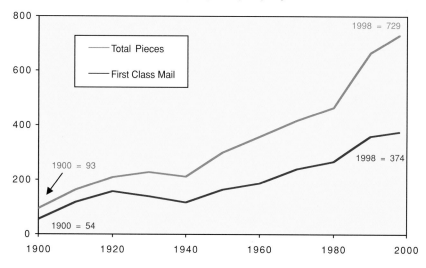

Total Pieces

First Class Mail

1998 = 729

1900 = 93

1900 = 54

1998 = 374

Telephone calls became ubiquitous in American life.

The telephone was invented in the United States in 1876. By 1900, 1.35 million telephone lines had been installed—about 18 lines for every thousand people. By 1997, 197 million telephones were in use in America—about 735 lines for every thousand people.

In 1900, almost 8 million calls were made every day—mostly for business purposes. This represented an average of 38 calls per year for every person in America. By 1940, the telephone had become ordinary household equipment. The number of calls per person rose rapidly—doubling from 1940 to 1960, doubling again from 1960 to 1980, and nearly doubling again from 1980 to 1997. In 1997, the number of phone calls per person totaled 2,325 per year or 6.4 calls per day. This figure did not include the vast number of business phone calls carried within organizations by private branch exchanges (PBXs).

A growing number of phone calls are no longer made from one person to another. Beginning with recorded messages decades ago, people have been dialing up to talk to machines. In the last decade of the century, machines were calling machines on the phone. Estimates indicate that less than half the phone calls in America involved a human voice: the bulk of calls were machine-to-machine transmissions, such as those initiated by credit card authorization machines at retail stores.

Like the automobile, the basic telephone evolved into a wide array of devices over the century. For sixty years, the telephone was a standard device made by Western Electric for the Bell System. It was tough and cheap, and underwent periodic improvements. Beginning in the 1960s, and especially after federal deregulation in the 1980s, various other types of phones appeared. By the end of the century, telephones were built to look like shoes, shotguns, and starships.

The fax machine, which uses phone lines to telecopy documents, is actually older than the telephone: the first fax machines were connected to telegraph lines in the middle of the nineteenth century.

But all these devices still plugged into the wall. Mobile phones were an expensive rarity until a new radio technology, cellular, made them inexpensive. The cellular phone was introduced in the mid-1980s. By 1999, more than 76 million Americans were cellular phone subscribers. Nearly every one of these subscribers already had a regular telephone. By the end of the century, cellular phones had radically tightened the social network in both time and space: automobile accidents were reported instantly, and business meetings involved people in subway cars and on beaches.

Telephone Calls
Per capita per year

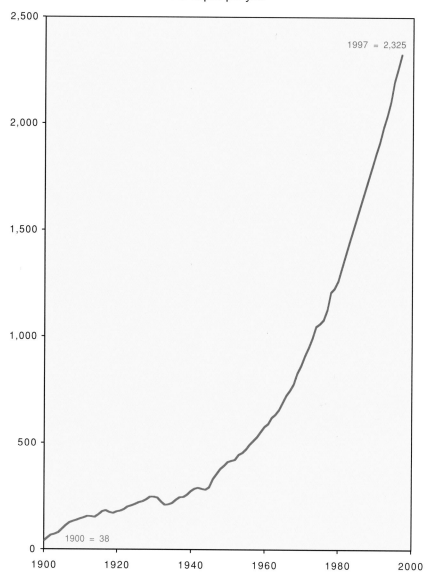

1997 = 2,325

1900 = 38

The number of personal computers in American homes escalated when the World Wide Web was developed.

Apple marketed the first fully assembled personal computers in 1977, but a mass market did not develop immediately. The operating systems, peripheral devices, and providers that made them useful were introduced piecemeal in the years that followed—MS-DOS in 1982, the Lotus spreadsheet in 1983, graphical user interfaces in 1984, laser printers in 1985, high-resolution monitors in 1986, and the first on-line services in 1988. Portable computers were introduced in 1981; laptops with high-quality displays came later. Because their speed and memory double in about eighteen months, personal computers become obsolete faster than almost any other appliance, their value plummeting to near zero in about four years.

When a Defense Department computer network unexpectedly evolved into the Internet in 1991 and the Internet spawned the World Wide Web in 1992, computer usage accelerated. By 1999, the Web contained an estimated 800 million pages, and about a third of the nation's households were connected to it for information, audio and video entertainment (including pornography), e-mail connections with the entire world, and on-line commerce of every kind.

The Web was qualitatively different from earlier computer applications such as the spreadsheet and word processing. The Web was first a communications medium, allowing ordinary persons to publish or discover vast quantities of material. It created entire social networks, such as the tens of thousands who play bridge interactively and the millions who buy from on-line auction sites.

A broad range of human activities migrated to the Web. Some were exotic, such as purchasing an asteroid of one's own or viewing spy satellite images of old Soviet air force bases. Mundane activities were also moving increasingly onto the Web: finding a mate, monitoring the behavior of children with a "Web cam," making airline reservations, getting a college education, deciding which movie theater to visit, reading the news, gambling, creating and investing in a 401(k) pension plan, selecting a physician, consulting the *Encyclopedia Britannica* or the card catalog of the Library of Congress, buying groceries, doing one's tax return and submitting it to the IRS, and voting. Many of these activities were either free or much cheaper than alternative methods. And by the end of the century, cellular phones provided access to the Web, making all of these activities portable.

Personal Computers
Percentage of households with a personal computer

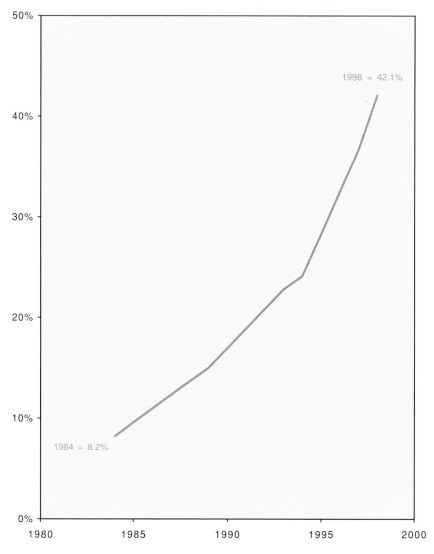

Notes

Abbreviations

HS	*Historical Statistics of the United States, Colonial Times to 1970,* Bicentennial Edition (Washington, D.C.: U.S. Census Bureau, 1975). Citations to HS are to the series number, such as A 6 ("Total Population"), not to the page number.
SA	*Statistical Abstract of the United States* (Washington, D.C.: U.S. Census Bureau, annual). Citations to SA are followed by the year and the table number, not the page number. References to SA 1998 are to the CD-ROM version, which includes more years for many of the tables.
CB	U.S. Census Bureau.
Middletown I	Robert S. Lynd and Helen Merrell Lynd, *Middletown: A Study in American Culture* (New York: Harcourt Brace, 1929).
Middletown II	Robert S. Lynd and Helen Merrell Lynd, *Middletown in Transition: A Study in Cultural Conflicts* (New York: Harcourt Brace, 1937).
Middletown III	Theodore Caplow led a team that replicated and extended the Lynds' two original studies in the late 1970s with the support of the National Science Foundation. The main findings were published in two books: Theodore Caplow, Howard M. Bahr, Bruce A. Chadwick, Reuben Hill, and Margaret Holmes Williamson, *Middletown Families: Fifty Years of Change and Continuity* (Minneapolis: University of Minnesota Press, 1982); and Theodore Caplow, Howard M. Bahr, Bruce A. Chadwick, Dwight W. Hoover, Laurence A. Martin, Joseph B. Tamney, and Margaret Holmes Williamson, *All Faithful People: Change and Continuity in Middletown's Religion* (Minneapolis: University of Minnesota Press, 1983).
Middletown IV	Theodore Caplow, Howard M. Bahr, Bruce A. Chadwick, and Vaughn R. A. Call replicated two surveys in Middletown in 1999,

	the High School Survey and the Community Survey.
GPO	U.S. Government Printing Office.
WA	*World Almanac and Book of Facts* (Mahwah, N.J.: World Almanac Books, annual). Citations to WA are followed by the year and the page number.
NYT	*New York Times Almanac* (New York: Penguin Reference Books, annual). Citations to NYT are followed by the year and the page number.
GSS	*General Social Survey* conducted roughly annually by the National Opinion Research Center; see www.norc.uchicago.edu/gss/home-page.htm and the information retrieval system at www.icpsr.umich.edu/GSS99/index.html.
HCS	Margaret Werner Cahalan, *Historical Corrections Statistics in the United States, 1850–1954,* Bureau of Justice Statistics, NCJ 102529 (Washington, D.C.: GPO, 1986).

Correction for Inflation.
All dollar figures were converted to 1999 dollars using Consumer Price Index conversion factors found at www.orst.edu/dept/pol_sci/fac/sahr/cv1999.pdf (accessed August 31, 2000).

Correction for Population Growth.
To standardize for population size, data from HS series A 6 and SA 1999, table 2, were used. In most cases, the total population, rather than resident population or civilian population, was used.

Preface

xii   James A. Garfield, *The Works of James Abram Garfield,* ed. Burke A. Hinsdale, vol. 1 (Boston: James R. Osgood and Company, 1882), pages 454–455.

Chapter 1. Population

2   **Population Size and Growth Rate.**
HS series A 6; SA 1999, table 2. The figure for 2000 is from "Population and Household Topics: Estimates" at www.census.gov/population/www/estimates/popest.html (accessed August 31, 2000). Projection for 2011 is from Population Estimates Program, Population Division, "Annual Projections of the Total Resident Population" at www.census.gov/population/projections/nation/summary/np-t1.txt (accessed August 18, 2000).

4   **Life Expectancy.**
HS series B 116–117 and B 122–123; SA 1999, table 129. For the racial difference in life expectancy, see SA 1999, table 1421.

6   **Age Structure.**
HS series A 119–134. See also CB, Population Estimates Program, Population Division, "Resident Population Estimates of the United States by Age and Sex" at www.census.gov/population/estimates/nation/intfile2-1.txt (accessed August 20, 2000).

8 **Centenarians.**

For 1950 to 2000, see Constance A. Krach and Victoria A. Velkoff, "Centenarians in the United States," *Current Population Reports* P23-199RV (1999). For 1900 to 1940, see Ira Rosenwaike, "On Measuring the Extreme Aged in the Population," *Journal of the American Statistical Association* 63 (March 1968): 29–40. For the difficulties involved in enumerating centenarians, see Jacob S. Siegel and Jeffrey S. Passel, "New Estimates of the Number of Centenarians in the United States," *Journal of the American Statistical Association* 71 (September 1976):559–566.

10 **Population Drift.**

HS series A 172; SA 1999, table 35.

12 **Urban/Rural/Suburban.**

HS series A 57 and A 69; SA 1999, table 46. For suburbs from 1910 to 1960, see Ben J. Wattenberg and Richard M. Scammon, *This U.S.A.: An Unexpected Family Portrait of 194,067,296 Americans Drawn from the Census* (Garden City, N.Y.: Doubleday, 1965). For suburbs from 1970 to 1990, see Mark Baldassare, "Suburban Communities," *Annual Review of Sociology* 18 (1992):475–494.

14 **Immigrants.**

HS series C 89–101; SA 1999, tables 5, 6, 8, 9, and 10. For 1998 data, see Immigration and Naturalization Service, Office of Policy and Planning, Statistics Branch, "Legal Immigration, Fiscal Year 1998" (May 1999).

16 **Foreign Born.**

HS series A 105, A 112, and A 6; SA 1999, tables 56 and 57; and A. Dianne Schmidley and Campbell Gibson, "Profile of the Foreign-Born Population in the United States: 1997," *Current Population Reports* P23-195 (1999). For 1999 figure, see CB Population Estimates Program, Population Division, "Quarterly Estimates of the United States Foreign-Born and Native Resident Populations: April 1, 1990 to July 1, 1999," at www.census.gov/population/estimates/nation/nativity/fbtab001.txt (accessed August 22, 2000).

18 **Minorities.**

Cary Davis, Carl Haub, and JoAnne Willette, "U.S. Hispanics: Changing the Face of America," *Population Bulletin* 38 (June 1983):8; HS series A 91–104; and SA 1999, tables 20, 37, and 38. The Hispanic proportions shown on the chart for 1950 and 2000 include only the roughly 90 percent of Hispanics who described themselves as white. This adjustment was made so that individuals who were members of two protected minorities (for example, black and Hispanic) would not be counted twice.

20 **Ethnicities.**

For 1900, see SA 1939, table 20, and CB, *Negro Population, 1790–1915* (1918). For 1950, CB, *Census of Population: 1960, Characteristics of the Population*, vol. 1, page 1-68, table 29. For 1990, *1990 Census of Population, General Population Characteristics, United States Summary*, table 276. See also St. Clair Drake and Horace R. Cayton, *Black Metropolis: A Study of Negro Life in a Northern City* (New York: Harcourt Brace, 1945). For the minority proportion of American cities in 1990, see SA 1999, table 48.

Chapter 2. Work

24 **Work Sectors.**
HS series D 199–215; SA 1999, table 675.

26 **Farmers.**
HS series K 1 and K 4; SA 1998, table 1101; and SA 1999, table 1102. For technological advances in agriculture, see Wayne D. Rasmussen, "The Impact of Technological Change on American Agriculture, 1862–1962," *Journal of Economic History* 22 (December 1962):578–591.

28 **Mine and Rail Fatalities.**
HS series M 271 and Q 398; SA 1987, tables 1054 and 1219; SA 1997, tables 681 and 685; SA 1999, table 716; and Bureau of Transportation Statistics, *National Transportation Statistics 1999*, table 3-7, at www.bts.gov (accessed September 19, 2000). We did not standardize employee fatalities on railroads and in mines for the declining number of railroad and mine employees. If we did standardize for the number of employees, then the decline would be much less steep. But this correction would partly miss the point: the American workplace became much safer during the twentieth century in part because fewer workers were working in dangerous occupations.

30 **Professionals.**
HS series D 255, D 267, and D 275; SA 1991, table 652; SA 1996, table 637; SA 1997, table 645; SA 1998, table 672; and SA 1999, table 675.

32 **Men's Work Longevity.**
HS series D 29 and D 35; SA 1997, tables 620 and 629; and SA 1999, tables 650 and 657.

34 **Work Hours.**
HS series D 803. Data for 1971–2000 from the Bureau of Labor Statistics data retrieval system at www.bls.gov/cesbtabs.htm (accessed September 4, 2000).

36 **Housework.**
Middletown I, III, and IV, Community Survey, items 23, 24, 31, and 33. For married women, see Middletown I, pages 169–170.

38 **Women in the Labor Force.**
HS series D 59, D 60, and D 62; SA 1984, table 683; and SA 1999, tables 658 and 659.

40 **Attitudes toward Wives Working.**
For 1936, see August 1936 poll in George H. Gallup, *The Gallup Poll: Public Opinion, 1935–1971* (New York: Random House, 1972). For 1972 and subsequent years, see the Internet archive of the *General Social Survey* at www.icpsr.umich.edu/GSS99/codebook/fework.htm (accessed August 24, 2000).

42 **Women's Occupations.**
HS series D 217–232; SA 1959, table 383; and SA 1999, table 675.

44 **Female and Black Professionals.**
For women, see HS series D 233; SA 1997, table 645; and SA 1999, table 675. For blacks, see Stephan Thernstrom and Abigail Thernstrom, *Black and White in*

America: One Nation, Indivisible (New York: Simon and Schuster, 1997), page 187; SA 1997, table 645; SA 1998, table 672; and SA 1999, table 675.

46 **Unemployment.**
HS series D 86; SA 1979, table 671; SA 1982–1983, table 654; SA 1998, table 677; and SA 1999, table 682. See also Bureau of Labor Statistics, *Labor Force Statistics from the Current Population Survey*, table A-1, at www.bls.gov/webapps/ legacy/cpsatab1.htm (accessed August 23, 2000).

48 **Unions.**
HS series D 4, D 14, D 927, and D 940; SA 1987, table 692; SA 1997, tables 624 and 688; and SA 1999, tables 649 and 718.

Chapter 3. Education

52 **Educational Attainment.**
SA 1999, tables 265 and 1426.

54 **Gender Balance of Graduates.**
For high school diplomas from 1900 to 1970, see HS series H 600 and H 601. From 1971 to 1983, see www.nces.ed.gov/pubs2000/Digest99/d99t104.html (accessed August 26, 2000). From 1984 to 1997, see SA 1999, table 307. Amazingly, the U.S. Department of Education has stopped publishing the number of high school graduates by gender in the *Digest of Education Statistics*; the 1999 edition lists male and female graduates only through 1983. The *Digest* does provide figures on high school completion (including about half a million GED completions per year), but it does not separate diplomas from alternative forms of completion. For bachelor's degrees from 1900 to 1960, see HS series H 753 and H 754. From 1961 to 2000, see www.nces.ed.gov/pubs2000/Digest99/ d99t249.html (accessed August 26, 2000). For master's degrees from 1900 to 1960, see HS series H 758 and H 759. From 1961 to 2000, see www.nces.ed.gov/pubs2000/Digest99/d99t249.html (accessed August 26, 2000). From 1900 to 1960, professional degrees such as M.D. and J.D. were counted with bachelor's degrees. From 1961 onward, they were counted separately. For academic doctoral degrees, see HS series H 758 and H 759. From 1961 to 2000, see www.nces.ed.gov/pubs2000/Digest99/d99t249.html (accessed August 26, 2000).

56 **Pupil-Teacher Ratio.**
The pupil-teacher ratio is generally calculated as the number of full-time teachers divided by the number of full-time students. It is an approximation of the average class size, but it is not exactly the same thing. Average class size is probably larger than the pupil-teacher ratio because at some point during the day, some teachers have preparation time and other nonclassroom duties. See HS series H 423 and H 425; SA 1998, table 269; and SA 1999, table 294. See also *Digest of Education Statistics 1999* at www.nces.ed.gov/pubs2000/digest99/ d99t065.html (accessed August 23, 2000). See the National Commission on Excellence in Education's report, *A Nation at Risk: The Imperative for Educational Reform: A Report to the Nation and the Secretary of Education* (Washington, D.C.: GPO, 1983). For information on the public school system, see Theodore Caplow, *Perverse Incentives: The Neglect of Social Technology in the Public Sector* (Westport, Conn.: Praeger, 1994), pages 47–75.

58 **Preschool Enrollment.**
HS series H 421; SA 1998, tables 258 and 266; and SA 1999, table 261. See also *Digest of Education Statistics 1998* at www.nces.ed.gov/pubs99/digest98/ d98t006.html (accessed August 25, 2000). For the characteristics of nursery schools, see Gladys M. Martinez and Jennifer C. Day, "School Enrollment: Social and Economic Characteristics of Students," *Current Population Reports* P20-516 (July 1999).

60 **Private School Enrollment.**
HS series H 422, H 424, H 427, and H 429; SA 1998, table 258; and SA 1999, table 261. For pupil-teacher ratio information, see SA 1999, table 275.

62 **Harvard College Tuition.**
Harvard tuition costs from Ruth Loescher, Harvard Public Relations Office, telephone conversation with T. Caplow, February 18, 1999. See also Harvard University web site, www.harvard.edu (accessed April 16, 2000), and "Money Income in the United States: 1999," *Current Population Reports* P60-209 (September 2000), table A.

64 **Graduate Degrees Conferred.**
For 1900 to 1960, see HS series H 752, H 757, and H 761. For 1961 to 2000, see *Digest of Education Statistics 1999* at www.nces.ed.gov/pubs2000/Digest99/ d99t249.html (accessed August 26, 2000), and SA, various years. On the value of the Ph.D. in literature for nonacademic occupations, see Elaine Showalter, "Regeneration," *PMLA* 114 (May 1999):318.

Chapter 4. Family

68 **Marriage Rate and Age.**
For marriage rate, see HS series B 214; SA 1979, table 117; SA 1988, table 126; SA 1998, table 156; and SA 1999, table 155. For marriage age, see HS series A 158 and A 159; and SA 1998, table 159. For the marital status of the adult population, see SA 1999, table 62.

70 **Premarital Sexual Activity.**
This series was created by combining data from several sources. See Edward O. Laumann, John H. Gagnon, Robert T. Michael, and Stuart Michaels, *The Social Organization of Sexuality: Sexual Practices in the United States* (Chicago: University of Chicago Press, 1994), page 327; Bruce A. Chadwick and Tim B. Heaton, *Statistical Handbook on Adolescents in America* (Phoenix: Oryx Press, 1996), tables 11-4 and 11-6; Charles E. Turner and Heather G. Miller, *AIDS: Sexual Behavior and Intravenous Drug Use* (Washington, D.C.: National Academy Press, 1989), page 89; and Charles F. Westoff and Robert Parke, Jr., "Sexuality, Contraception and Pregnancy Among Young Unwed Females in the United States," in *Demographic and Social Aspects of Population Growth* (Washington, D.C.: GPO, 1972), table 1. See also Alfred C. Kinsey, Wardell B. Pomeroy, and Clyde E. Martin, *Sexual Behavior in the Human Male* (Philadelphia: W. B. Saunders, 1948); Alfred C. Kinsey, Wardell B. Pomeroy, Clyde E. Martin, and Paul E. Gebhard, *Sexual Behavior in the Human Female* (Philadelphia: W. B. Saunders, 1953); and Julia A. Ericksen with Sally A. Steffen, *Kiss and Tell: Surveying Sex in the Twentieth Century* (Cambridge, Mass.: Harvard University Press, 1999).

72 **Cohabiting Couples.**
SA 1987, tables 54 and 55; SA 1998, tables 62 and 64; and SA 1999, tables 65 and 68. For possible reasons for the rise in cohabitation, see Andrew J. Cherlin, *Marriage, Divorce, Remarriage* (Cambridge, Mass.: Harvard University Press, 1992), pages 12–13. See also SA 1999, table 66. For differential rates of cohabitation by education and other factors, along with an overview of the literature on cohabitation, see Pamela J. Smock, "Cohabitation in the United States: An Appraisal of Research Themes, Findings, and Implications," *Annual Review of Sociology* 26 (2000):1–20.

74 **Married Persons with Extramarital Sexual Experience.**
For the Kinsey data, see page 585 of the volume on males and pages 416–417 of the volume on females (both cited in note for page 70). For the 1992 data, see table 5.9A of Laumann et al. (also cited in note for page 70).

76 **Attitudes toward Sex.**
GSS on premarital sex, questions 217 and 795A.

78 **Divorce.**
HS series B 217; SA 1997, table 145; and SA 1999, table 155. See also Conrad Taeuber and Irene B. Taeuber, *The Changing Population of the United States* (New York: John Wiley, 1958), page 155. On covenant marriage in Louisiana, see Steven L. Nock, James D. Wright, and Laura Sanchez, "America's Divorce Problem," *Society* 36 (May/June 1999):43–52. For the median duration of marriages, see Theodore Caplow, Howard M. Bahr, Bruce A. Chadwick, Reuben Hill, and Margaret Holmes Williamson, *Middletown Families: Fifty Years of Change and Continuity* (Minneapolis: University of Minnesota Press, 1982). For attitudes toward divorce, see GSS, questions 215A, 736I, and 755.

80 **Households Headed by a Married Couple.**
HS series A 288, A 293, and A 310; SA 1997, table 68; and SA 1999, table 73. See also Ken Bryson, "Household and Family Characteristics: March 1995," *Current Population Reports* P20-488 (October 1996).

82 **Married Women by Race.**
CB, *1930 Census General Report*, page 2. See also Douglas L. Anderson, Richard E. Barrett, and Donald J. Bogue, *The Population of the United States*, 3d ed. (New York: Free Press, 1997), page 196; SA 1997, table 58; and SA 1999, table 62.

84 **Fertility.**
For 1905, 1920, and 1930, see Michael R. Haines, "American Fertility in Transition: New Estimates of Birth Rates in the United States, 1900–1910," *Demography* 26 (February 1989):137–148. For 1940 to 1970, see HS series B 11. For subsequent years, see SA 1982–1983, table 85; SA 1997, table 93; SA 1998, table 97; and SA 1999, tables 96 and 1352. For abortion statistics, see SA 1999, table 114, and Stephanie J. Ventura, T. J. Matthews, and Sally C. Curtin, "Declines in Teenage Birth Rates, 1991–97: National and State Patterns," *National Vital Statistics Reports* 47 (December 17, 1998).

86 **Nonmarital Births.**
HS series A 26, A 27, B 9, and B10; SA 1997, table 97; and SA 1999, table 100. See also Ross Gregory, *Modern America, 1914–1945* (New York: Facts on File, 1995), page 159. See the Internet archives of Centers for Disease Control and

Prevention on out-of-wedlock births, at www.cdc.gov/nchs/fastats/unmarry.htm (accessed September 20, 2000). For an overview of premarital childbearing, see Amara Bacu, "Trends in Premarital Childbearing," *Current Population Reports* P23-197 (October 1999).

88 **Parent-Child Contact in Middletown.**
Middletown I, III, IV, Community Survey, items 34 and 35.

Chapter 5. Living Arrangements

92 **Size of the Household.**
HS series A 343–349; SA 1999, table 72. For information about eighth or later births, see HS series B 20–27, and SA 1999, table 98.

94 **Housing.**
HS series N 156 and N 159, and SA 1999, table 1199. For the average new house of 1998, see SA 1999, table 1201.

96 **Home Ownership.**
HS series N 243 and N 305; SA 1988, table 1224; and SA 1999, tables 1215 and 1219. For information on differences between rentals and owned houses and information on racial differences, see SA 1999, tables 1214 and 1215.

98 **Household Mechanization.**
SA 1959, tables 1110 and 1134; SA 1997, tables 1197 and 1207; and SA 1999, table 1428. See also Middletown I, pages 96–98.

100 **Automobiles and Televisions.**
HS series 152; SA 1979, tables 1096 and 1098; SA 1984, table 1063; SA 1991, table 1036; SA 1997, tables 1005 and 1009; and SA 1999, tables 1027, 1039, 1222, and 1439.

102 **Mobility.**
HS series C 3; SA 1982–1983, table xvii. See also the Internet archives of the Census Bureau, at www.census.gov/population/socdemo/migration/tab-a1.txt (accessed August 28, 2000). For percentages born in state of residence for 1990, see www.census.gov/population/socdemo/migration/pob-rank.txt (accessed August 25, 2000). For variation in mobility rates by social characteristics, see Carol S. Faber, "Geographical Mobility," *Current Population Reports* P20-520 (January 2000).

Chapter 6. Religion

106 **Churches.**
Alexis de Tocqueville, *Democracy in America*, ed. J. P. Mayer, trans. George Lawrence (New York: HarperCollins, 2000), page 291. HS series H 788, H 790, H 791, and A 6–8; SA 1959, table 70; SA 1979, table 77; SA 1988, table 76; SA 1997, table 86; and SA 1999, table 89.

108 **Protestants.**
HS series H 803 and H 805; SA 1976, table 76; SA 1988, table 88; SA 1996, table 87; SA 1998, table 89; and SA 1999, table 88. See also WA 2000, page 692; SA 1999, table 88; and WA 1999, page 684. See Theodore Caplow, *American Social Trends* (Fort Worth: Harcourt Brace, 1991), pages 66–75.

110 **Catholics.**
HS series H 800; SA 1970, table 51; SA 1988, table 77; SA 1989, table 79; SA 1991, table 78; SA 1993, table 88; SA 1995, table 84; SA 1997, table 85; SA 1998, table 89; SA 1999, table 88; WA 1999, page 406; and Eileen Lindner, ed., *Yearbook of American and Canadian Churches 2000: Religious Pluralism in the New Millennium* (Nashville: Abingdon Press, 2000). For the sustainability of Catholic growth, see Theodore Caplow, *American Social Trends* (Fort Worth: Harcourt Brace, 1991), pages 66–75. For decline in Catholic schools, see NYT 1999, page 360. For the Catholic priesthood, see Theodore Caplow, *American Social Trends* (Fort Worth: Harcourt Brace, 1991), pages 185–200. For the importance of American Catholics' disobedience of the church's teaching on birth control, see Andrew Greeley, *The Catholic Myth* (New York: Scribner, 1990). For the Catholic ascendance in education, income, and occupation, see Andrew Greeley, *Religious Change in America* (Cambridge, Mass.: Harvard University Press, 1989).

112 **Other Religions.**
HS series H 796 and H 797; SA 1922, table 47; SA 1951, table 52; and SA 1979, table 76. See also NYT 1999, page 684; and CB, *Census of Religious Bodies 1910* (Washington, D.C.: GPO, 1916). See also *Encyclopedia Britannica* at www.eb.com (accessed May 16, 2000).

114 **Church Attendance.**
Princeton Research Center for the Study of American Religion, *Religion in America* (Princeton, N.J.: Princeton University Press, 1982), page 44; SA 1999, table 89.

116 **Middletown Religious Attitudes.**
CB, *Census of Religious Bodies 1910* (Washington, D.C.: GPO, 1916), and Middletown I, III, and IV. See Theodore Caplow, Howard M. Bahr, and Bruce A. Chadwick, *All Faithful People* (Minneapolis: University of Minnesota Press, 1983), pages 12–13. For the decline in religious ethnocentrism, see Gallup Poll at www.gallup.com/polls/indicators/indreligion4.asp (accessed September 14, 2000).

Chapter 7. Active Leisure

120 **Professional Sports.**
HS series H 868, H 869, and H 870; SA 1979, table 407; SA 1988, table 373; SA 1997, table 417; SA 1999, table 441; and faxed communications from National Football League, the National Basketball Association, and the National Hockey League, January 1999. For information on salaries, see Thomas Heath, "Redskins Sold in Record Deal," *Washington Post,* January 11, 1999, sec. A, p. 1. See also Suman Bandrapalli, " Major League Baseball Teams Tap into Latin American Talent," *Christian Science Monitor* at www.csmonitor.com/durable/1997/11/17/ feat/sports.2.html (accessed September 19, 2000).

122 **Men's Track.**
WA 1900–1999; NYT 1990 and 1999; and *ESPN Sports Almanac* (1999). For the world record holders over the century, see WA 1999, pages 911–912.

124 **Yellowstone National Park.**
National Park Service, at www2.nature.nps.gov/stats/decademain.htm (accessed

August 25, 2000). For establishment and components of the park, see NYT 1999, pages 56–58. For the most visited sites in 1999, see WA 1999, page 565.

126 **Boy Scouts of America.**
Boy Scouts of America at www.scouting.org/nav/about.html (accessed May 7, 2000). For information on the history of Boy Scouts, see *Columbia Encyclopedia*, 3d ed., s.v. "Boy Scouts."

128 **Land Speed Records.**
WA 1999, page 979. See also *Guinness Book of World Records* (New York: Sterling, 1965), page 302. See also "List of world land speed record holders" at www.cnn.com/TECH/9710/15/brits.land.speed/list.reu.html (accessed August 25, 2000). For improvements of oval and other tracks, see WA 1999, pages 978–979, and *Guinness Book of World Records* (New York: Sterling, 1965), pages 302–303.

130 **Overseas Travelers.**
HS series H 921 and H 941. See also SA 1974, tables 355 and 357; SA 1980, table 427; SA 1988, tables 389 and 390; SA 1991, tables 421 and 423; SA 1998, table 455; and SA 1999, table 459.

Chapter 8. Health

134 **Infant Mortality.**
CB, *Abstract of the 1900 Census,* table 97; HS series B 142; SA 1922, table 53; SA 1959, table 73; SA 1980, table 200; SA 1997, tables 213 and 1336; and SA 1999, tables 133 and 226.

136 **Adult Diseases.**
HS series B 149, B 159, B 160, and B 157; SA 1974, table 86; SA 1977, table 104; SA 1979, table 110; SA 1980, table 116; SA 1982–1983, table 113; SA 1984, table 109; SA 1988, table 118; SA 1989, table 117; SA 1991, table 116; SA 1993, table 126; SA 1995, table 125; SA 1996, table 129; and SA 1997, table 127. For the influenza epidemic of 1918, see Alfred W. Crosby, *America's Forgotten Pandemic: The Influenza of 1918* (New York: Cambridge University Press, 1989). See also American Medical Association, *Home Medical Encyclopedia* (New York: Random House, 1989), s.v. "influenza" and "pneumonia," and *Encyclopedia Britannica*, 14th ed., s.v. "influenza."

138 **Sexually Transmitted Infections and AIDS.**
HS series B 292 and B 293; SA 1997, tables 133 and 213; SA 1999, tables 2 and 226; WA 1998, page 391; and WA 1999, page 887. For AIDS information, see WA 1999, page 887, and SA 1998, tables 144 and 224; see also National Center for Health Statistics at www.cdc.gov/nchs/fastats/aids-hiv.htm (accessed August 31, 2000). See also American Medical Association, *Home Medical Encyclopedia* (New York: Random House, 1989), pages 898 and 900. For the downturn in AIDS after 1996, see Centers for Disease Control and Prevention, "Trends in the HIV and AIDS Epidemic 1998" at www.cdc.gov/hiv/stats/trends98.pdf (accessed September 29, 2000).

140 **Suicide Rates.**
HS series H 980; SA 1988, table 117; SA 1997, table 127; and SA 1999, table 137. For adolescent suicides, see Lawrence Steinberg, *Adolescence,* 5th ed. (New

York: McGraw-Hill, 1996). For regional variation, see SA 1979, table 111. For other information, see SA 1997, tables 130–132, 139, and 1339.

142 **Alcohol.**
SA 1959, table 1071; SA 1979, table 1431; SA 1988, table 186; SA 1995, table 227; SA 1998, tables 237 and 249; and SA 1999, table 252. For information on effects of alcohol, see National Institute on Alcohol Abuse and Alcoholism, "The Economic Costs of Alcohol and Drug Abuse in the United States—1992" at www.nih.gov/EconomicCosts/Chapter1.html#1.3 (accessed September 18, 2000).

144 **Smoking.**
SA 1959, table 1073. See also Epidemiology and Statistics Unit, American Lung Association, *Trends in Cigarette Smoking* (December 1999), at www.lungusa.org/data (accessed July 15, 2000); R. T. Ravenholt, "Tobacco's Global Death March," *Population and Development Review* 16 (June 1990):213–240; SA 1979, table 201; and SA 1998, table 238. For the life expectancy of thirty-year-old smokers, see G. H. Miller, Charles E. Chittenden, and Robert J. Myers, "Life Expectancy at Age 30: Nonsmoking versus Smoking Men," *Contingencies* (May/June 1990):30, at www.contingencies.org/query.asp (accessed September 19, 2000).

146 **Drugs.**
National Household Survey on Drug Abuse, tables 41–45, at www.samhsa.gov/OAS/NHSDA (accessed April 18, 2000). For cocaine seizures in 1998, see SA 1999, table 361.

148 **Accidents.**
HS series B 164 and B165; SA 1979, table 110; SA 1982–1983, table 113; SA 1987, table 114; SA 1998, table 148; SA 1991, table 116; and SA 1999, table 137. For the rate of drowning, see SA 1971, table 76; SA 1980, table 116; and SA 1999, table 146.

150 **Hospitals.**
HS series B 361 and B 373, and SA 1999, table 204. For hospital use and outpatient surgery performed, see SA 1997, tables 187 and 194. For changes in hospital use, see American Hospital Association, *Hospital Statistics* (Health Forum, annual).

152 **Health Care Costs.**
SA 1999, table 1422. For the hospital share of health care costs, see SA 1999, table 168. For the proportion of the population covered by health insurance, see SA 1999, table 185.

154 **Mental Patients.**
HS series B 423–427 and B 428–443; SA 1959, table 93; SA 1979, table 184; SA 1987, tables 158 and 159; and SA 1997, tables 204 and 205. For the number of patients in institutions, see Philip Bean, ed., *Mental Illness: Changes and Trends* (New York: John Wiley, 1983).

156 **Disabilities.**
HS series H 356 and H 357; SA 1922, table 43; SA 1974, table 471; SA 1977, table 543; SA 1979, table 566; SA 1987, table 619; SA 1989, table 604; SA 1991, table 612; SA 1993, table 604; SA 1998, table 625; and SA 1999, table 631.

Chapter 9. Money

160 **Earnings.**
HS series D 802; SA 1998, table 692; SA 1999, table 698; and Ben J. Wattenberg, *Values Matter Most* (New York: Free Press, 1995), page 83. See also employment cost trends from the Bureau of Labor Statistics, at www.bls.gov/ecthome.htm (accessed September 21, 2000). For a more thorough discussion of the dispute among economists about trends in real compensation, see Herbert Stein and Murray Foss, *The Illustrated Guide to the American Economy*, 3d ed. (Washington, D.C.: AEI Press, 1999), pages 104–111. For the CPI's overestimation of inflation, see Senate Finance Committee, *Toward A More Accurate Measure Of The Cost Of Living*, report prepared by the Advisory Commission to Study the Consumer Price Index (The Boskin Commission Report), December 4, 1996, at www.ssa.gov/history/reports/boskinrpt.html#exec (accessed July 29, 2000).

162 **Female and Black Wages.**
SA 1998, tables 696, 697, and 745; and SA 1999, tables 702 and 703. See also June O'Neill and Solomon Polacheck, "Why the Gender Gap Narrowed in the 1980s," *Journal of Labor Economics* 11, no. 1 (1993):205–228, table 1; James P. Smith and Finis R. Welch, "Black Economic Progress After Myrdal," *Journal of Economic Literature* 27 (1989):519–564, table 1; and Diana Furchtgott-Roth and Christine Stolba, *Women's Figures* (Washington, D.C.: AEI Press, 1999), page xvii.

164 **Middle Income.**
HS series G 328. See also CB, "Historical Income Tables," table F3, at www.census.gov/hhes/income/histinc/f03 (accessed August 31, 2000). For the rise in GNP from 1900 to 1929, see HS series F 1. On the importance of new and improved goods to rising standards of living, see W. Michael Cox and Richard Alm, *Myths of Rich and Poor: Why We're Better Off than We Think* (New York: Basic Books, 1999).

166 **Household Expenses.**
HS series G 460–469 and G 495–563; SA 1999, table 729. For a review of Ernst Engel's famous law, see H. S. Houthakker, "An International Comparison of Household Expenditure Patterns, Commemorating the Centenary of Engel's Law," *Econometrika* 25 (October 1957):532–551.

168 **Philanthropy.**
HS series H 398–402; SA 1977, table 559; SA 1984, table 665; SA 1991, table 627; and SA 1998, table 641.

170 **Personal Debt.**
HS series F 8, F 393, and F 413; SA 1974, table 744; SA 1979, table 877; SA 1988, tables 678 and 817; SA 1998, tables 721, 816, and 817; and SA 1999, tables 820 and 824. For home equity loans, see CB, "Home Equity Lines of Credit—A Look at the People Who Obtain Them," *Statistical Brief* SB/95-15 (1995).

172 **Income Shares.**
HS series G 319, G 323, G 326, and G 330. See also table F-3, "Mean Income Received by Each Fifth and Top 5 Percent of Families (All Races), 1966 to 1998"; table H-2, "Share of Aggregate Income Received by Each Fifth and Top 5 Percent of

Households (All Races): 1967 to 1999"; and table H-3C, "Mean Income Received by Each Fifth and Top 5 Percent of Households of Hispanic Origin: 1972 to 1999," at www.census.gov/hhes/income/histinc (accessed August 31, 2000). Also see table F-2, "Share of Aggregate Income Received by Each Fifth and Top 5 Percent of Families (All Races): 1947 to 1998," at www.census.gov/hhes/income/histinc/f02.html (accessed August 31, 2000). See also John Cassidy, "Who Killed the Middle Class," *New Yorker,* October 16, 1995, pages 113–115.

174 **Poverty.**
Joseph Dalaker and Bernadette D. Proctor, "Poverty in the United States 1999," *Current Population Reports* P60-210 (2000). See also SA 1998, tables 756–766. For the individual duration in poverty, see Mary Naifeh, "Dynamics of Economic Well-Being, Poverty, 1993–94: Trap Door? Revolving Door? Or Both?" *Current Population Reports* P70-63 (1998).

176 **Inflation.**
HS series E 135; SA 1998, table 772; and SA 1999, table 776. See also the Bureau of Labor Statistics web site at www.bls.gov/cpifaq.htm (accessed October 19, 2000). See also Robert Sahr, "Inflation Conversion Factors for Dollars, 1800 to Estimated 2000," at www.orst.edu/dept/pol_sci/fac/sahr/sahr.htm (accessed August 31, 2000). For the Consumer Price Index and extreme cases, see SA 1998, table 772. For producer prices, see SA 1998, tables 772 and 777, and HS series E 23.

Chapter 10. Politics

180 **Presidential Vote.**
Estimates of the percentage of eligible voters who vote are available from two sources: a biennial report of the Clerk of the U.S. House of Representatives and the Census Bureau's Current Population Reports. HS series Y 27 and Y 79–83; SA 1960, table 468; SA 1987, table 418; SA 1988, table 418; and SA 1997, tables 462 and 464. For states banning felons, see "Five States Consider Easing Ban on Felons Voting" at www.cnn.com/2000/US/02/12/felon.voting/index.html (accessed September 21, 2000).

182 **Congress.**
Norman J. Ornstein, Thomas E. Mann, and Michael J. Malbin, *Vital Statistics on Congress: 1999–2000* (Washington, D.C.: AEI Press, 2000), table 1-19.

184 **Women in Congress.**
Norman J. Ornstein, Thomas E. Mann, and Michael J. Malbin, *Vital Statistics on Congress: 1999–2000* (Washington, D.C.: AEI Press, 2000), table 1-18.

186 **Black Elected Officials.**
SA 1998, table 480, and SA 1999, table 483. See also "Data Bank Fact Sheet," at www.jointcenter.org/databank/BEO.htm (accessed September 3, 2000), and WA 1999, page 522.

188 **Middletown Attitudes.**
Middletown I, III, and IV, High School Survey, items 306 and 506.

Chapter 11. Government

192 **Government Expenditures.**
HS series F 1 and Y 457; SA 1974, table 398; SA 1977, table 456; SA 1980,

table 481; SA 1987, table 428; SA 1998, table 499; and SA 1999, tables 503 and 698.

194 **Government Employees.**
HS series Y 308; SA 1987, table 471; SA 1997, tables 537 and 634; SA 1999, table 539. For federal expenditures exceeding state and local expenditures, see SA 97, tables 484 and 518. For a breakdown of federal expenditures, see SA 97, tables 518–521.

196 **Entitlements.**
SA 1959, tables 354 and 372; SA 1979, table 522; and SA 1997, tables 518, 580, and 582. See also WA 1998, pages 154 and 160.

198 **Federal Judiciary.**
HS series H 1097 and Y 308–317; SA 1988, table 501; SA 1998, table 559; and SA 1999, table 566. For judicial employees, see SA 1979, table 460; SA 1998, table 559; and NYT 1999, page 130. For trials, see SA 1998, table 68.

200 **Military Personnel.**
HS series Y 904; SA 1997, table 557; and SA 1999, table 587. See also the Department of Defense's Military Personnel Statistics web site at web1.whs.osd.mil/mmid/military/miltop.htm (accessed August 31, 2000).

202 **Blacks in the Armed Services.**
HS series B 1443, Y 906, and Y 907; WA 1998, page 150; and the Department of Defense's Military Personnel Statistics web site at www.defenselink.mil/pubs/almanac/almanac/people/minorities.html (accessed October 1, 2000). See also Harry A. Ploski and James Williams, *The Negro Almanac* (New York: Bellwether, 1967), pages 539–571; Morris J. MacGregor, Jr., *Integration of the Armed Forces, 1940–1965* (Washington, D.C.: U.S. Army Center of Military History, 1979), pages 7, 33, and 522; and Morris Fletcher, *The Black Soldier and Officer in the United States Army, 1891–1917* (Columbia, Mo.: University of Missouri Press, 1974).

204 **Women in the Armed Services.**
HS series Y 906 and Y 907; SA 1959, table 313; SA 1979, table 605; SA 1987, table 545; and WA 1998, page 150. See also the Department of Defense's Military Personnel Statistics web site at web1.whs.osd.mil/mmid/military/miltop.htm (accessed August 31, 2000). See also Jeanne Holm, *Women in the Military: An Unfinished Revolution,* rev. ed. (Novato, Calif.: Presidio, 1992).

206 **Battle Deaths.**
HS series Y 857, Y 859, Y 860, Y 879, and Y 880; WA 1998, page 149.

208 **Veterans.**
HS series A 119–134 and Y 856–903; SA 1987, table 563; and SA 1999, table 601.

210 **Middletown Patriotism.**
Middletown IV, High School Survey, items 513, 514, 517, and 519.

Chapter 12. Crime

214 Homicide.
HS series H 972; Bureau of Justice Statistics, *Sourcebook of Criminal Justice Statistics 1997* (Washington, D.C.: GPO, 1998), table 3.111; WA 2000, page 905; SA 1977, table 273; SA 1984, table 285; SA 1991, table 292; and SA 1999, table 342. For 1999 figure, see FBI web site, at www.fbi.gov (accessed September 4, 2000). For differential homicide rates, see Bureau of Justice Statistics, *Sourcebook of Criminal Justice Statistics 1997* (Washington, D.C.: GPO, 1998), section 3.

216 Robbery Rate.
HS series H 956; SA 1998, table 335; WA 2000, page 906; and the *Uniform Crime Reports* web site at www.fbi.gov/ucr.htm (accessed September 1, 2000). For the incidence of robbery, and for information on its surge after 1960, see HCS, section 2. See also Adam Dobrin, Brian Wiersema, Colin Loftin, and David McDowall, eds., *Statistical Handbook on Violence in America* (Phoenix: Oryx Press, 1996).

218 Executions.
HS series H 1155, H 1159, H 1162, and H 1165; SA 1987, table 311; SA 1997, table 362; and HCS, table 2.1. See also Paul Duggan, "Another Day, Another Execution: At Texas Death House, They Have It Down to a Science," *Washington Post,* December 9, 1998, sec. A, p. 11. The chart shows executions "under civil authority." It does not include 160 executions by the Army and Air Force (the Navy has had no executions since 1849) or the illegal executions called lynching.

220 Police.
HS series H 1013; SA 1987, table 286; and SA 1999, table 504. For the most consequential growth, see SA 1997, table 645. For the number of correctional officers, see HCS, section 1.20. For the number of police officers, see *Occupational Outlook Handbook* at the Bureau of Labor Statistics web site at stats.bls.gov/oco/ocos159.htm (accessed July 26, 2000).

222 Prisoners.
SA 1959, table 2, and SA 1997, tables 1 and 2. See HCS, table 3.2. See Bureau of Justice Statistics web site at www.ojp.usdoj.gov/bjs (accessed May 19, 2000). Figures for 1980 and 1990 from SA 1999, table 382. For an overview of prison population trends, see Theodore Caplow and Jonathan Simon, "Understanding Prison Policy and Population Trends," *Crime and Justice* 26 (1999):63–120. For the characteristics of prisoners, see Allen J. Beck and Christopher J. Mumola, *Prisoners in 1998,* Bureau of Justice Statistics, NCJ 175687 (Washington, D.C.: BJS, 1999).

224 Offenses of New Prisoners.
HCS, table 5.1; Jodi M. Brown and Patrick A. Langan, *State Court Sentencing of Convicted Felons,* Bureau of Justice Statistics, NCJ 164614 (Washington, D.C.: GPO, 1988), table 2.8; and BJS web site at www.ojp.usdoj.gov/bjs (accessed September 1, 2000). For the rates of property offenses and rates of larceny and fraud, see SA 1979, table 291, and SA 1998, table 343. For the rise in drug sentences, see Bureau of Justice Statistics, *Drugs and Crime Facts: Drug Law Violations: Pretrial, Prosecution, and Adjudication,* from the Bureau of Justice

Statistics web site at www.ojp.usdoj.gov/bjs/dcf/ptrpa.htm (accessed September 1, 2000). For the distribution of felony sentences, see Jodi M. Brown and Patrick A. Langan, *Felony Sentences in the United States,* Bureau of Justice Statistics, NCJ 175045 (Washington, D.C.: GPO, 1999).

226 **Juvenile Offenders.**
SA 1949, table 163; SA 1959, table 183; SA 1970, table 224; SA 1979, table 310; SA 1988, table 279; and SA 1998, table 355. See also Office of Juvenile Justice and Delinquency Prevention, *Statistical Briefing Book,* at www.ojjdp.ncjrs.org/ojstatbb/qa251.html (accessed August 25, 2000).

Chapter 13. Transportation

230 **Passengers.**
HS series Q 6, Q 69–81, and Q 284–312; SA 1984, table 1099; and SA 1999, table 1014.

232 **Freight.**
For value of shipments, see HS series Q 148–162, Q 251–263, Q 331–345, and Q 530–541; SA 1999, table 1014 and 1017. For UPS and the Internet, see www.ups.com (accessed October 1, 2000).

234 **Traffic.**
HS series Q 56, Q 152, and Q 199; SA 1984, table 1051; SA 1997, tables 996 and 1010; and SA 1999, tables 1020 and 1439. For the size of the transportation network, see Bureau of Transportation Statistics, *Transportation in the United States: A Review* (1997), page 2, at www.bts.gov (accessed September 26, 2000). For the average daily travel and paved roads, and the use of public transportation versus privately owned cars, see SA 1997, tables 1014 and 1016.

236 **Traffic Deaths.**
HS series Q 230 and Q 232; SA 1997, tables 1017 and 1019; and Bureau of Transportation Statistics, *Statistical Handbook,* at www.bts.gov (accessed September 1, 2000). For the decline in traffic deaths, see SA 1997, tables 1017–1019.

238 **Bicycles.**
HS series P 298; SA 1976, table 406; and SA 1992, table 395. See also CB, "Motorcycle, Bicycle, and Parts: Manufacturing," *Economic Census 1997,* at www.census.gov/prod/www/abs/a7ecmani.html (accessed September 18, 2000).

Chapter 14. Business

242 **Gross Domestic Product.**
HS series A 23 and F 2, and Brent R. Moulton, "Improved Estimates of the National Income and Products Accounts for 1929–99: Results of the Comprehensive Revision," *Survey of Current Business* (April 2000), at the Bureau of Economic Analysis web site, www.bea.doc.gov (accessed April 2000). GDP for 1999 is from the same web site (accessed May 20, 2000). From 1900 to 1928, the data are based on retrospective estimates and are actually Gross National Product (GNP), not GDP. For our purposes, there is little difference between GNP and GDP during that period.

244 **Gross Domestic Product Fluctuations.**
HS series F 3, and Brent R. Moulton, "Improved Estimates of the National Income and Products Accounts for 1929–99: Results of the Comprehensive Revision," *Survey of Current Business* (April 2000), at the Bureau of Economic Analysis web site, www.bea.doc.gov (accessed April 2000). GDP change for 1999 from the same web site (accessed May 20, 2000). As on page 242, data from 1900 to 1928 are actually GNP figures.

246 **Business Receipts.**
HS series V 5, V 8, and V 11; and SA 1999, table 862.

248 **NYSE and NASDAQ.**
HS series X 531; SA 1979, table 894; SA 1984, table 871; SA 1988, tables 808 and 810; SA 1993, tables 834 and 835; SA 1998, tables 839 and 840; SA 1999, tables 843 and 844; and the NYSE web site, www.nyse.com (accessed May 20, 2000). See also *The Nasdaq Stock Market Five-Year Statistical Review* at www.marketdata.nasdaq.co/asp/Sec1fiveYrs.asp (accessed September 4, 2000).

250 **Dow Jones.**
SA 1959, table 465, and Phyllis S. Pierce, *The Dow Jones Averages, 1885–1990* (New York: McGraw-Hill, 1991). See also *Dow Jones Indexes: The Markets' Measure* at indexes.dowjones.com (accessed September 4, 2000). For dividend yields and price-earnings ratios, see Council of Economic Advisers, *Economic Report of the President 2000* (Washington, D.C.: GPO, 2000), table B-93. For the number of equity funds, see U.S. Industry Total, section 1, at www.ici.org (accessed September 28, 2000).

252 **Stockholders.**
SA 1953, table 592; SA 1959, table 594; SA 1970, tables 2 and 684; SA 1988, tables 2 and 592; SA 1998, table 842; and Louis Hacker, *The United States: A Graphic History* (New York: Modern Age Books, 1937), page 170. See also Lewis Kimmel, *Share Ownership in the U.S.* (Washington, D.C.: Brookings Institution, 1952), and Robert J. Lampman's review of *Trends in the Distribution of Stock Ownership* by Edwin Burk Cox, *Journal of the American Statistical Association* (June 1964):606–607. For the average, long-term return on equities, see Jeremy J. Siegel, *Stocks for the Long Run: The Definitive Guide to Financial Market Returns and Long-Term Investment Strategies,* 2d ed. (New York: McGraw-Hill, 1998).

254 **Petroleum.**
HS series M 138–142; SA 1988, table 925; SA 1998, table 1177; SA 1999, table 1178; and NYT 1999, page 365. For the importance of petroleum in the twentieth century, see Daniel Yergin, *The Prize: The Epic Quest for Oil, Money, and Power* (New York: Simon and Schuster, 1991).

256 **Energy.**
HS series F1 and M 76–92; SA 1998, table 948; and SA 1999, tables 722 and 954. The quote about economic output is from R. Buckminster Fuller et al., "Document 1: Inventory of World Resources, Human Trends and Needs," in *World Design Science Decade 1965–1975* (Carbondale, Ill.: Southern Illinois University, 1965–1967), pages 29–30.

258 **Patents.**
HS series W 100–102. See U.S. Patent and Trademark Office, *TAF Special Report:*

All Patents, All Types, January 1977–December 1999, at www.uspto.gov/web/offices/ac/ido/oeip/taf/reports.htm#PSR (accessed September 1, 2000). For patents issued to the U.S. and foreign governments, see SA 1998, table 886. A tiny fraction (less than 1 percent in 1999) of patents are issued to the U.S. government and to foreign governments. These patents are not included in the charts.

260 **Trade Balance.**
HS series U 187–200. See also International Trade Administration, Office of Trade and Economic Analysis, "U.S. International Trade in Goods and Services," at www.ita.doc.gov/td/industry/otea/usfth/aggregate/H99t01.txt (accessed September 1, 2000).

262 **International Investment.**
HS series U 26 and U 33; SA 1987, table 1389; SA 1993, table 1331; and SA 1999, table 1310. For the consequences of the increased value of foreign investment, see Herbert Stein and Murray Foss, *The Illustrated Guide to the American Economy,* 3d ed. (Washington, D.C.: AEI Press, 1999), pages 268–269.

Chapter 15. Communications

266 **Books.**
HS series R 192; SA 1999, table 938. Also see Renee Richards, "Books: Their Place in America: 1900 to 1995" (unpublished manuscript, University of Virginia, 1998), quoting R. R. Bowker, *Annual Library and Trade Almanac:* 1982, page 385; 1992, page 503; and 1998, page 522. For the quotation on the literate nonreader, see Theodore Peterson, "The Literate Nonreader, the Library, and the Publisher," in *The Future of General Adult Books and Reading in America,* ed. Peter S. Jennison and Robert N. Sheridan (Chicago: American Library Association, 1970), pages 90–102.

268 **Newspapers.**
HS series R 246–249; SA 1988, table 892; SA 1999, table 942; and NYT 1999, pages 389–390. On the *Post's* move to the Internet, see Jeffrey Toobin, "The Regular Guy," *New Yorker,* March 2000, pages 94–101.

270 **Advertising.**
HS series T 444; SA 1998, table 2; and NYT 1999, page 354.

272 **Post Office.**
HS series R 163 and R 174; and SA 1999, table 946.

274 **Telephones.**
SA 1991, table 922; and SA 1999, table 926. For cellular phones in 1999, see Federal Communications Commission, *Statistical Trends in Telephony,* at www.fcc.gov/Bureaus/Common_Carrier/Reports/FCC-State_Link/trends.html (accessed September 12, 2000).

276 **Computers.**
Robert Kominsky, *Computer Use in the United States: 1984* (Washington, D.C.: Bureau of the Census, 1988). See also Eric Newburger, *Computer Use in the United States,* at the CB web site, www.census.gov/population/www/socdemo/computer.html (accessed September 20, 2000). For a chronology of the computer revolution, see NYT 1999, pages 787–789.

Index

Poverty, factors affecting, 174
Pneumonia, 136
Prayer, 114
Pregnancy among teenagers, 86
Premarital sexual activity, 70, 76, 138
Preschool education, 58
Presidential elections, 180
Prisoners, 218
    characteristics of, 222
    offenses of new, 224
Prisons
    local, state, and federal, 222, 224
    for military personnel, 224
Private
    express companies, 272
    philanthropy, 168
    police, 220
    schools, 60
Production technology, changes in, 28
Products and services, quantity and qual-
        ity, 246
Professional credentials, 64
Professions, women and blacks in, 44
Property crimes, 224, 226
Proprietorships, share of business rev-
        enues, 246
Protestant ethic, 188
Protestants, 14
    denominations, 108
Psychotropic substances, 146
Public schools, 52, 56
Pupil-teacher ratio
    in private schools, 60
    in public schools, 56

Railroads, 230, 232
    safety, 28
Rankin, Jeannette, 184
Rape, executions for, 218
Reading (books), 266
Real incomes, 164
Refrigerators, 98
Religion
    auspices for private schools, 60
    ethnocentrism, 116
    diversity in organized, 112
    membership in organizations, 106
    weekly attendance, 114
Remarriages, 78
Rental housing, 96

Republicans, 180, 182
Residential mobility, 102
Retail store workers hours, 34
Revenues, business
    new sources of, 246
    share of, 246
Road system, 234
Robberies, 216, 226
Robertson, Pat, 106
Robinson, Jackie, 120
Roe v. Wade, 84
Roman Catholic Church, *see* Catholics
Roosevelt, Theodore, 180
Rural areas, 12

Safety, 28, 148
St. Louis, 20
San Antonio, 20
San Diego, 20
Schools
    public, 56
    private, 60
Segregation, in armed services, 202
Selective Service Act of 1940, 202
Senate, 182
    women in, 184
Servants, domestic, 36, 42, 92
Services, imports and exports of, 260
Seton, Ernest Thompson, 126
Sexual activity, 70, 74, 76, 138
Sexual Behavior in the Human Female, 70
Sexual Behavior in the Human Male, 70
Sexually transmitted diseases, 138
Shares, trading volume of, 248
Short-term hospitals, 150
Siegel, Jeremy, 252
Single-family detached homes, 94
Single-parent families, 80
Smith, Margaret Chase, 184
Smokers, percentage of population, 144
Smoking, cause of death, 144
Social issues, adolescent attitudes toward,
        188
Social Security, 192, 194, 196
South, 10, 20, 60, 186
South Dakota, 214
Southern Baptists, 108
Speaker of the House of Representatives,
        182
Special education classes, 56

Speed, land, world record, 128
Sports, 122
    professional, 120
    and television, 120
Standard of living, 256
Standard and Poor's 500, 250
States
    decisions of voting eligibility, 180
    employees of, 194
    and executions, 218
    share of health cost, 152
    spending of, 192
Stein, Herbert, 160, 262
Stockholders, as percentage of population,
    252
Stocks
    broadening of ownership, 252
    market, 248, 250, 252
    prices, 262
    transactions, 248
Stokes, Carl B., 186
Strikes, 48
Suburbs, 12, 94
Suicide rates, 140
Sunday newspapers, 268
Supreme Court, 60, 84, 186, 218
Syphilis, 138

Taxing power, 192
Tax-sheltered savings, 250
Taylor, Frederick, 28
Teaching, 42, 56, 60
Technological advances, 30, 256
    in agriculture, 26
    in production technology, 28
Telephones, 272, 274
Television, 268, 270
    effects on American life, 100
    and sports, 120
Texas, 10, 218
Third parties, 180, 182
Tocqueville, Alexis de, 106
Tourists, and destinations, 130
Track and field performance, 122
Trade balance, 260
Trading volume (stocks), 248, 250
Traffic, 100, 232, 234
    death rate, 236
Tranquilizers, 154
Transportation, costs, 166

Travel
    modes of, 230
    overseas, 130
Trial marriage, 72
Trucks, 100, 232
Tuberculosis, 136
Tuition and fees, college, 62
Two-party system, 180
Typhoid fever, 136

Unemployment rate, 46
Uniform Crime Reports, 216
Unionization, 28, 48
United Parcel Service, 232
Universities, *see* Colleges
Urban areas/corridors, 12
USA Today, 268

Veterans, 196, 208
Veterans Administration, 150, 208
Vice president of U.S., 182
Vietnam War, 46, 200, 206, 208, 236
    educational deferments, 52
Violent crimes, 224, 226
Virginia, 70, 218
Voter participation, 180

Wages, 160, 162
Wallace, George, 180
Wall Street Journal, 268
Wars
    battle deaths in, 206
    blacks in, 202
    numbers of personnel in, 200
    veterans of, 208
Washing machines, 98
Washington, D.C., 20
Washington Post, 268
Washington Redskins, 120
Waterways, inland, 232
Wattenberg, Ben, xiii
Welfare grants, 196
West, 10, 20
Western Hemisphere, immigration from,
    14
White-collar jobs, 24, 28
    and unemployment, 46
Whooping cough, 134
Wine, 142
Women

About the Authors

Theodore Caplow is Commonwealth Professor of Sociology at the University of Virginia, where he has taught for three decades. Prior to 1970, he was a professor at Columbia University. He has been a visiting professor at the Universities of Bordeaux, Aix-Marseilles, Utrecht, Stanford, Puerto Rico, Bogota, Paris, Rome, and Oslo. He has served as president of the Tocqueville Society and as secretary of the American Sociological Association. In 1987, he cofounded the International Research Group for the Comparative Charting of Social Change, a consortium of social scientists studying social indicators in ten nations, and he currently coordinates its U.S. activities. He was the principal investigator of the National Science Foundation-funded Middletown III project in the 1970s and the Middletown IV project in 1999.

Mr. Caplow is the author or coauthor of 18 books and more than 160 research papers. His works have been translated into every European language, as well as Japanese and Chinese. Mr. Caplow's books about social change include *American Social Trends* (Harcourt Brace Jovanovich, 1991) and *Recent Social Trends in the United States, 1960–1990* (McGill-Queen's, 1991).

Louis Hicks is a research fellow at AEI and an associate professor of sociology at St. Mary's College of Maryland, where he has taught since 1993. Before coming to St. Mary's College, he worked as a researcher on two volumes about social change: *American Social Trends* (Harcourt Brace Jovanovich, 1991) and *Recent Social Trends in the United States, 1960–1990* (McGill-Queen's, 1991). He is a Fellow of the Inter-University Seminar on Armed Forces and Society, and a member of the U.S. team of the International Research Group for the Comparative Charting of Social Change.

Mr. Hicks is the author of "Normal Accidents in Military Operations," *Sociological Perspectives* 36 (Winter 1993), and coauthor of *Systems of War and Peace* (University Press of America, 1995).

Ben J. Wattenberg is a senior fellow at AEI and moderator of *Think Tank*, seen weekly on PBS. He is the host-essayist of the three-hour PBS prime-time documentary, "The First Measured Century."

Mr. Wattenberg's many books include one about each decennial census from 1960 to 1990: *This U.S.A.: An Unexpected Family Portrait of 194,067,296 Americans Drawn from the Census* (Doubleday, 1965); *The Real America: A Surprising Examination of the State of the Union* (Doubleday, 1974); *The Good News Is the Bad News Is Wrong* (Simon and Schuster, 1984); and *Values Matter Most: How Republicans or Democrats or a Third Party Can Win and Renew the American Way of Life* (Free Press, 1995). He is also the author of *The Birth Dearth* (Pharos, 1987) and coauthor, with Richard Scammon, of *The Real Majority* (Coward-McCann, 1970).

His twenty-five-year career in public television includes three series—*In Search of the Real America, Ben Wattenberg's 1980*, and *Ben Wattenberg at Large*—along with recent specials such as "The Grandchild Gap," "America's Number One—Now What?" and "The Stockholder Society."

His syndicated column appears in 200 newspapers. He worked as speechwriter/assistant for President Lyndon Johnson, Senator Hubert H. Humphrey, and Senator Henry M. "Scoop" Jackson. He was cofounder and chairman of the Coalition for a Democratic Majority.

Supplementary Resources

PBS Documentary on Videocassette

The First Measured Century is the companion book to the three-hour PBS documentary "The First Measured Century," a special from the producers of *Think Tank with Ben Wattenberg*. To order the two-tape set of "The First Measured Century" documentary on videocassette, call 1-800-PLAY-PBS. The cost is $29.98 for personal use and $89.95 for classroom use (including the cost of rebroadcast rights). Credit cards are accepted.

Interactive Web Site

For additional educational and program information, visit "The First Measured Century" web site at www.pbs.org/fmc. You'll find extensive transcripts from the PBS documentary, historical timelines, interactive charts and graphs, biographies of contributing experts, downloadable teacher's materials, a discussion forum, and more.

A Note on the Book

This book was edited by Juyne Linger of the AEI Press.

Kenneth Krattenmaker of the AEI Press designed the book and set the type.

Nancy Rosenberg prepared the index.

The text was set in Berkeley and Helvetica Condensed.

Fontana Lithograph, Inc., of Cheverly, Maryland, printed and bound the book, using permanent acid-free paper.

The AEI Press is the publisher for the American Enterprise Institute for Public Policy Research, 1150 Seventeenth Street, N.W., Washington, D.C. 20036; *Christopher DeMuth,* publisher; *Montgomery Brown,* director; *Juyne Linger,* editor; *Ann Petty,* editor; *Leigh Tripoli,* editor; *Kenneth Krattenmaker,* art director; *Mark Fisher,* senior typesetter; and *Jennifer Morretta,* production editor. The AEI web site is located at *www.aei.org.*